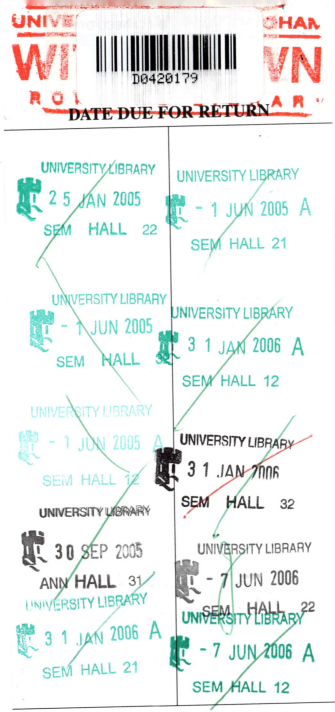

Chinese Women – Living and Working

This book presents significant new findings on new domains of employment for women in China's burgeoning market economy of the 1990s and the twenty-first century. Experts in gender, politics, media studies and anthropology discuss the impact of economic reform and globalization on Chinese women in family businesses, management, the professions, the prostitution industry and domestic service. Significant themes include changing marriage and consumer aspirations and the reinvention of domestic space. The volume offers fresh insights into changing definitions of 'women's work' in contemporary China and questions women's perceived 'disadvantage' in the market economy.

Anne E. McLaren is a Senior Lecturer in Chinese literature, language and cultural studies at the Melbourne Institute of Asian Languages and Societies, University of Melbourne. She has published extensively on the popular culture of late imperial China, women's performance narratives, gender studies and Chinese marriage systems.

Chinese Women – Living and Working

Edited by Anne E. McLaren

RoutledgeCurzon
Taylor & Francis Group
LONDON AND NEW YORK

First published 2004
by RoutledgeCurzon
11 New Fetter Lane, London EC4P 4EE

Simultaneously published in the USA and Canada
by RoutledgeCurzon
29 West 35th Street, New York, NY 10001

RoutledgeCurzon is an imprint of the Taylor & Francis Group

Typeset in Times by LaserScript Ltd, Mitcham, Surrey
Printed and bound in Great Britain by
Antony Rowe Ltd, Chippenham, Wiltshire

British Library Cataloguing in Publication Data
A catalogue record for this book is available from the British Library

Library of Congress Cataloging in Publication Data
A catalog record for this book has been requested

ISBN 0–415–31217–5

Contents

Illustrations

Plates

Tables

Contributors

Stephanie Hemelryk Donald is Associate Professor and Head of Film and Television at the Queensland University of Technology, Brisbane. She has edited *Media in China: Content, Consumption, and Crisis* (Curzon 2001) (with Michael Keane); *Picturing Power in the People's Republic of China: Posters of the Cultural Revolution* (1999) (with Harriet Evans); and *Belief in China; Art and Politics, Deities and Mortality* (1996) (with Robert Benewick). She has also authored the *Global Media Atlas* (2001), *The State of China Atlas* (1999), and *Public Secrets, Public Spaces; Cinema and Civility in China* (2000).

Louise Edwards teaches Chinese and Asian Studies at the Australian National University, Canberra. She is PhD graduate from Griffith University; her publications include *Men and Women in Qing China* (E.J. Brill 1994, University of Hawaii, 2001), *Censored by Confucius* (M.E. Sharpe, 1996) (with Kam Louie) and *Women in Asia: Tradition, Modernity and Globalisation* (Allen & Unwin, University of Michigan Press, 2000) (with Mina Roces).

David S. G. Goodman is Director of the Institute for International Studies, University of Technology, Sydney. Recent publications include *Social and Political Change in Revolutionary China* (2000); *Shanxi in Reform: Everyday Life in a North China Province* (2000); and *China's Communist Revolutions* (2002). He is currently completing a book on social and political change in Shanxi Province during the 1990s.

Elaine Jeffreys lectures in Chinese Studies at the University of Technology, Sydney. She obtained her doctorate from the University of Melbourne, Department of Political Science. Forthcoming is a book, *China, Sex and Prostitution*, from Routledge. She has published widely on issues relating to the nature of Chinese studies, feminist theory and activism, and the 'selling and buying of sex' in present-day China.

Anne E. McLaren is a Senior Lecturer in Chinese literature, language and culture at the University of Melbourne. Her research interests include popular culture in late imperial China, oral and literate culture and Chinese marriage systems. Publications include *Chinese Popular Culture and Ming Chantefables* (Leiden: Brill, 1998), *Dress, Sex and Text in Chinese Culture* (co-edited with Antonia Finnane, Monash Asia Institute, 1999) and *The Chinese Femme Fatale: Stories from the Ming Period* (University of Sydney East Asia Monographs, 1994).

Sally Sargeson is a Senior Lecturer in the Institute of Contemporary Chinese Studies at the University of Nottingham. Her research focuses on local governance, labour and property relations in China. Her publications include *Reworking China's Proletariat* (1999) and the edited volume *Collective Goods, Collective Actions in Asia* (2002).

Wanning Sun is a native of Anhui Province, China. She teaches Media and Communication Studies at the Faculty of Media, Culture and Society at Curtin University of Technology, Western Australia. Sun Wanning is the author of *Leaving China: Media, Migration, and Transnational Imagination* (Rowman & Littlefield, 2002). She is currently working on gender, internal migration and social change in China. Other research interests are Chinese media, media theory and analysis, gender and media.

Clodagh Wylie completed a Master of Arts degree (2002) at the University of Melbourne on the subject of Chinese women in the private sector. She was awarded scholarships to study in Shanghai at both the East China Normal University and Fudan University, in 1996 and 1998 respectively. In 1999 she conducted fieldwork on Chinese women in Shanghai and Beijing. Currently she works for the Australian Consulate in Shanghai.

Series editor's foreword

The contributions of women to the social, political and economic transformations occurring in the Asian region are legion. Women have served as leaders of nations, communities, workplaces, activist groups and families. Asian women have joined with others to participate in fomenting change at the micro and macro levels. They have been both agents and targets of national and international interventions in social policy at the level of the household and family. In the performance of these myriad roles women have forged new and modern gendered identities that are recognisably global and local. Their life experiences are rich, diverse and instructive. The books in this series testify to the central role women play in creating the new Asia and re-creating Asian womanhood. Moreover, these books attest to the resilience and inventiveness of women around the Asian region in the face of entrenched and evolving patriarchal social norms.

Scholars publishing in this series demonstrate a commitment to promoting the productive conversation between Women's Studies and Asian Studies. The need to understand the diversity of experiences of femininity and womanhood around the world increases inexorably as globalisation proceeds apace. Lessons from the experiences of Asian women present us with fresh opportunities for building new possibilities for women's progress the world over.

The Asian Studies Association of Australia (ASAA) sponsors this publication series as part of its ongoing commitment to promoting knowledge about women in Asia. In particular, the ASAA women's caucus provides the intellectual vigour and enthusiasm that maintains the Women in Asia Series (WIAS). The aim of the series, since its inception in 1992, is to promote knowledge about women in Asia to both academic and general audiences. To this end, WIAS books draw on a wide range of disciplines, including anthropology, sociology, political science, cultural studies and history.

Louise Edwards
Australian National University

Acknowledgements

This book owes its inspiration to the Editorial Board of the Women in Asia Publication Series of the Asian Studies Association of Australia. The series editor, Louise Edwards, also a contributor to this volume, has continued to play a dynamic role in the promotion of the studies of Chinese women and feminist scholarship in general. I am grateful to her for her ongoing enthusiasm and assistance throughout this project.

I would also like to thank the contributors to this project, who with considerable good will responded to various deadlines and requests to revise and proofread. Thanks go also to Susan La Marca, of the University of Melbourne, who spent many hours in formatting and proofreading the draft volume. Peter Sowden of RoutledgeCurzon was a prompt and helpful correspondent and we are grateful to him for ensuring the timely completion of this book.

The chapter by David S. G. Goodman was first published in *Asian Studies Review*, vol. 26: 3 (Sept. 2002), 331–53. We thank Blackwell Publishing for allowing us to reproduce it here.

Introduction

Anne E. McLaren

In twenty-first century China, women take on managerial roles in the private sector, acquire technological skills in the professions, attempt to enter the innermost sanctums of political power, work as maids in the homes of the affluent and ply their trade as prostitutes in the tent cities of the migrant workers. It is a complex picture of opportunity, challenge, disadvantage and abuse. The focus of this book is on the 'new' domains in which women are finding employment in the reform era (post-1978), on the reinvention of 'old' domains and on the intersection between notions of 'women's work' and the market economy. In brief, it deals with 'Chinese women – living and working'.

The chapters in this volume, commissioned from scholars in such fields as anthropology, gender studies, media studies, politics and social history, offer fresh insights into the 'new' areas of employment for women. Most of the 'new' areas are in fact 'old' ones revamped in the contemporary era, such as domestic service and prostitution. Another 'new' domain is the emergence of wives as the financial managers of household businesses run, at least nominally, by their husbands (see David S. G. Goodman, this volume). This too has parallels with the situation of late imperial China, when women traditionally took on the role of 'domestic bursar' in affluent households (McDermott 1990). More genuinely 'new' domains for women (at least compared with imperial China) would include leadership positions in foreign joint ventures or in major companies (Clodagh Wylie) or in positions of authority within the Chinese Communist Party or China's political structure (Louise Edwards).

The reappearance of a form of 'concubinage' for women represents another 'new' domain that springs organically from China's traditional marriage system (Elaine Jeffreys). In the educational sphere, woman teachers are gaining skills in information technology and in the process transforming notions of the politically 'virtuous' teacher (Stephanie Donald). Women's continuing interest in, or even dominance of, domestic space is the subject of studies by Sally Sargeson (the building of mansions in Zhejiang) and Anne McLaren (women's ritual work and domestic space).

Other significant themes explored by authors in this volume include the integration of China into the globalised economy (Sargeson, Wylie), the increasing influence of United Nations definitions of labour within China

(Jeffreys), and the rhetorical use of women's emancipation to assert the superiority of 'socialism' and enhance national legitimacy (Edwards). To what extent are women disadvantaged by the reform years? This is an important subject in Goodman's study of women's agency in household businesses in Shanxi, where he argues they appear 'invisible' but play a significant role, and also in Edward's historical perspective on women's participation in politics, where she points to a picture of stagnation for women in the reform era. The occupations of maid and prostitute bring differential benefits to women so engaged. Notions of gender inequality, or conversely, notions of women's agency, are underlying themes of all chapters in this volume. The dismal picture of women's political power painted by Edwards contrasts strongly with the image of female agency in Donald's study of the techno-literate woman teacher.

This volume has been divided into three sections: '"New" Domains in the Chinese Market Economy', 'Women in the Professions' and 'Reinventing Domestic Space'. While no comprehensive coverage can be achieved in a volume of this size, the contributors have drawn on fieldwork from a vast swathe of territory in China, ranging from urban and coastal areas such as Beijing, Shanghai, Anhui and the lower Yangtze delta, to Jiangxi and the northwestern province of Shanxi. This territory includes some of China's wealthiest regions, but also some of its poorest. This study seeks to build on recent scholarly work on gendered patterns of work in China (notably Croll 1994, 1995; Entwisle and Henderson 2000; Davis and Harrell 1993; Gates 1996; Jacka 1997; Judd 1994; Rofel 1999) by opening up new areas of enquiry in less studied fields. These include women's employment in the private sector and in marginalised or stigmatised occupations such as domestic service and prostitution. The impact of information technology on women working in the professions and the emergence of Chinese-language women's websites are emerging new issues discussed in the contributions of Donald and Wylie. McLaren argues that women's 'ritual work' constitutes a little-known but nonetheless significant symbolic dimension to notions of 'women's work', both in the imperial and contemporary periods. Sargeson's study of housing trends in Zhejiang breaks new ground in its provocative exposé of how the marriage preferences of young women have led to startling economic consequences, including the promotion of labour migration within China, changes in the transmission of property across the generations, and the growth of conspicuous consumption in coastal China.

In 'Why Women Count', David S. G. Goodman tackles the issue of women's perceived relative 'disadvantage' in employment during the reform period and argues that this is not necessarily borne out in practice. Women most disadvantaged by the reforms appear to be those in former state-owned enterprises. However, new opportunities have emerged for mainly younger women in household-based enterprises. His extensive survey of 279 individuals from elite cadre or 'new rich' circles in Shanxi Province demonstrates that, contrary to the received wisdom, women do indeed exercise 'leadership' in household enterprises. The wife may suffer from 'an inherent invisibility' in popular perceptions but her role as financial or business manager is critical for the success of the enterprise. Goodman not only surveyed entrepreneurs about their activities but also questioned men about the roles played by their wives in their enterprises. He was able to identify three categories of women amongst the Shanxi elite: wives of the 'new rich' entrepreneurs; wives of leading cadres; and women who were themselves leading cadres or entrepreneurs.

Goodman argues that, based on his survey group, the nuclear family is the engine of growth in the private sector in Shanxi Province – specifically, the husband and wife team. The wives were of roughly comparable educational background to the husbands. Many had received higher education, although more men were university graduates. Many 'new rich' couples had met for the first time in the classroom (some had met in kindergarten) and they worked closely together in their enterprise. The wives of the 'new rich' are often very 'professionally active' and the majority had professional or white-collar work. Of the small band of women entrepreneurs in the survey, all were members of the Chinese Communist Party (CCP) or had parents who were. Half of their number had a husband who was a leading CCP cadre. For Goodman, this suggests the 'centrality' of the Party in the national reform process. Goodman also points to the intense 'parochialism' of family connections in Shanxi and close connection between new-rich elites and the party-state as a factor in the emergence of married couple enterprises.

Another finding is that these elite families had a slightly larger number of children than the average in the region. The 'one-child policy' established after 1979 appears to have had little impact among this group. Women entrepreneurs were all mothers, and some had relatively large families. Having children did not appear to have been an impediment to their careers. Most of the marriages were not exogamous – that is, the couple came from the same region in contrast to the traditional practice for women to marry out of their native place. He hypothesises that women who married within their home town or village had occupational advantages in terms of networking and local knowledge.

The reform period has thrown up new definitions of work among the elite in Shanxi. For example, a distinction is made between a 'wife who does not work' (because the husband is rich) and a so-called 'housewife'. Women in these two categories do not engage in remunerated work. However, the former is regarded as the privileged wife of a member of the 'elite' or 'new rich', and the latter as a woman of low skills who cannot find employment.

Goodman demonstrates that women who work with their husband as his 'business manager' play a significant but largely unacknowledged role in the success of these enterprises. He notes these findings may not hold as well for other regions that are less parochial in nature than Shanxi. He concludes that 'the family is potentially a most important source of social power and influence for women' and the family itself now exercises important power both economically and politically.

Clodagh Wylie takes us deeper into the issues of women's adaptation to the world of the entrepreneur, this time in an urban milieu. Goodman notes the relative 'invisibility' of women when working with their husbands. What happens when women are not working in household enterprises, but in major companies and joint ventures? In her micro-study of women in Beijing and Shanghai, Wylie hypothesises that women in this sector might well suffer from the traditional stereotype that management and entrepreneurship are perceived as 'male' domains and might feel uncomfortable with positions of leadership or authority. They might also experience problems in their ability to network, a skill of fundamental importance in business.

Goodman's study relies heavily on husbands' perceptions of their wives. Wylie's study, by contrast, focuses on the women's self-perceptions. She carried out a qualitative survey of a small group of women in managerial positions, including directors or deputy managers in the hospitality trade, international business and human resources. A quarter of her sample were accountants or business managers and another quarter were professional workers in marketing and pharmaceuticals. The small numbers involved (twenty) mean that this is a preliminary survey, but nonetheless it offers valuable insights into the self-images of women in positions of authority.

Wylie questioned the women about their experience of working in positions of authority, including their attitude towards networking (*guanxi*). Her findings extend the earlier work of Mayfair Yang (1994), who distinguished between women's use of *guanxi within* an organisation and men's use of *guanxi* to establish relations *between* organisations. Intra-relational networking is encapsulated in the term *youhao* (warmth and friendliness), the term used by women in the survey group to describe the relations they sought to cultivate with colleagues in their own workplace. A *youhao* relationship was not seen as incompatible with an authoritative role, on the contrary, for women in leadership roles, 'friendly' relations tended to enhance authority. Some of the survey group spoke frankly of the underside of the *youhao* ethos, that of flattering one's superiors (*haohua* 'good talk'). Women who were recipients of *haohua* from subordinates could find it distasteful and insincere. A minority found the demands of *guanxi* somewhat distasteful. For example, one woman working in an American joint-venture automotive company spoke of her feelings of discomfort at the external networking required in her job. Women, even those in senior roles, agreed that it was important to use *guanxi* and exercise authority in a 'non-threatening' way.

Women in the survey group aspired to be a 'modern woman'. For most, this primarily meant being independent in decision-making at work and enjoying economic independence in their life-styles. Adaptability, confidence and resourcefulness were also qualities mentioned frequently. Traditional 'feminine' qualities such as proper deportment, good appearance, empathy with colleagues and a non-threatening manner were also perceived to be important. For these women, work in the private sector was associated with high pay, occupational challenge, career flexibility and relative freedom of choice. Negatives of work in the private sector were said to be the reduced job stability, work pressure and longer working hours.

Most women were regular users of the Internet, although one-third claimed they had never used the Internet. This is a higher level of use than suggested by statistics on Internet use in China generally. Wylie also examines a number of websites designed specifically for the Chinese woman, including women entrepreneurs. The current scope of the influence of these websites is unknown, but they offer enormous potential to construct women's domains, allow for women's networking, and promote new fashions and dialogue between a transnational community of Chinese-speaking women from China, Singapore, Taiwan and Hong Kong.

For uneducated rural women, entry into urban domestic service has opened up new opportunities. Wanning Sun, an anthropologist, explores the re-emergence of the maid in affluent households in Beijing. Maids were a common feature of wealthier households in twentieth-century China, before the founding of the People's Republic. During the decades of the Maoist era (1949–76) only senior party cadres were able to retain maids. Maids for non-cadre well-off households re-emerged in the 1980s and 1990s with the changing conditions of the reform period. The return of the maid (commonly called 'nanny' or *baomu*) thus represents the reinvention of an 'old' domain of female employment. Sun argues that the arrival of the maid as a new element in the urban workforce 'has dramatically altered the cultural landscape of Chinese cities'.

The arrival of maids in urban areas such as Beijing followed the usual pattern of migration based on local connections. According to Sun, it was women from Wuwei village in Anhui Province who were among the very earliest to migrate to other regions in search of a better economic future. She notes that domestic service offers opportunities for job mobility denied many rural women. Some use their earlier jobs in Beijing as a base from which they step forth to other opportunities. For example, they may study part-time, accumulate capital and then eventually start up their own enterprises. Others seek out money-making opportunities in the city for their children and family members. In providing employment opportunities for others in her own village, the maid thus 'becomes a conduit between home and the city . . . an initiator and a vital link in the chain of rural–urban migration'.

Once the maids have been in the city for a long time, it becomes harder to return to rural life. Sun notes the ambivalence many feel for their native place. They experience feelings of nostalgia but also revulsion at the 'backward' state of their home villages. She describes this as part of the process whereby the rural woman becomes 'modern'. In the urban environment they become 'civilised'; they learn about equality, privacy, freedom, modern household technology and modern sanitation and practices. In this way the rural maid becomes 'the object of the modernizing process'.

During the reform period maids from a number of regions have competed for work in the Beijing market. Beijing employers tend to categorise maids by place of origin, a process Sun describes as a type of commercial 'branding'. Provincial stereotypes play a role in this competition: the Sichuan maid is perceived as better-looking than her Anhui counterpart and more docile. The Wuwei maid has now come to be thought of as less desirable because of her alleged tendency to congregate, relate gossip about her employers and tutor novice maids on the tricks of the trade. The Chifeng maid, who came from a poor region in Inner Mongolia, brought further competition. According to Sun, the effect of the 'branding' of migrant maids in urban areas is to further confirm stereotypes concerning social stratification between urban regions and provinces.

One of the most interesting changes in the later reform period is the arrival of the local urban maid – that is, the Beijing maid. This is a much more recent phenomenon, forced on some women due to the downsizing of state enterprises. Local maids are likely to be older women 'stood-down' (*xiagang*) from state enterprises. As Sun notes, the trend of local Beijingers to enter the despised occupation of maid 'represents a fundamental shift in people's values regarding work, self-worth and money'. Local *baomu* cost more but they have good 'brand' attractiveness. They are seen as possessing more local knowledge, as more 'modern' and 'civilised' (they know how to programme a microwave) and are much less likely to abscond with goods from the households of their employers.

The association between poverty, rural origin and criminality has spurred the Chinese state to intervene in the originally casual and autonomous arrangements made between employer and employee. The state-operated Women's Federation was charged with regulating the industry from 1983 on. The Federation works directly with agencies in more than ten provinces to recruit domestic workers for the Beijing market. In this process, the maid has gained a new and imposing title, 'household domestic worker' (*jiazheng fuwu yuan*), a ponderous word strikingly different from the intimacy of the term 'nanny' (*baomu*) with its implications of kinship relations. In this way state intervention has also led to the professionalisation of the occupation of maid.

Together with the reappearance of the maid, the reform period was also marked by that of the prostitute in Chinese society. As with the market for maids, it took the state some time to recognise publicly that prostitution existed and to attempt to police it. Unlike the maids, now registered by the state as 'domestic workers', the prostitute has continued to be an illegal element in the body politic. Prostitution remained largely underground and hence unrecognised in the 1980s. However, from the early 1990s, with growing concerns about the links between prostitution, sexually transmitted diseases, criminality and official corruption, the Chinese state has increasingly sought to control and regulate prostitution and to lay criminal charges against 'the buyers and sellers of sex'.

Drawing from her own fieldwork and from police and legal reports, Jeffreys offers us a fascinating overview of the structure of the sex industry in China. She argues that prostitution in China is practised within a complex seven-tier hierarchy. At the top are the long-term mistresses ('second wives') of wealthy and influential men, especially government officials and entrepreneurs from within China and other East Asian countries. The women 'actively solicit' men who can provide them with an allowance and accommodation. Beneath them in popular perceptions of status one finds the 'hired wife' who accompanies a man for a limited time – for example, on a business trip – for a set payment. The third type of prostitute works for the hospitality industry and receive funds from the men they 'accompany' as 'hostess' as well as a share from the profits of the site where they work (for example, a karaoke venue or a bar). A fourth category, the 'doorbell girls', actively solicit customers in hotels, and the fifth tier are the 'hairdresser sisters' who work in massage or beauty parlours, gym centres and similar. The final two categories have the lowest status because the only service provided is a sexual one; these are the 'street women' who solicit men in public spaces and the women of the transient labour camps. The latter service the needs of 'migrant workers' from China's provinces who flock to the city to work in urban construction projects.

State intervention in the sex industry has become complicated with the introduction into China of new ideas from the West that prostitution should be considered as a commercial business transaction or a civil rights issue, not as a matter of the victimisation of women or of criminality. The new trend in the West is best summed up in the nomenclature for the individual who sells sexual services – a 'sex worker', not the pejorative 'prostitute'. Jeffrey's focuses on the cross-currents of the debate in China about the nature of the selling of sex as a form of 'labour': is it a criminal act, proof of the exploitation of women, or a consciously chosen career option – 'a form of labour like any other'?

At stake are issues not just of women's rights but also of public health, particularly control of the spread of the HIV/AIDS virus, and of China's position with regard to new UN frameworks favouring the legalising and regulating of prostitution as 'sex work'. Domestic interests in public health, public security and taxation, as well as various international non-governmental organisations (NGOs) are all lobbying the Chinese government to legalise the sex industry. However, these attempts are meeting sustained resistance from the All China Woman's Federation, an arm of the Chinese state, which continues to put forward its historical position that the commercialisation of sex is 'exploitation', 'harmful' to women's rights and completely inappropriate in a socialist state. The Women's Federation has further lobbied the government to prohibit the paid mistresses, calling it a type of 'concubinage', which should be banned in line with the Marriage Law of 2001.

China's stance on prostitution has been subject to explicit criticism by the UN Convention on the Elimination of All Forms of Discrimination against Women for failing to adequately tackle the problem of 'enforced' prostitution, on the one hand, and for its failure to legalise 'voluntary' prostitution, on the other. Internally, the Chinese government meets with criticism from its own public health sector, sociologists and some women studies scholars who argue that current Chinese policy in this field is 'gender biased and discriminatory' and leads to 'human rights abuses'.

As Jeffreys reports, the Chinese government has tried various strategies to control prostitution, particularly in the hospitality and entertainment industries. These campaigns have exposed direct links between the sale of sex in these industries and governmental corruption, particularly the collusion of local governments in the running of these sorts of enterprises. In response to these problems, the disciplinary committees of the Chinese Communist Party and the State Auditing Administration have conducted audits to monitor the situation. These audits reveal that vast amounts of public sector funds have been expended in the hospitality and entertainment industries in recent decades, including an unknown portion in the provision of sexual services to government employees. In the late 1990s and the year 2000 large-scale crackdowns were carried out by the state aimed at closing 'unregulated' enterprises in the hospitality and entertainment industries. The importance of prostitution to national economic growth became apparent when this official crackdown was followed by a slump in China's GDP of 1 per cent.

Jeffreys argues that the Western 'pro-sex work' position is simply inappropriate to the Chinese context. First, the 'liberal underpinning' of the pro-sex lobby is alien to historical understandings and practices in China. Second, even if prostitution was recognised as a form of 'paid labour', the general lack of independent trade unions and of civil rights in occupational health and safety issues would ensure that the 'sex worker' remained highly vulnerable to abuse and exploitation. Finally, in the Chinese case the complex interpenetration of governmental regulation, on the one hand, and governmental corruption, on the other, makes for a very distinctive social context for the practice of prostitution.

Among the implications of Jeffreys' study is that Chinese 'modernity' is of a different cast from that of the West. The distinctive nature of the sex industry in China undercuts the liberal Western notion that 'the organisation of modern societies is to all extents and purposes identical'. In its audits and crackdowns, the punitive force of the Chinese state has drawn attention to the (usually male) proprietors of businesses selling sexual services and on officials who have misappropriated public funds. Jeffreys concludes that, contrary to the views of 'pro-sex work' advocates, and notwithstanding the anomalies and imperfections in the current system, the Chinese state has come up with a particularly Chinese solution to this egregious problem. Instead of relying on Western notions of the rights of the individual and civil liberties, the Chinese state has chosen instead to exploit the ambiguities of a situation where the sale of sex in China is considered as neither a 'crime' nor 'an accepted social practice'.

With the study of 'Women in the Professions', we turn from China's new private sector and market competition to the public sector, the realm of the Communist Party and the Chinese state. In her chapter, Louise Edwards deals with women's agency in a very public domain – that of politics. In imperial China politics was almost entirely the domain of men, the rare Empress, Empress-Dowager or favoured consort of the Emperor excepted. The late nineteenth century marks the emergence of women into the political arena of a modernising state. As Louise Edwards argues here, the relative visibility of women as politicians has become one of the most important signifiers of 'the relative status of women internationally'.

After 1949 women's political work, like that of men, was inevitably party political work, the party in question being the Chinese Communist Party.

Edwards describes in detail what this 'subordination' of feminist activists to Party discipline meant in terms of women's political interests and influence. In a country where traditions of male work (in public space) and women's work (in domestic space) were deeply ingrained, it is perhaps not surprising that women's work in the political arena was delimited by the term 'women's work' (*funü gongzuo*). The effect of the notion of 'women's work' was to limit women's political influence to the mobilisation of women to work for the good of the Party. Care was taken by the Party leadership not to alienate men with the threat of women's emancipation. For this reason women activists worked within separate women's departments within the Party. This suggested that the agenda for women 'would remain contained as women's business and not spill over into the broader social and political scene'.

For much of the socialist period, Edwards argues, women followed the shifting campaigns of the Party leadership without demur, serving as no more than 'political wives to the male Party machine'. She discerns a shift, however, by the late twentieth century. 'Women's work' within the Party retains its importance not so much to mobilise the masses for the latest campaign but to demonstrate the 'superiority' of socialism and to give the appearance that the Party leadership still maintains 'close relations' with the people it governs. China's international reputation, as with the case of debates about prostitution, is also of concern to the central government. In 1995 the State Council brought out its Program for the Development of Chinese Women (1995–2000), which called for an expansion in the numbers of women in leadership positions in state posts. In 2001 a further ten-year plan was released with a similar set of ambitious goals for women's political participation. By the turn of the century the rhetoric of women's emancipation had changed significantly from the pre-reform period stress on subordination to Party goals to one of self-expression and self-actualisation. Participation in politics is now said to enhance women's self-respect, self-confidence, self-reliance and self-improvement.

Nonetheless, Edwards argues, women's participation in Chinese politics and the cause of women's emancipation generally is still constrained by the historical burden of 'women's work'. It is still very difficult to set up a feminist movement independent of the Party bureaucracy. 'Women's work' still remains the type of work accorded low status and remuneration. The result is that women politicians are 'overwhelmingly concentrated' in areas such as culture, education and health, not in the 'masculine' areas of finance, economics and industry. With regard to the number of women representatives to the National People's Congress (NPC), these have remained relatively stable during the reform period at around 21 per cent. However, the representation of women at the State Council and Standing Committee of the NPC has not advanced.

In China it is the Party central organisations that possess the greatest power. Very few women have been elected to the Party's Politburo and none has ever been elected to its innermost sanctum, the standing committee of the Politburo. A hopeful sign, however, is the election in 2002 of female industrialist, Wu Yi, to the Politburo, the first woman to hold this position who is not married to a

Party leader. With regard to the general membership of the Chinese Communist Party, only 17 per cent of the band of 66.3 million Party members are female. Internal female commentators argue that these woeful numbers are due to a residue of 'sexual inequality' and the tenacity of traditional notions about women's roles in societies. Rural women are particularly disadvantaged. Women's political participation is also suffering from a backlash against the pro-women policies of the Cultural Revolution, which was perceived to have led to an influx of poorly prepared women to leadership positions.

The teaching profession is another area that is subject to increasing reinvention in the reform period. The ability to use new media technology has become one of the touchstones for assessing the new 'modern' teacher. In the Chinese tradition, the teacher represents not just academic expertise and competence but also 'traditional' virtues and personal integrity. Most importantly, he or she should be able to convey 'a sense of continuity in culture and social behaviours'. It is exactly this cultural transmission, from the revolutionary past to the modernised, reformist present, that is one of the hardest duties of the contemporary teacher. As Stephanie Donald, an expert in Chinese media education points out: 'Teachers say (off the record) that the history of revolution ... has less and less currency with the young.'

Women comprise almost half of China's primary schoolteachers and over a third of its secondary schoolteachers. Entry to the profession of teaching for women was a major step forward in the revolutionary and socialist periods, because teaching had been traditionally regarded as a leadership role more suitable for men than women. Chinese films of the earlier decades of socialist China tended to stress the role of male models in inspiring young women. The exception to the generally male models promoted by these films were teachers, who were typically female and served as role models of professional virtue. During the Cultural Revolution teachers, many of them female, were attacked as 'bad class elements'. This was the 'nadir' of the status of the teaching profession in China. Subsequently, Donalds argues, the importance of teachers in China's modernisation project has improved the status of teachers to that of 'a professional class of educators'. Compulsory continued training and upgrading of teachers, especially in the use of new technological media, has further bolstered their position.

In recent years the Chinese state has set very ambitious goals for the technologisation of education. One goal is to network virtually all schools by 2003. Students are now taught information technology, especially in such areas as English language teaching. Teachers increasingly rely on the computer as an aid to teaching. PowerPoint presentations are replacing the old 'chalk and talk' methods. With the increased technologisation of learning, the teacher increasingly takes on the role of 'a technologically skilled communicator'.

How is the woman educator faring in the emergence of the technologically literate teacher? In various encounters with women educators, Donald noted the high level of competence displayed and the goal of providing self-enrichment and a happy ('fun') learning environment for the students. This impression of competence was confirmed by case studies drawn from two schools. In one case study, a teacher in a school in Jiangxi Province, a teacher used the story of Robinson Crusoe to organise field trips to rural regions so as to allow the students to re-create the Crusoe story by 'surviving' in the countryside. The students made their own film of this event and relayed it back to the class through PowerPoint and video. In this case, one could say that the woman teacher was using a radically new method to transmit some 'traditional' Chinese values (endurance, fortitude, 'collective endeavour') to a group of students perceived to be mollycoddled, 'spoilt' single children. Donald concludes on a note of optimism: although teaching in China, as elsewhere, is a 'feminised profession' with 'minimal career prospects' and low remuneration, nonetheless, the emergence of the IT-competent woman teacher in the Chinese classroom augurs well for her strengthening professional status and a growing recognition of her role within 'the modern landscape of Chinese society'.

The final chapters return to issues of the family and domestic space, traditionally the paramount domain of 'women's work' in China. Anthropologist Sally Sargeson's study of house construction and domestic space in Zhejiang Province provides a dramatic insight into the relationship between the construction of multi-storey mansions in Zhejiang villages, household work patterns, internal labour migration, inheritance of property, and the marital choices made by young women of the region. As she demonstrates, the configuration of new housing in this region, not to mention the 'embedding' of Zhejiang villages within a global economy, is based around one prime social fact: a young woman will only marry a man who owns a mansion.

During the reform period, Zhejiang has seen a huge boom in household construction. Per capita living space of Zhejiang villagers is reaching unheard sizes of 40 square metres or more in the 1990s. Sargeson carried out a survey of 296 households in Zhejiang, followed up by detailed interviews with forty households. She found that over half had built at least one new house from 1990 to 2000. Some families had even demolished and rebuilt several times. For the people in the region, the boom in household construction can be explained very simply: 'No woman would marry a man without a new house.' The young women interviewed by Sargeson confirmed this image of the power of bridal choice. Furthermore, the young women wanted a particular sort of configuration of space within the new residence. Their standard requirements were for a space for the young couple to enjoy marital intimacy and a separate space for the parents-in-law. Multi-floor residences often combine a series of self-contained units for the couple, the parents-in-law, and empty space for the children to be.

Her findings concerning the motives for the boom in household construction in this region have important implications for our understanding of how China's market reforms have changed marriage customs and traditional methods of the transmission of property within families. The economic consequences are startling: as Sargeson argues, 'women's housing aspirations are also propelling credit circulation, rural–urban migration and the redistribution of family wealth'. The burden of providing the mansion for the bride falls very heavily on her parents-in-law. Sargeson interviewed elderly parents who hasten from one job to another, working double shifts to pay for their son's mansion. Young men migrate from rural to urban areas in search of lucrative work and remit funds back to their family for housing. When the multi-storey mansion is built, the parents might well move into the ground floor and live within 'unpainted concrete walls' while the son and his wife inhabit a grandly furnished unit on an upper floor.

Young women are also increasingly dictating the architectural style, internal design and furnishing of their mansions. New housing reflects a flamboyant pastiche of different styles, ranging from an echo of the curled-up tile roofs of the past to baroque architraves, courtyards, water features and garden beds modelled on Western suburban 'utopias'. In spite of the expense lavished on the external appearance of the dwelling, construction safety and sanitation regulations are rarely observed. Villagers appear to feel little nostalgia for the courtyards and verandahs of the past, which provided for intimate interaction with their neighbours. Inside the mansions, the 'ritual and social-structural hierarchies' that governed the demarcation of domestic space in the Chinese tradition have been transformed into spatial arrangements that prioritise the residents as consumers rather than as producers and that divide public from private space. The 'modern' mansions of Zhejiang are bereft of the ancestral altars of the past and instead are stocked with sofas, VCR, karaoke, TV, exercise equipment, aquariums and the like.

Sargeson argues that the major beneficiary in this massive investment in housing by the family is probably the son rather than the married couple. Chinese property legislation tends towards the 'individualisation' of property rights; that is, property brought into a marriage remains the personal property of the individual unless the couple sign a written agreement to the contrary. However, she notes that the adverse effect on the wife is mitigated somewhat by other legislation which prioritises the right of spouses to inherit property over children and other family members. The issue of who benefits most is thus a complex one. The parents of the groom benefit from preservation of the patriline, but often at the expense of their own personal interests. Sargeson concludes that the remarkable bargaining power that young women exercise in the Zhejiang marriage market gives the lie to the usual assumptions that women are simply 'the objects of marital exchange' and 'victims' of exploitation in the patrilineal marriage system.

In her study of women's labour in the home and ritual space in China, Anne McLaren returns to the issue of shifting notions of 'women's work' in the imperial and contemporary periods. She notes that notions of work done by women have been understood narrowly as the production of goods and services, with little attention paid to the symbolic aspects of women's work, which included the power to protect the family through ritual means and 'mediation between the household and supernatural forces'. Much ink has been spilt about what women gained from the revolution and socialist reforms. Very rarely has the question been asked about what women may have lost in the process of modernisation. McLaren argues that when women departed from their homes and farms for factories and collective enterprises, they commonly lost a fellowship with a community of women, with whom they had laboured and enjoyed a rich oral and ritual culture. In the new work units (*danwei*) run by the socialist state, leadership positions were held by male cadres, not older women. Government campaigns against 'superstition' also robbed communities of traditional marriage and funeral ceremonies, where women had often played powerful roles as ritual lamenters.

Once one examines popular perceptions of women's work through the lens of women's oral and ritual culture, a more nuanced picture of gendered notions of labour emerges. McLaren examines four case studies that illustrate 'the intersection between oral arts, ritual culture and the daily tasks defined as "women's work" in rural China'. These case studies reveal a surprising level of female agency in the ritual organisation of domestic space and, in some cases, of village communities.

In the bridal laments examined by McLaren in Nanhui, a coastal county belonging to the jurisdiction of Shanghai, the bride constructs notions of female labour that project a strong sense of the importance of her work for the family. The Chinese marriage system relied on the transfer of the bride's labour from her natal home to the household of her parents-in-law. It was crucial to the face of her natal family that the young woman acquire appropriate domestic skills in spinning, weaving, cooking and the diplomatic skills necessary in serving a large household. The bride fears not the judgement of the groom but the harsh words of her mother-in-law, his sisters and aunts. It is clear that the domestic space of her husband's household is in the control not of the menfolk but of the senior women. The bride's goal is to acquire the sort of skills that will allow her to dominate the household in her turn, as the mother-in-law ages and she acquires maturity. It is by her household skills and knowledge of correct protocols that she will be assessed.

The cult to the Maiden of the Lavatory (*Keng San guniang*), investigated by Chen Qinjian, is a fascinating example of another ritual performance also practised by young girls. The cult was based around the removal of barrels of human waste to a manure pit located at the back of the residence. This was a humble task, commonly carried out by women, but one of great importance in the production of fertiliser for use on crops. The ritual involved calling on the Keng San Maiden to descend from the manure pit into an empty wicker basket, carrying the (invisible) deity back to the main room of the house, and calling on the deity to 'write' on rice bran scattered on the dining table. The girls would ask questions of the deity relating to their future husbands, their married life and future children, all matters of burning interest to unmarried women in China. One could speculate that the cult allowed these girls a sense of control over their own destiny, or provided a source of consolation in a situation where they appear to be the powerless objects of a patriarchal marriage system. McLaren concludes that this cult 'shows how even very humble activities, such as the removal of human waste, were infused with ritual significance in traditional village settings'.

These two examples offer insights into the very little studied world of women's 'ritual work' in pre-modern China. The next two case studies, however, provide dramatic evidence of women expanding their ritual power to areas such as ancestral and community rituals traditionally denied to them. In Jiayuan village, Guangdong, the reform era has allowed affluent families compete to build lavish tombs and memorial stones for their ancestors. Women preside over these rituals, in a dramatic turnaround of past practices, which expressly prohibited women from taking part in the ancestral cult. The wives of Communist Party cadres are heavily involved. The cadres turn a blind eye or even aid their wives but find it impolitic to play a leading role. In Dazuo village in Fujian, women play a leading role in religious activities at an individual, household, lineage and regional level. Economic circumstances too have shaped this surprising emergence of the ritually powerful woman. Women do most of the heavy work of the village, even heavy construction work done elsewhere by men, while the men engage in the more lucrative occupations of fishing and stone-carving. These occupations often take the men far away from the village, thus leaving a communal space in which women have seized ritual control over ancestral worship, propitiation of ghosts and the supernatural protection of households. Women serve as spirit mediums and preside over the birthday celebrations of the major village deities. One could conclude here that the strict gender divisions of labour have 'opened up a public and private ritual space in which women could find new forms of agency'.

Overall, the chapters in this volume contribute to the impression of women's opportunity and agency in the reform period rather than to their disadvantage. However, it is clear too that women at the lower levels of domestic service and the hierarchy of prostitution are at risk of abuse. In this volume we have chosen to focus on 'new' and emerging occupations for women rather than on the plight of the middle-aged woman who has been stood down from her post in the state sector, or the rural girls removed from schools to work in the fields, while their brothers are sent on to further education or lucrative jobs in the townships. Nor have we dealt with the kinds of women who have suffered victimisation as a result of rampant discrimination, such as the sad cases described so eloquently in Xinran's *The Good Women of China* (2002).

This snapshot of women in the reform era is obviously partial and incomplete. Nonetheless, the women discussed here are representative of an important cross-section of Chinese women, those whose life-styles, marriage patterns and careers are intextricably shaped by the forces of globalisation and the internationalisation of definitions of labour. The maid in the homes of affluent Beijingers is the object of the 'civilising' project of 'modernity' and is pulling her family and kin into broad circuits of labour migration and exchange. The girl in the massage parlour or the karaoke bar may not be a legal 'sex worker' from the point of view of the Chinese government, but she is a type of quasi-legal 'prostitute' whom the Chinese state alternately nurtures and prohibits. The demanding brides of Zhejiang Province are stimulating powerful currents of consumer aspiration, internal labour migration and the transfer of property between generations. The mansions they require are elaborations of suburban 'utopias' derived from Western consumption patterns and are designed with the decor and spatial configuration appropriate for the 'modern' nuclear family. The age of information technology has brought new opportunities for the managerial woman to network with transnational Internet communities of women across the Chinese-speaking realms of Asia. Women educators too adopt professional models based on competence in new media technologies.

New ideas, together with new patterns of labour, now shape the consciousness of these women. Village women, now serving as domestic workers in urban centres learn to value independence from their natal family and the relative privacy of their new occupations. Domestic critics of the Chinese government's ambivalent policy towards prostitutes are influenced by Western arguments about human rights, private sexual acts and individual choice. Women managers in the private sector relish the challenge of greater occupational choice and income than before, while seeking to adapt to a workplace defined as inherently 'masculine'. Women educators, when working with multi-media, base their teaching on Western pedagogic models and Western content. 'Spoilt' products of the One Child Policy are taught to survive like Robinson Crusoe in the countryside.

As for the role of the state, in many cases examined here it has intervened in a developing market after the event rather than seeking to regulate it from inception. For example, the trade in maids went from being a casual street encounter to one where the state set up regulation and training agencies. In the case of prostitution, the role of the state is more complex. It cannot regulate what must remain illegal but periodically seeks to shut down enterprises that engage in activities deemed to be 'non-regulated'. Issues of public security and government corruption have spurred the state to take action. Women play a minimal role in China's Communist Party and political system but the state has ambitious goals to increase their numbers. As in the past, the rhetoric of women's emancipation is of signal importance to the state, which relies for its legitimacy on perceptions that under 'socialism', especially 'socialism with Chinese characteristics', the equality of men and women is better protected than in the rampant capitalism of the West.

References

Croll, E. J. (1994) *From Heaven to Earth: Images and Experiences of Development in China*, London: Routledge.

—— (1995) *Changing Identities of Chinese Women: Rhetoric, Experience, and Self-perception in Twentieth-century China*, Atlantic Highlands, NJ: Zed Books.

Davis, D. and Harrell, S. (1993) *Chinese Families in the Post-Mao Era*, Berkeley: University of California Press.

Entwisle, B. and Henderson, G. E. (2000) *Re-drawing Boundaries: Work, Households, and Gender in China*, Berkeley and Los Angeles: University of California Press.

Gates, Hill (1996) *China's Motor: A Thousand Years of Petty Capitalism*, Ithaca, NY: Cornell University Press.

Jacka, T. (1997) *Women's Work in Rural China: Change and Continuity in an Era of Reform*, Cambridge, New York and Melbourne: Cambridge University Press.

Judd, E. R. (1994) *Gender and Power in Rural North China*, Stanford, CA: Stanford University Press.

McDermott, J. P. (1990) 'The Chinese Domestic Bursar', *Ajia Bunka Kenkyū* (Nov.): 15–23.

Rofel, L. (1999) *Other Modernities: Gendered Yearnings in China after Socialism*, Berkeley: University of California Press.

Xinran (2000) *The Good Women of China: Hidden Voices*, trans. E. Tyldesley, London: Chatto & Windus.

Yang, Mayfair (1994) *Gifts, Favors and Banquets: The Art of Social Relationships in China*, Ithaca, NY: Cornell University Press.

Part I

'New' domains in the Chinese market economy

1   Why women count

Chinese women and the leadership of reform

David S. G. Goodman

Since the end of the 1970s, and the introduction of an incremental series of measures that have sought to reform the previously existing system of state socialism, the People's Republic of China (PRC) has experienced a sustained period of rapid economic growth, and dramatic social change. The clear winners in this process have been those in the new rich socio-economic categories, who have emerged with and driven much of the change. They include those who have established new kinds of enterprise that reach beyond the previous economic structures, as well as those who have provided new services to meet the demands of both the state and society in a period of rapid economic restructuring and subsequent social change (Goodman 1996). The clear losers have been the peasantry in the poorer rural areas, especially those located in the interior provinces of China's West.[1]

Although during the 1980s and early 1990s some external academic observers raised concerns that the processes of change might leave women amongst the most disadvantaged, the impact of reform has clearly been more mixed, and not susceptible to such ready analysis. Certainly the absence of state protection for women economically and the withdrawal of affirmative action supporting their participation in politics have resulted in lower income, the loss of any substantive share of positions of formal political power, and even weaker conditions of employment (Honig and Hershatter 1988; Hooper 1984: 317; Maurer-Fazio *et al.* 1999: 55–8; Rosen 1994). However, more recent research since the mid-1990s has highlighted the more complex picture that emerges with the disaggregation of women by various social, political, economic and cultural criteria, including socio-economic category, region, generation, and interaction with the networks of relationships that bind family and locality with national and international processes of production.

Some women have clearly been disadvantaged by reform, and often quite explicitly because they were women. For example, those women workers in former state-owned and -operated enterprises have found themselves the first put out of work as a result of economic restructuring and down-sizing, on the grounds that women should not be regarded as the principal income-earner in each family. At the same time, it is also clear that the development of production lines in new light industrial enterprises in South and East China has provided other women with new employment opportunities, and again often explicitly because they were women. In this case the argument of their employers has been some variation on a theme that women are more likely to be suited to this kind of work, as well as cheaper, and less likely to make trouble in the workplace. Of course, even successful negotiation of the opportunities that have emerged with reform may mean simultaneously dealing with difficulties, as in this case where the circumstances and consequences of factory employment may be little more than wage slavery.[2] While a few commentators have continued to highlight only the disadvantages to women (Hooper 1998: 167–93; Org 2001), it has become more usual to consider the double-sided impact of reform on women in general, and even more, on women in specific situations and on specific groups of women, in particular.[3] It is even clear that some women – such as the cultural workers described by McLaren (1998) in the Lower Yangtze Delta – have been able to negotiate their ways successfully through the dramatically changing social currents to stake out territory for their own development.

All the same, at leadership levels the evidence would seem at first sight to be relatively clear cut. Two decades of reform have considerably reduced the number and proportion of women serving in senior positions of political leadership. There remain, as before, few women who are senior leaders of the Chinese Communist Party (CCP), ministers of the central government, or provincial leaders of the party-state. While women continue to serve as deputy mayors in China's cities, and hold a number of ministerial appointments, and while every provincial leadership group has a required woman, their numbers remain low and the proportion of women on the CCP's Central Committee has fallen.[4] This lack of leadership responsibilities also seems to have been mirrored in the ranks of the emerging new entrepreneurs, exceptionally few of whom are women. Indeed, most of the academic analysis of the developing private sector of the economy or of the new-style capitalists readily acknowledges this gender imbalance (Gold 1989; Pearson 1997; Guthrie 1999).

In contrast, the results of a survey of the local elite in Shanxi Province, North China, during the late 1990s suggests that women's lack of participation even in the leadership of reform may have been more apparent than substantial. It was certainly the case that in Shanxi women did not fill the positions regarded as those of economic or political leadership in any significant numbers. At the same time the survey suggests that many women played significant roles in the leadership of the new economy. Most significantly, the new enterprises of the reform era were often family affairs, at least to the extent that they were based on the joint efforts of husbands and wives. Where the husband was presented as the designated entrepreneur, the wife was frequently also active in the same enterprise, in many cases acting as its bookkeeper and business manager. To some extent the apparent lack of participation was a matter of definition, with women's role in the leadership of reform rarely if ever acknowledged within the PRC, and as a result less likely to be reflected in any account of the process of change.

There was an inherent invisibility to this role of women in the leadership of reform that is of course not confined by any means to the PRC. The invisibility of women in the work-force, of specific kinds of 'women's work', and of women whose domestic workload is discounted (both those employed for wages outside the family home, and those who are not) are all topics that have begun to be examined in the context of many societies around the world, and not just by those who regard themselves as feminist economists (Waring 1988, 2nd ed. 1999; Ferber and Nelson 1993). At the same time the prevalence of the family in enterprise development, and the related invisibility of women's work within family enterprises are also not new themes in the history of Chinese culture.

There is much in common with many, though not all, of the enterprises that were described by interviewees in Shanxi during the late 1990s and those identified by Hill Gates as examples of 'petty capitalism' both in China's pre-1949 past and more recently on Taiwan: essentially family-based and male-dominated enterprises, whose transactional activities were characterised by personalism even when operating in an open market (Gates 1996). Necessarily, in those enterprises, amongst other related qualities, women were for the most part also economically invisible, even when, as in Taiwan after 1950, they came to play a major role in the development of such enterprises alongside their husbands, often too as business managers and book-keepers.[5] Moreover, commentators on the development of the Taiwan economy have highlighted the extent to which working women, even when not invisible, had their work, regardless of whether it was inside or outside the household, defined as an extension of family duties.

Social change in Shanxi

The information on Chinese women presented here is drawn from a survey of social change in Shanxi Province undertaken during the period 1996–98.[6] Shanxi is a North China province that in 1998 had 31.7 million people, a GDP of 160 million yuan RMB, and a GDP per capita of 5,072 yuan RMB.[7] Although it is, and has been for the previous seventy years, one of the country's major heavy industrial bases, with exceptionally large and high-quality resources of coal, its reputation within China is one of peasant radicalism. It was the site of the major front-line base areas against Japanese invasion during the War of Resistance of 1937–45; and the later Mao-era model production brigade of Dazhai is located in its east. Since the 1920s Shanxi has been an established major centre for heavy industry, and it currently produces large proportions of China's coal, coke, aluminum, electricity and specialist steels. The lack of understanding of Shanxi's local conditions more generally is not too surprising given its mountainous topography and lack of transport links with the rest of China. Other Chinese were effectively hindered from visiting Shanxi, let alone doing business there, until a massive road-building programme made the province more accessible during the mid-1990s.[8]

Until the 1990s, provincial economic development had depended heavily on central government investment, growing fastest during the mid-1950s and mid-1980s: it was only during the mid-1990s that sustained, though still only moderate, above-national-average rates of growth were achieved without that support. This less spectacular economic profile, and other aspects of its economy, means that

Shanxi has more in common with many of China's provinces – particularly those inland – than the more economically advanced coastal provinces of Guangdong, Zhejiang and Jiangsu; as well as the large municipalities of Beijing and Shanghai.

In the 1990s Shanxi's economic structure ceased to revolve solely around the central state sector, though it still played a sizeable role in provincial development. There was relatively little foreign interaction with the province though there was considerable domestic investment from and trade with other parts of China, particularly in the development of the collective and private sectors of the economy. By 1997, 32 per cent of the province's Gross Value of Industrial Production (GVIO) was produced by the state sector, all of which was in heavy industry, compared to a national average of 25.5 per cent. The derivation of 37.1 per cent of provincial GVIO was from the collective (or local government) sector of the economy, based predominantly on coal industry support activities and by-products, compared to a national average of 38.1 per cent. Production of 17.9 per cent of GVIO came nationally from the private sector of the economy, whereas in Shanxi a much higher 26.8 per cent of provincial GVIO came from the private sector, with production based in the new technologies, foodstuffs and textiles ('Shanxi Jianhang' 1996: 9). In 1997, only 4.1 per cent of GVIO was derived from the foreign-funded sector of the economy, compared to a national average of 18.5 per cent.[9] In 1998, industrial production was 47.5 per cent of GDP in Shanxi, agricultural production was 13 per cent of GDP, whilst the retail and other service sectors were (and remain) dominated by private entrepreneurs (Shanxi tongji nianjian 1998: 19).

Two hundred and seventy-nine members of the provincial and local elite were interviewed in Shanxi Province during the period 1996–98. Although it would be hard to argue that those selected for interview were statistically representative or randomly chosen, interviewees were drawn from all over the province, and from a variety of industries, occupations and types of location. Of those interviewed, 54 were leading cadres and 225 were identified as members of the 'new rich' – the essential leaders of economic reform in the province.

The category of the new rich is defined by position in the economy, as well as by wealth and patterns of expenditure (Robison and Goodman 1996a; esp. Robison and Goodman 1996b: 1–16). In particular, in the China of the 1990s it included all those entrepreneurs who had benefited from the changed economic environment of the reform era to develop new types of enterprises. While large numbers of these new rich were owner-operators from the private sector, the concept also includes managers of various kinds from different parts of the economy, including a few in the private sector, who, although they may often own equity in the enterprise they manage, also gain their status from a position of leadership. It even includes managers in the state sector of the economy who had reformed the enterprises for which they were responsible to take advantage of the new economic environment. However, the majority of managers among the ranks of the new rich were to be found in collective (urban and rural), equity-based and foreign-funded enterprises, many of which had developed from originally private enterprises.[10] While many are far wealthier, a convenient guideline is to expect members of the new rich to receive a monthly income at least equivalent to the average annual income per capita in their locality. In Shanxi this would indicate that members of the new rich had an income in excess of 60,000 yuan RMB a year during 1998.

Table 1.1 provides summary information on those leading cadres and members of the new rich who were interviewed by levels of administration (for cadres), category of enterprise (for members of the new rich), and by gender. As Table 1.1 indicates, those interviewed were overwhelmingly male. Unsurprisingly, and in keeping with the expected gender difference, very few of the leading cadres were women: only 2 of the 54 interviewed. As a regular practice, the provincial committee of the CCP includes amongst its leadership only one woman, who is usually a Vice Governor of the Provincial Government, and who equally usually has responsibilities for education, health care and social services. Of the 225 entrepreneurs who were identified and interviewed as examples of the province's new rich, only 12 were women. By far the largest concentration of these was the 9 interviewees who were owner-operators of private sector enterprises.

While the 12 women entrepreneurs and 2 women cadres who were interviewed may provide some information about the role of women in contemporary China, the interviews with the 201 married male entrepreneurs and the 52 married leading cadres[11] also reveal information about their wives that can additionally and possibly more usefully (because of the larger number involved) be interrogated. This information is clearly not comprehensive – there is, for example, almost no detail available about the social or political background of the parents of the interviewee's wives, unlike that for their husbands, and details of the CCP membership of interviewees' wives are patchy at best. Moreover,

Table 1.1 Women in leadership positions: cadres and the new rich (number and percentage of interviewees in Shanxi, 1996–98, by category)

Category	Interviewees (no.)	Women (no.)	%
Leadership cadres	54	2	3.7
Provincial administration	18	0	
District-level	12	1	
County	12	1	
Section	12	0	
New rich entrepreneurs	225	12	5.3
State-sector managers	50	0	
Urban collective managers	33	2	
Rural collective managers	32	0	
Equity-based enterprise managers	26	0	
Joint-venture and private-sector managers	17	1	
Private-sector owner-operators	67	9	

there are clear methodological difficulties in asking husbands about their wives and their activities. Only occasionally in the course of the interviews were wives in attendance and even more rarely was it possible to interview or talk to them as well. Nonetheless, in the absence of alternative sources of information, these interviews do provide an indication of the background and roles of those women, and particularly their involvement in the development of both reform in general, and more specifically the new enterprises that have been at the heart of the process of change. While the survey was not specifically designed to extract information about women's role in reform, its findings on this topic are so interesting that it seemed worthwhile articulating these results, albeit as preliminary results and suggesting further research agendas.

Information about women in Shanxi's elite under reform derived from the interviews is considered in terms of three broad groups: the wives of the new rich entrepreneurs; the wives of leading cadres; and those few women who are either leading cadres or entrepreneurs in their own right. Although the detail is by no means as rich, the profile of the women that emerges is largely similar to that of the men who were more widely presented as local and provincial leaders. In particular, the latter were characterised by their intense localism, and the ties that bound them in various ways to the party-state (Goodman 2001: 132–56). There is, however, one crucial difference that characterises the women at the centre of Shanxi's elite: in addition to being the wives of the new rich and the wives of cadres, occasionally women entrepreneurs, and even more occasionally leading cadres, they were all almost without exception also mothers.[12] Moreover, the size of family was by no means as restricted as might be thought to have resulted from the implementation of the 'one-child policy'. There is no suggestion that the women who appear as having been economically, or for that matter politically, active either had small families in order to return quickly to the workforce, or forwent having children for whatever reason.

The numbers presented in Table 1.2, on the average number of children per family for different categories of the local elite, indicates that small families were not the norm. Exactly comparable figures for either the Shanxi population as a whole, or those who were neither members of the new rich nor cadres, are not available. However, in 1998 the average size of family in Shanxi was 3.63 people, just slightly above the national average of 3.58 people. In comparison, as can be readily calculated from Table 1.2, the various categories of Shanxi's elite had an average family size that ranged from at least 3.79 to 4.7 people (*Zhongguo tongji nianjian* 1999: 99, Table 4–5, 'Household, Population and Sex Ratio by Region'). Perhaps even more remarkably, these indicators of family size are not significantly different if calculations are made in terms of those couples who married before, and those who married after, the introduction of the 'one-child policy' in 1979.

Wives of the new rich

Contemporary magazines and television programmes in the PRC are prone to portray the life-styles of the new rich and occasionally famous in terms of their

Table 1.2 Children of interviewees (number, 1996–98, by category of interviewee)

Category of interviewee	Average size of family (no. of children)
Cadres	2.19
Managers	
State sector	1.79
Urban collective	1.90
Rural collective	2.50
Equity-based enterprise	1.90
Joint venture and private sector	2.70
Owner-operators	1.90

houses, expenditure patterns and leisure activities.[13] The wives play such a central role in this process that the reader or viewer could be forgiven for thinking that most if not all of the wives of the new rich were 'non-working wives,' a description preferred by the new rich themselves to that of 'housewife'.[14] This is not an unimportant distinction. 'Work' in this context is very much conceptualised as paid employment outside the home. A non-working wife (*meigongzuo de furen* or more colloquially *meigongzuo de laopo*) is seen as someone who has the ability to obtain work, and may at some time have been in the workforce, but now because of the family's wealth (it is implied) chooses not to work. A housewife (*jiating zhufu* or more locally in Shanxi, *jiating funü*) is regarded as someone of considerably lower status, who has no experience of or ability to obtain work outside the home. On those few occasions when interviewees indicated that their wife was 'just a housewife', the voice dropped, and there was a hint of shame.

There certainly were wives of the new rich who were non-working and others who were housewives. However, this is by no means the dominant characterisation of the wives of the new rich in the Shanxi local elite that emerges from the survey of 1996–98. On the contrary, the non-working wife appears as a minority in every one of the various different categories of the new rich. The wives of the new rich were more usually professionally active, often alongside their husbands.

Two important, and related, keys to understanding the involvement of the wives of the new rich in reform are the extreme parochialism and the family basis of much of social and economic development. The wives of the new rich not only came from similar backgrounds to that of their husbands, but they often also came from the same location, grew up together, and at least partly in consequence ended up working together. Particularly as far as rural society is concerned this finding indicates considerable change from earlier insistences on exogamous marriage (Stacey 1983: 218). At times that emphasis had even extended to a ban on marriages between people with the same surname regardless of lineage relationships, despite the consequences given the limited number of Chinese family names (Croll 1981: 80ff.). Although such restrictions on the definition of exogamy and its operationalisation were modified by the Marriage Law of 1950, and although practices have clearly varied across China and with changes in the wider political and socio-economic environments,[15] it remained the norm for women to move away from their native place to get married. Collectivisation was built around and reinforced patrilocal lineages, and at least in part native village exogamy was identified as a major check on women's ability to attain local positions of economic and political leadership since they would subsequently lack the necessary local knowledge and access to networks of influence (Diamond 1975: 25; Johnson 1983: 220ff). All the same, the social emphasis on exogamy had clearly begun to change somewhat by the 1970s and 1980s, when studies of rural areas in both South and North China indicated that in contrast to previous practices it was not unusual for about a third of all peasants to be married within the village. [16]

The evidence from the interviews conducted in Shanxi is certainly that much of economic development was family-centred, or perhaps more accurately husband-and-wife-centred. Larger, sometimes extended, families still existed, but as other research has clearly identified, particularly in the rural sector economic success had led to a decline in household size and to a greater focus by peasants on the role of the nuclear family.[17] Especially in the private sector of the economy, husbands and wives worked together. However, it is also clear that husbands and wives also worked in the same enterprise in other sectors of the economy./

A distinct pattern of family management is suggested from interviews with entrepreneurs who were either owner-operators (in the private sector) or, to a lesser extent, running enterprises that had grown from originally private-sector enterprises. The husband was the managing director of the enterprise and its external face, whose name appeared on the formal documentation associated with the enterprise. He was responsible for the establishment of the enterprise; all aspects of negotiations with local (and where appropriate superior) governments; and the production process, if specialist staff were not also employed.

In most cases the wife was presented as essentially the business manager. She was described as most usually being responsible for the administrative infrastructure of the enterprise, and in particular its financial management. Depending on the size of the enterprise, her responsibilities might also have included personnel and related matters. However, a primary concern was clearly looking after the books. It was quite common to find that in the development of the enterprise the wife had found the need to acquire both basic book-keeping and sometimes more advanced accountancy skills and qualifications through further study, usually at a local technical college, though there were three cases where a wife had decided to move further afield (and even, in one instance, to Beijing) in order to acquire an undergraduate degree in commerce.

Studies of the process of reform in other parts of China, while tending to focus on the role of local government rather than the family, nonetheless emphasise the extent to which social and economic development is local and characterised by a rhetoric of parochialism (White 1998; Oi 1999; Whiting 2001). Parochialism in Shanxi may indeed be no stronger a force in the process of change than elsewhere in China. However, it is also possible that there are particularly provincial forces at work in this case. Until the mid-1990s, communications around the province and with the rest of China were extremely limited. Social mobility was consequently low, and the localism of marriage patterns was reinforced by the particularities of local languages that tend to be county specific.

The impressions of parochialism and family-based enterprise are certainly reinforced by other demographic and career indicators of the wives of the new rich. Table 1.3 provides information on the age and educational background of the wives of the new rich and cadres, as well as parenthetically of their husbands. It indicates that the wives of the new rich were most usually a couple of years younger than their husbands. The exception was those who are married to owner-operators, who were more usually the same age. This particular statistic reflects other characteristics of those couples who established private-sector enterprises, notably the high probability that they had grown up together.

Table 1.4 details the birthplace of the wives of the new rich and cadres. Almost three-quarters of the wives of the new rich were born in the same place as their husbands. 'Place' in this case is operationalised as town or county. While these are fairly broad operational categories, later evidence will indicate the narrowness of the identification rather than its breadth. For all categories of the new rich, except that of state sector managers, the majority of wives were born in the same place as their husbands. Even for the category of state sector managers the proportion is only just under half. This and other differences in the proportion of wives of the new rich with the same birthplace as their husbands

Table 1.3 Wives of the new rich and cadres: age and education

	Average age of wives at year's end 1998	Highest educational level				
		University (%)	College (%)	Middle school (%)	Primary (%)	None (%)
Cadres	50 (51)	40 (49)	34 (41)	23 (10)	3	
State-sector managers	46 (48)	17 (49)	33 (21)	44 (27)	3 (3)	3
Urban collective managers	45 (48)	19 (31)	19 (34)	55 (34)	7 (1)	
Rural collective managers	44 (47)	4 (6)	7 (19)	75 (69)	14 (6)	
Equity-based enterprise managers	38 (42)	15 (40)	23 (7)	62 (47)	(6)	
Joint-venture and private-sector managers	43 (45)	16 (45)	34 (37)	50 (18)		
Private-sector owner-operators	42 (41)	5 (16)	22 (16)	66 (59)	7 (9)	

Note: Figures in parentheses are equivalents for husbands in each category.

Table 1.4 Wives of the new rich and cadres: birthplace (number and percentage in Shanxi, 1996–98, by category of interviewee)

	Interviewee							
	Manager					*Owner-operator*	*Total new rich*	*Cadre*
	State sector	*Collective*		*Equity-based enterprise*	*Joint venture & private*			
		urban	*rural*					
Birthplace of wife:								
Same as husband	19	23	22	12	10	42	128	28
Not same as husband	20	6	8	7	2	6	49	21
Not known	11	2	2	2	1	6	24	3
Total	50	31	32	21	13	54	201	52
% of wives born in same place as husband	48.7	79.3	73.3	63.2	83.3	87.5	72.3	57.1

were presumably a function of social mobility. Managers of state sector enterprises usually have a career pattern that sees them move away from home at an early age, with the opportunities often denied others to meet spouses from another location.[18]

As Table 1.3 indicates, while the wives of the new rich were generally less educated than their husbands, from the perspective of the distribution of the highest level of education achieved, the difference was certainly not great. Fewer wives had graduated from university, but the numbers of husbands and wives who had participated in higher education of all kinds was roughly equal. In the case of private-sector entrepreneurs, the proportion of wives who were graduates from higher education (university and college combined) was actually higher than that of their husbands.

The educational link, and particularly at an early age, is clearly important for understanding some of the dynamics of husband and wife interaction in the new economy. Table 1.5 lists husbands and wives who first met through being in class together in the formal system of education. Almost half of the new rich couples had first met this way. Remarkably, almost four in every ten couples had first met in kindergarten. Given the high proportion of couples who, as already noted, had married within their county, this might have been an expected consequence of the emergence of enterprises in the rural collective and private sectors of the economy, where development was fuelled by a rhetoric of local identification and motivation (Goodman 2003). However, the proportion of couples who met in kindergarten was not low in any category of the new rich.

Table 1.6 provides information on the workplace of the wives of the new rich, and Table 1.7 on the occupation of the wives of the new rich and cadres, as revealed through the interviews with their husbands. As Table 1.6 indicates, almost half of all wives and husbands worked together in the same enterprise.

Table 1.5 The new rich and cadres: education as a meeting place for marriage (number and percentage in Shanxi, 1996–98, by category of interviewee)

	Interviewee									
	Manager					*Owner-operator*	*Total new rich*	*(%)*	*Cadre*	*(%)*
	State sector	*Collective*		*Equity-based enterprise*	*Joint venture & private*					
		urban	*rural*							
Original meeting place: spouses met in										
Kindergarten	10	7	11	7	3	20	58	39.5	13	29.6
Secondary school	2	1	–	–	–	–	3	2.0	2	4.6
Higher education	1	2	–	–	5	–	8	5.4	4	9.1
Did not meet spouse through kindergarten, secondary school or higher education	22	7	16	7	6	20	78	53.0	25	56.8
Unknown	15	16	5	7	0	23	66	–	10	–
Total	50	33	32	21	14	63	213	–	54	–

Table 1.6 Wives of the new rich: workplace (number and percentage in Shanxi, 1996–98, by category of interviewee)

	Interviewee						
	Manager					Owner-operator	Total new rich
	State sector	Collective		Equity-based enterprise	Joint venture & private		
		urban	rural				
Workplace of wife:							
Same as husband	18	6	11	8	4	43	88
Not same as husband	25	25	19	12	7	4	94
Not known	7		2	1	2	7	19
Total	50	31	32	21	13	54	201
Per cent of wives working in same enterprise as husband	41.8	19.4	36.7	40.0	36.4	91.5	48.4

Necessarily, there were different proportions of husbands and wives in the same workplace across the different categories of the new rich. In the private sector, owner-operators and their wives almost always worked together; elsewhere the proportion was more usually four in every ten. The exception was the urban collective sector where only one in five couples worked in the same enterprise.

As the information presented in Table 1.7 suggests, wives were often employed as accountants and bookkeepers, not only, as already noted, in the running of family concerns in the private sector but also in other types of enterprise. Because of their interchangeable usage in contemporary Shanxi, and mostly elsewhere in China (though it would seem that this started to change somewhat during the late 1990s), no distinction has been made between 'bookkeeper' and 'accountant'.

The notion that the wives of the new rich were 'non-working' is flatly contradicted by Table 1.7. Not only were a quarter of the wives of the new rich employed as bookkeepers and accountants, but goodly proportions were also employed as teachers and cadres. Altogether, professional or white-collar work accounted for 67 per cent of the occupations of the wives of the new rich. The number of wives who were teachers are distributed across all categories of the new rich, but those who were cadres were largely wives of managers of state sector enterprises, reinforcing the role of that kind of enterprise as socially a part of the party-state, even when reformed (Steinfeld 1998). Indeed, regardless of their occupation, many of those who were the wife of a manager in the state sector were also members of the CCP themselves.

Cadre's wives

While there were very few women appointed to leadership positions as cadres in Shanxi, the wives of those who were the leading cadres also played an important

Table 1.7 Wives of the new rich and cadres: occupation (number and percentage in Shanxi, 1996–98, by category of interviewee)

Occupation of wife:	Interviewee									
	Manager			Equity-based enterprise	Joint venture & private	Owner-operator	Total new rich	(%)	Cadre	(%)
	State sector	Collective								
		urban	rural							
Professional	2	4	–	–	–	1	7	3.8	4	8.2
Doctor	1	3	–	–	–	–	4	2.2	5	10.2
Accountant or bookkeeper	3	1	3	3	1	35	46	25.0	6	12.2
Teacher	5	6	2	2	1	3	19	10.3	4	8.2
People's Liberation Army	–	–	–	–	–	–	–	–	1	2.0
Cadre	14	1	–	4	3	3	25	13.6	17	34.7
Manager	5	–	–	4	1	–	10	5.4	1	2.0
Technician	2	1	1	–	–	–	4	2.2	3	6.1
Administrative work	4	3	1	2	–	2	12	6.5	1	2.0
Worker	4	6	8	–	2	–	20	10.9	2	4.1
Unemployed	–	1	1	–	–	–	2	1.1	–	–
Retired	2	4	2	–	1	2	11	6.0	2	4.1
Non-working (house)wife	1	1	12	4	3	3	24	13.0	3	6.1
Unknown	7	–	2	2	1	5	17	–	3	–
Total	50	31	32	21	13	54	201		52	

role in the reform process. Unlike their counterparts among the wives of the new rich, they were almost certain, by virtue of their husband's work, not to have worked together. However, by the same token, they were also likely to be better educated and to be professionally employed. Their role in reform was not as leading cadres but rather as the professionals and managers who provided state, social and enterprise support services for economic development: as engineers, lawyers, doctors, accountants, teachers, managers, administrators and cadres.

As Table 1.3 indicates, the age and educational profile of leading cadres' wives and those of their husbands were very similar. The overwhelming majority of cadres' wives had received some form of higher education. Indeed, were graduation from the political party schools to be excluded from the calculation, it might be possible to mount an argument that leading cadres' wives had higher levels of education than their husbands.

Moreover, in this and other respects, there were clear differences among the wives of cadres at different levels of the system, and in particular, between those of leading cadres within the provincial administration on the one hand, and those of the local leading cadres at county level and within the county on the other.[19] Local leading cadres were less likely to have been university educated and more likely to have received higher education only through a Party school. The wives of local leading cadres were similarly likely to have received less education, while the wives of cadres at the provincial level were more likely to have been university graduates.

The selection and training processes that attended the careers of leading cadres (as opposed to other less politicised cadres) usually took them away from their roots. Moreover, while the CCP has in general no 'law of avoidance' such as existed under the imperial system of rule, in Shanxi at least it was rare to find a leading cadre below the provincial level serving in their home county or district. Under these circumstances it might be assumed that the extreme localism noted in the marriage patterns of the new rich was not repeated for couples where the husband was a leading cadre. However, this was not entirely the case. The leading cadres at the district and county levels and within the county replicated those characteristics to a high degree.

Table 1.4 suggests that in general just over half of all couples where the husband was a leading cadre were born in either the same town or the same county. Table 1.5 suggests that a quarter of all the leading cadres interviewed and their wives met for the first time in kindergarten. The exceptions to both these characterisations were the leading cadres in the provincial administration and their wives. Though some of the leading cadres from the provincial administration and their wives came from the same location and met early on in their educational careers, it was more usual for them to have been from different parts of China and to have met later. Indeed, the only leading cadres who were revealed in interviews as having met their wives at university were those working at the provincial level of the administration.

Information on the employment of the wives of leading cadres is provided in Table 1.7. There are, once again, differences between the wives of the local cadres and the wives of those in the provincial administration. Many of the latter were themselves members of the CCP, and worked as cadres in various other offices of the party-state. Over a third of leading cadres' wives were employed as cadres, though interestingly the wives of provincial-level leading cadres were equally likely to have been employed in some professional occupation such as an engineer or doctor. At the county level and within the county, leading cadres' wives were more likely to be employed as teachers and accountants, in addition to serving as cadres. Of the wives of leading cadres interviewed 83.5 per cent were employed in professional or white-collar jobs. Almost all the wives of provincial-level leading cadres were members of the CCP.

Women cadres and women entrepreneurs

Twelve women entrepreneurs and two female leading cadres do not really provide an adequate sample for any kind of generalisation about the role of women leaders in reform. It was precisely for this reason that information was sought in interviews with husbands about their wives' economic and political behaviour. Nonetheless, any attempt at analysis must clearly include their experience.

The two female leading cadres interviewed represented two very different social backgrounds and careers. One was the daughter of a revolutionary cadre, who had joined the CCP forces during the War of Resistance to Japan at the very heart of a major Communist border region. Her father had gone on to become a leading cadre himself after the establishment of the PRC. A graduate of the Central Party School, his daughter had become a leading cadre after working in the hierarchy of the Youth League. Her husband was also a CCP member and a technical worker, and the family were able to live together. The other female leading cadre had been recruited to the CCP when a university student in Shanxi, and had worked as a researcher in a technological area before moving on to become a leading cadre at district level. Her husband was also a leading cadre, though at provincial level, thus requiring them to live apart.

The twelve women entrepreneurs interviewed were active in a wide variety of economic activity. The companies they ran were involved in transportation; automotive engineering; retail (a beauty shop, a clothes shop); a hotel; the manufacture of furniture, clothes, office fittings and leather products; and seed production. Only one of the women entrepreneurs was not married, and ten were long-term members of the CCP. Only one of the women entrepreneurs was a university graduate, though two others had also received higher education. All the rest had completed middle school.

The evidence from the interviews of the twelve women entrepreneurs suggests the centrality of the party-state in the process of economic development, as was the case more generally for the new rich (Goodman 1998: 39–62). Only two of the women entrepreneurs interviewed were not members of the CCP, and in every case membership predated the involvement in enterprise management or development. The two women entrepreneurs who were not CCP members themselves had parents who were not only Party members but also leading cadres. Moreover, six of the eleven married women entrepreneurs had husbands who were leading cadres, all within Shanxi.

The place of localism as part of the explanation of economic development is much less certain for these female entrepreneurs, though it clearly played a role in determining the marriage prospects for the interviewees. Of the eleven married women entrepreneurs, eight had married a husband from their birthplace, and three of the couples had first met at school. However, unlike the evidence from the interviews with the male members of the new-rich about their wives, it would seem that husbands of women entrepreneurs did not work with their spouses to the same extent as the couples to be found working together where the husband was identified as the entrepreneur. Only three of the husbands of new rich women entrepreneurs worked in the enterprise established by their wives; though necessarily too much of a conclusion cannot be drawn from such a small sample. All the same, none of the women entrepreneurs had a husband who was employed as an accountant or bookkeeper.

Women in the leadership of social change

A survey of predominantly male entrepreneurs and leading cadres in Shanxi might at first sight seem to be a most unpromising place to start looking for evidence of the role of women in the leadership in reform. Clearly, there are methodological problems in interviewing husbands about their wives' activities, whatever those might be, and any conclusions must consequently necessarily be kept in perspective. Nonetheless, the results from that survey point not only to the importance of localism and the party-state in social and economic change, but also to the role of the family in enterprise development and to the roles of women in the leadership of reform.

Shanxi Province is usually regarded by Chinese as a socially conservative part of the PRC, as well as less economically developed. These two features may necessarily be mutually reinforcing, not least because in Shanxi itself they are recognised not without some pride. Regardless of such considerations, it was clearly the case that in Shanxi few women were to be found publicly identified as the leaders of either local politics or economic development during the late 1990s. However, this does not mean that women might not have had a role to play in reform, or even in the leadership of reform, albeit less publicly acknowledged.

In Shanxi Province during the 1990s social and economic change was characterised by an intense parochialism. It was manifested most obviously from a social perspective by the numbers of leading cadres and members of the new rich who married spouses from their own backgrounds, and even from their own birthplaces. One important consequence was that this parochialism then contributed to the operation of the party-state's central role in both promoting economic development and providing the social and political networks to support reform in general and enterprise development in particular. Another, equally important consequence was that this parochialism was associated with the emergence of family enterprises in which husbands and wives worked together. It is these consequences of parochialism that highlight the role of women in reform, and that placed many women in effective if not formal positions of leadership in economic development.

The evidence of the survey is that the wives of the new rich played a leading role in the development of the enterprises for which their husbands were better known. This was true across most of the different types of new enterprise generated by reform, but particularly the case for private sector enterprises, where it was the norm for the husband to become the operations manager and the wife to become the business manager. Of course while structurally these women might have been in positions of leadership, there was no symbolic recognition of their roles, so it would be doubtful that even they would think of themselves other than as wives.

Of less significance, although cadres' wives were less likely to play effective leadership roles of that kind, they nonetheless also played a central role in reform. In particular, cadres' wives ensured the provision of essential services to the processes of social and economic change. Many were either cadres or professionals such as doctors, engineers, accountants and teachers. While by 1998 very few had been selected by the CCP – of which many cadres' wives were members – to go on and become leading cadres themselves, they almost all contributed to the development and maintenance of the human and physical infrastructure for reform.

An explanation of women's role in reform based on parochialism, essentially a cultural argument, does not of course mean that there has been no change, or for that matter that there is no potential for further change. It is clear, for example, that the divorce rate for urban women even in Shanxi has increased as women have come to find their own economic and social independence. To take another example: in the past in Shanxi it was more usual in many parts of the province for wives to be at least two years older than their husbands at marriage. Yet the evidence from the comparative age of husbands and wives in the current provincial elite (Table 1.3) indicates that is no longer the case. The larger questions for the future are about the timing and speed of change, and the consequences not only for husbands and wives, but also gender relations more generally.

Necessarily, a micro-level study is limited in the conclusions that can be drawn, and is likely to raise more detailed questions for further investigation. In the first place, Shanxi has been examined in isolation. It has not been proposed as representative of China as a whole, and comments about the characteristics of its development – such as, notably, its parochialism – are offered in that context, not as relative descriptions compared to the rest of the country. Further research is clearly required to locate Shanxi's experience in that of China as a whole, and preferably not simply through a process of replicating the interviews of 1996–98 in other provinces.

The evidence of interviews in Shanxi during the late 1990s points very strongly to the need to investigate further the relationships between women, power and work at the level of the individual enterprise in greater detail, including interviewing the women involved themselves. Some women may indeed be capable negotiators of their new and complex circumstances, despite the sustained strengths of both patriarchy and family ties, as the Shanxi study suggests. However, there is also a need to go beyond those findings and the statistics, to enquire in greater detail about the gendered dimensions of leadership in management, production and marketing, as well as divisions of responsibility and decision-making within enterprises.

The family's centrality to these questions highlights another and related focus for further research, of general significance for understanding the processes of change in China, as well as a determinant of women's participation in public affairs. Studies of social and economic change in the PRC have tended to concentrate disproportionately on the state's initiatives and actions. The Shanxi study suggests not only that the family is potentially a most important source of social power and influence for women, but that it may also serve that function more generally. Under the system of state socialism, formal state structures used to be the only locus for public activity. It would seem at least possible that with reform and the increasing complexity of society other forums – such as the family – have come to be important for the exercise of power economically and politically. This aspect of socio-political change indicates the need to enquire in greater detail about the interactions between the family, lineage and local politics.

Notes

1 In March 2000, Zhu Rongji (*Government Work Report for 2000* to the 3rd session of the 9th National People's Congress, 5 March 2000) publicly acknowledged that average GDP per capita in the West was half that in the eastern and coastal provinces: in *China Daily*, 6 March 2000. By late 2000 average income per capita in the poorest province, Guizhou, was only 8 per cent of that in the richest provincial-level unit, Shanghai. According to Wang Shaoguang and Hu Angang, 'Measured by such human development indicators as education, life expectancy, and infant mortality, for instance, the difference between China's most developed and least-developed provinces is comparable to that between the Western industrial countries and the poorest countries in the world' (Wang and Hu 1999–2000).

2 Wang (2000: 62) provides a recent and excellent summary of the various trends in employment as far as women are concerned. See also Lee 1998a and 1998b.

3 Edwards (2000: 59–84) provides an outstanding overview of the interactions between women and reform. See also Jacka (1997); Rofel (1998); Evans (1997).

4 Rosen (1995: 315–41). On past practices, see Lamb (1984) and Goodman (1986). Details of the current political leadership may be found in the *China Directory 2002* (2001), Kawasaki.

5 To quote Norma Diamond: 'Women in the peasant sector and in the traditional business class of small shopkeepers ... work, though the significance and burden of this work is obscured by its being done within the framework of the family ... In business families, wives and daughters work in the shop, keep an eye on the apprentices and clerks, serve as loan agents, and help in the decision-making' (1973: 216).

6 It is part of a project to investigate the emergence of political communities and the negotiation of identity in Shanxi under reform. The project has been supported by a research grant from the Australian Research Council. Professor Tian Youru of the Modern Shanxi Research Institute, and Li Xueqian of Shanxi University provided help and assistance without which this project would not have taken place. Neither

they nor indeed anyone else in Shanxi who has contributed to this project, including those interviewed for this study, is in any way responsible for the interpretation or views expressed here.

7 Because the survey reported in the following discussion refers to the years 1996–98, data are provided for those years rather than the most recently published. Economic development statistics for 1998 are taken from *1949–1999 Shanxi wushi nian* (1949–1999 Fifty Years of Shanxi) 1999: 160 (GDP) and 168 (population.) A report on Shanxi's development during the 1990s may be found in Governor Sun Wensheng's speech to the 9th Shanxi Provincial People's Congress on 8 January 1998 (Sun 1998). Note that 8.3 yuan [dollar] RMB [*Renminbi* or People's Currency] = 1US$. By the national census of 1 November 2000, the provincial population had grown to 32.97 million (Zhang Wei 2001). In 2000 GDP per capita was 5,085 yuan RMB (Shanxi Statistical Bureau, 2001).

8 For further information on the development of Shanxi, see Breslin 1989: 135; Gillin 1967; and Goodman 1999.

9 Statistics for 1997 are calculated from *Zhongguo tongji nianjian 1998* [China Statistical Yearbook 1998] 1998: 435. These national figures are used for comparative purposes as provincial and national compilations of statistics are often inconsistent. See Herrmann-Pillath (1995: esp. 35).

10 Private-sector entrepreneurs who wished to grow in scale were frequently required either to establish new collective sector enterprises based on their original companies, or to share equity in other ways with local government in the development of new enterprises. See Chen (1998), Parris (1996); Oi (1995: 1132), Goodman (1995), Lin (1995); Walder (1995) and Young (1995).

11 Twelve of the new-rich entrepreneurs interviewed were not married.

12 Of the 201 married couples in the survey, only one had no children.

13 For an example from Shanxi, see Yu (2000: 75).

14 As indeed was also the case in Taiwan during the 1960s, as the new rich emerged there with economic development. See Diamond (1973: 217).

15 Chan *et. al* (1984: 188–91), for example, note an increase in intra-village marriage to 70–80 per cent of all marriages during the famine that followed the Great Leap Forward; Mark Selden charts the consequences of market closure and restrictions on other wider social interactions on the increased incidence of intra-village marriage (Selden 1993: 152ff.).

16 Parish and Whyte (1978: esp. 171, 246) considers Guangdong, in South China; Wolf (1985, esp. 167) examined Shandong, in North China. In single village studies, the Potters found that intra-village marriage had risen to 20% by the early 1980s (Potter and Potter, 1990: 271). Selden (1993: 155) notes a rate of 45% during the period 1970–84 and 68% during that of 1984–86.

17 Croll (1994, esp. 171). Despite the mythic power of the notion of an extended family of 'five generations under one roof' even well before 1949 the overwhelming majority of households consisted of a married couple and their children, with probably one surviving parent of the husband in the early stages of the couple's family life.

18 State-sector enterprise managers clearly have some characteristics in common with cadres. For a recent comparison of professional and political career paths, see Walder *et al.* (2000: 191–209).

19 Further details from the survey of leading cadres are presented in Goodman (2000: 159–83).

References

Breslin, S. (1989) 'Shanxi: China's Powerhouse', in D. S. G. Goodman (ed.) *China's Regional Development*, London: Routledge, 135–52.

Chan, A., Madsen, R. and Unger, J. (1984) *Chen Village: The Recent History of a Peasant Community in Mao's China*, Berkeley: University of California Press.

Chen, W. (1998) 'The Political Economy of Rural Industrialization in China: Village Conglomerates in Shandong Province', *Modern China*, 24, 1: 73–96.

China Directory 2002 (2001), Kawasaki.

Croll, E. (1981) *The Politics of Marriage in Contemporary China*, Cambridge: Cambridge University Press.

—— (1994) *From Heaven to Earth: Images and Experiences of Development in China*, London: Routledge.

Diamond, N. (1973) 'The Status of Women in Taiwan: One Step Forward, Two Steps Back', in M. B. Young (ed.) *Women in China*, Michigan Papers in Chinese Studies No. 15.

—— (1975) 'Collectivization, Kinship and the Status of Women in Rural China', *Bulletin of Concerned Asian Studies*, 7: 1, 9–21.

—— (1979) 'Women and Industry in Taiwan', *Modern China*, 5, (July) 3: 317–40.

Edwards, L. (2000) 'Women in the People's Republic of China: New Challenges to the Grand Gender Narrative', in L. Edwards and M. Roces (eds) *Women in Asia: Tradition, Modernity and Globalisation*, Sydney: Allen & Unwin, 59–84.

Evans, H. (1997) *Women and Sexuality in China*, New York: Continuum.

Ferber, M. A. and Nelson, J. A. (eds) (1993) *Beyond Economic Man*, Chicago: University of Chicago Press.

Gates, Hill (1996) *China's Motor: A Thousand Years of Petty Capitalism*, Ithaca, NY, and London: Cornell University Press.

Gillin, D. G. (1967) *Warlord Yen Hsi-shan in Shansi Province 1911–1949*, Princeton, NJ: Princeton University Press.

Gold, Thomas B. (1989) 'Guerrilla Interviewing among the Getihu', in P. Link, R. Madsen and P. G. Pickowicz (eds) *Unofficial China: Popular Culture and Thought in the People's Republic*, Boulder, CO: Westview Press.

Goodman, D. S. G. (1986) *China's Provincial Leaders, 1949–1985*, Cardiff: University College Press.

—— (1995) 'Collectives and Connectives, Capitalism and Corporatism: Structural Change in China', *The Journal of Communist Studies and Transition Politics*, 11 (March) 1: 915–42.

—— (1996) 'The People's Republic of China: The Party-state, Capitalist Revolution and New Entrepreneurs', in R. Robison and D. S. G. Goodman (eds) *The New Rich in Asia: Mobile Phones, McDonalds and Middle Class Revolution*, London: Routledge.

—— (1998) 'In Search of China's New Middle Classes: The Creation of Wealth and Diversity in Shanxi during the 1990s', *Asian Studies Review*, 22, 1: 39–62.

—— (1999) 'King Coal and Secretary Hu: Shanxi's Third Modernisation', in C. Feng and H. Hendrrischke (eds) *The Political Economy of China's Provinces: Competitive and Comparative Advantage*, London: Routledge.

—— (2000) 'The Localism of Local Leadership: Cadres in Reform Shanxi', in *Journal of Contemporary China*, 9, 24: 159–83.

—— (2001) 'The Interdependence of State and Society: The Political Sociology of Local Leadership', in C. Chao and B. J. Dickson (eds) *Remaking the Chinese State: Strategies, Society and Security*, London: Routledge.

—— (2003) 'Localism and Entrepreneurship: History, Identity and Solidarity as Factors of Production', in B. Krug (ed.) *China's Rational Entrepreneur*, London: Routledge.

Guthrie, D. (1999) *Dragon in a Three-Piece Suit: The Emergence of Capitalism in China*, Princeton, NJ: Princeton University Press.

Herrmann-Pillath, C. (ed.) (1995) *Wirtschaftliche Entwicklung Chinas Provinzen und Regionen, 1978–1992* [The Economic Development of China's Provinces and Regions], Baden-Baden: Nomos.

Honig, Emily and Hershatter, Gail (1988) *Personal Voices: Chinese Women in the 1980s*, Stanford, CA: Stanford University Press.

Hooper, Beverley (1984) 'China's Modernisation: Are Young Women Going to Lose Out?', *Modern China*, 10 (July) 3: 317–32.

—— (1998) '"Flower Vase and Housewife": Women and Consumerism in Post-Mao China', in K. Sen and M. Stivens (eds) *Gender and Power in Affluent Asia*, London: Routledge.

Jacka, T. (1997) *Women's Work in Rural China: Change and Opportunity in an Era of Reform*, Cambridge: Cambridge University Press.

Johnson, K. A. (1983) *Women, the Family and Peasant Revolution in China*, Chicago: University of Chicago Press.

Lamb, M. (1984) *Directory of Officials and Organizations in China*, New York: M.E. Sharpe.

Lee, C. K. (1998a) *Gender and the South China Miracle: Two Worlds of Factory Women*, Berkeley: University of California Press.

—— (1998b) 'The Labor Politics of Market Socialism', *Modern China*, 24, 1 (Jan.): 3–33.

Lin, N. (1995) 'Local Market Socialism: Local Corporatism in Action in Rural China', *Theory and Society*, 24: 107–21.

McLaren, A. E. (1998) 'Chinese Cultural Revivalism: Changing Gender Constructions in the Yangtze River Delta', in K. Sen and M. Stivens (eds) *Gender and Power in Affluent Asia*, London: Routledge.

Maurer-Fazio, M., Rawski, T. and Zhang, W. (1999) 'Inequality in Rewards for Holding Up Half the Sky: Gender Wage Gaps in China's Urban Labour Market, 1988–1994', *The China Journal*, 41: 61–93.

Oi, J. C. (1995) 'The Role of the Local State in China's Transitional Economy', *The China Quarterly*, 144 (Dec.): 1132–49.

—— (1999) *Rural China Takes Off: Institutional Foundations of Economic Reform*, Berkeley: University of California Press.

Org, M. (2001)'The Women China is Leaving Behind'. Available online at <http://www.societypolitics.chicklick.com/articles/3536p1.html> (accessed July 2001).

Parish, W. and Whyte, M. K. (1978) *Village and Family in Contemporary China*, Chicago: University of Chicago Press.

Parris, K. (1996) 'Private Entrepreneurs as Citizens: From Leninism to Corporatism', *China Information*, 10, 3/4: 1–28.

Pearson, M. M. (1997) *China's New Business Elite: The Political Consequences of Economic Reform*, Berkeley: University of California Press.

Potter, S. H. and Potter, J. M. (1990) *China's Peasants: The Anthropology of a Revolution*, Cambridge: Cambridge University Press.

Robison, R. and Goodman, D. S. G. (eds) (1996a) *The New Rich in Asia: Mobile Phones, McDonalds and Middle Class Revolution*, London: Routledge.

—— (1996b) 'The New Rich in Asia: Economic Development, Social Status and Political Consciousness', in R. Robison and D. S. G. Goodman (1996a), *The New Rich in Asia: Mobile Phones, McDonalds and Middle Class Revolution*, London: Routledge.

Rofel, L. (1998) *Other Modernities: Gendered Yearnings in China after Socialism*, Berkeley: University of California Press.

Rosen, S. (1994) 'Chinese Women in the 1990s: Images and Roles in Contention', in M. Brosseau and Lo C. K. (eds) *China Review 1994*, Hong Kong: Chinese University Press.

—— (1995) 'Women and Political Participation in China', *Pacific Affairs*, 68, 3: 315–41.

Selden, M. (1993) 'Family Strategies and Structures in Rural North China', in D. Davis and S. Harrell (eds) *Chinese Families in the Post-Mao Era*, Berkeley: University of California Press.

'Shanxi Jianhang xindai zhanlue he zhizhu chanye xuanze (1996) ['The Shanxi Construction Bank's Credit Strategy and Selection of Industries for Support'] *Touzi daokan* [Investment Guide], 1, 1 Feb.: 9.

Shanxi Statistical Bureau (2001) '"Jiuwu" shiqi wosheng guomin jingji heshehui fazhan huigu' ['An Overview of National Economic and Social Development in Shanxi during the Ninth Five-Year Plan'] *Shanxi ribao* [Shanxi Daily], 10 Feb.

Shanxi tongji nianjian (1998) [Shanxi Statistical Yearbook 1998] Beijing: Zhongguo tongji chubanshe.

1949–1999 Shanxi wushi nian [1949–1999 Fifty Years of Shanxi], Editorial Committee on Fifty Years of Shanxi, Beijing: Zhongguo tongji chubanshe.

Stacey, J. (1983) *Patriarchy and Socialist Revolution in China*, Berkeley and Los Angeles: University of California Press.

Steinfield, E. S. (1998) *Forging Reform in China: The Fate of State-owned Industry*, Cambridge: Cambridge University Press.

Sun, W. (1998) 'Quanmian guanche dangde shiwuda jingshen baxingjin fuminde hongwei daye duixiang ershiyi shiji' ['Push Forward the Great Task of Invigorating and Enriching Shanxi into the 21st Century'] *Shanxi zhengbao* [Shanxi Gazette], Feb.: 32.

Walder, A. G. (1995) 'Local Governments as Industrial Firms: An Organizational Analysis of China's Transitional Economy', *American Journal of Sociology*, 10, 2: 263–301.

Walder, A. G., Bobai Li, and Treiman, Donald J. (2000) 'Politics and Life Chances in a State Socialist Regime: Dual Career Paths into the Urban Chinese Elite, 1949 to 1996', *American Sociological Review*, 65: 191–209.

Wang, S. and Hu, A. (1999) *The Political Economy of Uneven Development: The Case of China*, Armonk, NY: M.E. Sharpe.

Wang, Z. (2000) 'Gender, Employment and Women's Resistance', in Elizabeth J. Perry and Mark Selden, *Chinese Society: Change, Conflict and Resistance*, London and New York: Routledge, 62–82.

Waring, M. (1999) *Counting for Nothing: What Men Value and What Women are Worth*, 2nd edn, University of Toronto Press. (Originally published in the USA under the title *If Women Counted* (1988), San Francisco: Harper & Row.)

White III, L. T. (1998) *Unstately Power*, vol. 1: *Local Causes of China's Economic Reforms*, New York: M.E. Sharpe.

Whiting, S. H. (2001) *Power and Wealth in Rural China: The Political Economy of Institutional Change*, Cambridge: Cambridge University Press.

Wolf, M. (1985) *Revolution Postponed: Women in Contemporary China*, Stanford, CA: Stanford University Press.

Young, S. (1995) *Private Business and Economic Reform in China*, Armonk, NY: M.E. Sharpe.

Yu, T. (2000) 'Wo gongzuode yitian' ['A Day in My Work'] *Huohua* [Spark], October, 75.

Zhang, W. (2001) 'Quansheng diwuci renkou pucha zhuyao shuju' ['The Key Figures of the Fifth National Census for Shanxi'] in Shanxi wanbao [Shanxi Evening News] 23 May.

Zhongguo tongji nianjian 1998 [China Statistical Yearbook 1998] (1998) Zhonghua renmin gongheguo guojia tongji ju. Beijing: Zhongguo tongji chubanshe.

Zhongguo tongji nianjian 1999 [China Statistical Yearbook 1999] (1999) Zhonghua renmin gongheguo guojia tongji ju. Beijing: Zhongguo tongji chubanshe.

Zhu, R. (2000) 'Government Work Report for 2000 to the 3rd session of the 9th National People's Congress, 5 March', in *China Daily*, 6 March.

2 Femininity and authority

Women in China's private sector

Clodagh Wylie

China has undergone rapid economic and social changes since the beginning of the reform period in 1978. The growth of the private sector is one significant change that has been the subject of considerable study. Women's participation in this expanding sector, however, has received relatively little attention (Gates 1991: Kitching 2001). In the complex environment of China's burgeoning private sector, women are renegotiating gender stereotypes and constructing their own space. These educated, urban professional women are also playing an important part in shaping business networking practices by discovering and developing the tools with which they can most successfully negotiate relationships in the workplace. This study, based on a survey of women in Beijing and Shanghai, examines how women are responding to the pressures to conform to female stereotypes in their professional and domestic lives and how they express agency through their interpretation of and resistance to mass-media models of femininity.

Described as white-collar ladies, office misses and female bosses, these women form a unique and privileged sector of society and are redefining notions of modern femininity. Members of this group appear to show little desire to be perceived as anything 'special' or out of the ordinary, yet their access to education – and therefore employment opportunities, as well as their potential for promoting changes in gender role subscriptions – prove that they are indeed a 'unique' group.

It is not easy to establish how many women are working in the Chinese private sector and definitions of 'private sector' often vary. According to the Pan Pacific East Asian Women's Association, in 1997 there were 20 million private entrepreneurs in China, 25 per cent of whom were women (Buscombe 1997). According to the State Industry Bureau, in 1998 more than 18 million women were registered as private enterprise owners, making up just over 40 per cent of the total (Wang 2000: 72). This figure could include women registered as private business owners who are selling goods on the streets or in small shops. A considerably lower figure is given in the China Statistical Yearbook for 1999, which records a figure of 7.5 million women employed in enterprises of ownership other than state-owned or urban collective-owned (2000, 132–3).

Another useful indicator is the number of women in professional associations. For example, the Beijing-based China Association of Women Entrepreneurs, established in 1985, has 7,000 national members (Smith 2000: 1). The Shanghai Women Entrepreneurs Association was established in the late 1990s and more than 100 female enterprise managers attended the founding meeting, coming from such sectors as industry, commerce, finance, agriculture, construction and tourism (*Shanghai Evening Post* website).

As with other Chinese women, women in the private sector are faced with the conflicting demands of both family and work. Many find it difficult to balance the two. The media's persistent promotion of 'ideal' womanhood and the general perception of the private sector as a particularly male space also confront these women. Operating in a space perceived as masculine (Rofel 1999: 96–103), women in the private sector pose a challenge to the still firmly held belief in a clear distinction between feminine and masculine in Chinese society. This is partly due to the fact that these women have assumed positions of legitimacy in an environment that is widely constructed as male territory: not suitable for women, who by their very nature, are seen to lack the necessary (male) qualities to succeed. Male entrepreneurs or those involved in some form of market activity, on the other hand, are seen as good husband material because of their access to goods and 'proven masculinity' (Rofel 1999: 233).

Ellen Judd (1990) found a negative perception of female managers during interviews in three Shandong villages in the late 1980s. Women are also subject to discriminatory practices in professional settings (Hilderbrandt and Liu 1988: 306, 309; Croll 1995: 117–24). Beverley Kitching (2001), who surveyed business women in Kunming in 1998, found that women had less 'access to capital and security of investment' (2001: 48). She concludes that women's interests have been sidelined in China's reformed period and it is more difficult for them to reach positions of seniority than men. She points to the case of women choosing to own their own businesses rather than climb the corporate ladder of a large enterprise (Kitching 2001: 49). Nonetheless, the women she surveyed believed that women had superior skills in establishing personal relationships (Kitching 2001: 48). This positive perception of the strengths of women is undermined by another common perception: namely, that women lack access to the well-established male dominated business networks (Korabik 1994: 121–2). Consequently, women may find themselves at a severe disadvantage in business if they are unable to foster *guanxi* – relationships/connections – in order to facilitate business success.

It is important to note briefly the historical context in which notions of femininity are now being renegotiated. In revolutionary and socialist China, notions of women's gender identity were dramatically reshaped. Traditional female values were rejected and replaced with Western notions of gender equality. However, following the upheavals of the Cultural Revolution (1966–76) and a backlash against the 'Iron woman' images of that era (Honig 2000), many women have since recounted feelings of loss in regard to their feminine identities: see the personal histories of Jung Chang, (1991) and Anchee Min (1994). These personal histories express a longing for the freedom to express one's femininity not only in dress, but also in terms of relationships with family and wider society. Since 1978 women have increasingly expressed a need for recognition of women's different qualities and needs (Woo 1994: 291–5; Croll 1995: 153–5).

In the earlier reform period, women took part in the burgeoning private sector in great numbers. These were generally women who started small street businesses to make ends meet after being laid off. They were commended not as glamorous models of the private sector, but rather as heroic examples of ingenuity and perseverance. However, when the sector proved to be highly profitable as well as risky, men's and women's experiences diverged greatly. The uncertainties of the private sector required the sorts of cunning and people skills thought unbecoming of women. According to Rofel's study of Hangzhou workers, by the 1990s, the main qualities associated with the private sector included the ability to take risks, to mix with a wide array of people, to travel and make contacts. All of these were identified as male attributes (Rofel 1999: 102–3).

This refeminisation of women in favour of a more 'traditional' gender balance finds parallels with the experience in post-communist Eastern Europe, where we find a similar destabilising of gender roles, followed by a later public rejection of these models and a return to 'traditional' sex stereotypes. According to Verdery, because socialist regimes customarily required large labour forces, gender equality within the family was promoted in order to free up women from clearly defined domestic roles within the home and to liberate them from participation in the public workforce. She also argues that women's increased participation in the workforce and the state promotion of gender equality led to their greater power within the family, while various state controls undercut male familial authority (Verdery 1996: 65). However, in post-socialist Europe, the state's previous usurpation of familial patriarchal authority has given way to policies and attitudes aimed at recovering men's lost authority in nuclear families. Now nationalist politics aim to reverse the debilitating 'mothering' of socialism by 'compelling women back into their nurturing and care-giving roles "natural" to their sex, and restoring to men their "natural" family authority' (Verdery 1996: 79–80).

Verdery's theory that post-socialist systems reinvent femininity and masculinity in the wake of revolutionary gender equality can help to explain the focus in many women's magazine articles in China on the importance of women maintaining and protecting their feminine qualities, particularly when working in business. It could also help to explain the ambivalence expressed by many women interviewed about the negotiation of femininity in Chinese business and managerial contexts. It is inferred that by working in the private sector or in a business that a woman is at risk of lessening or even forfeiting her femininity. The private sector and particularly entrepreneurialism are seen as inherently masculine and hence 'risky' spaces. Young single men are believed to be the most suitable candidates for work in these fields, whereas women are aligned with the more feminine space of the state sector (Rofel 1999: 97).

When a woman enters the uncertain and masculine arena of private enterprise there are a number of barriers to her success. First, discrimination is still a serious hindrance for many women seeking employment in the private sector. Second, women are often the first to be targeted when employers begin downsizing surplus labour. Additionally, some organisations put pressure on their female employees to take longer maternity leave, thus making it difficult for them to compete in the workplace. Finally, many women are being encouraged into retirement at an earlier age than is stipulated by the state (Liu and Rong 1995: 194; Wang 2000: 65).

Following the downfall of socialism in Eastern Europe, housework has become classified as non-work and thus receives no payment, the state no longer supports this work and it falls back into the feminine domain (Verdery 1996: 81–2). In China both housework and childcare are once more promoted as women's work.[1] There are private childcare centres but these are only available to the small number who can afford it. As a result, even women who hold positions equal with those of their husbands find that they have a very heavy burden indeed compared with men.

My intention here is to continue exploring the issue of perceptions of women in the 'masculinised' private sector in China. My focus will be on how women working in this sector perceive themselves rather than how others perceive them. How do these women compete with men in the art of networking? Is *guanxi* in business contexts gender sensitive? To what extent do these women perceive themselves as 'modern women' in the sense portrayed in the Chinese mass media? To what extent do these women use the Internet for networking and information and what is the impact of websites designed specifically for women? What do they think of work in the private sector as a career option and what do they regard as the attributes necessary for success in the private sector?

Survey of women in Beijing and Shanghai

In September 2000 I travelled to China to conduct interviews with female managers and employees working in private-sector enterprises. I conducted nineteen interviews in Shanghai and Beijing with women from a variety of private sector jobs (one state-sector employee was also included) and ranging in age from their mid-twenties to early fifties. The women I interviewed were contacted via friends and through the Shanghai American Chamber of Commerce membership directory. Interviews were conducted in places of work, teashops, eateries, shopping centres and private homes. The interviews lasted for up to one and a half hours depending on the convenience of the participant. During the interviews, I supplied participants with a questionnaire to look through while I worked through the questions with them. At other times, participants chose to fill in the questionnaire on their own after our discussion. Interviews were conducted in Chinese and English, depending on the preference of the participant. In several cases, I was assisted by a translator.

A limited timeframe meant that I was unable to interview participants more than once and this made it difficult to establish a genuine sense of trust. Moreover, despite their willingness to participate, many of the women displayed a degree of reservation in their responses while being interviewed or answering the supplied questionnaire. The women interviewed displayed a surprising level of modesty about their achievements, an ambivalence noted also by Elisabeth Croll, who discovered confusion among Chinese women in the light of an 'absence of a single rhetoric defining proper female needs and interests appropriate to a modern woman' (Croll 1995: 171). She also suggested that women lacked direction and were looking for 'cues, guidance and models in making sense of the new opportunities for women's social and self-expression in cosmopolitan China of the 1990s' (Croll 1995: 174, 176).

The women surveyed in Shanghai and Beijing worked in a variety of industries, and all but one worked in private enterprises.[2] The term 'private enterprise' is used here to include privately run businesses, joint ventures and wholly foreign-owned companies operating in China. Of the participants, three worked in the restaurant and hospitality sector, two of them in management positions. Five of the participants were accountants or responsible for financial affairs. Two were managers with international companies, one was the director of a small Chinese trade and shipping company, one was a deputy manager, two were consultants with international companies, one was a vice-director of a Chinese human resource company. There were two product marketers, one chief pharmacist and one teacher.

The majority of women interviewed (over 60 per cent) were 30 years of age and older. Only two women in the sample were in the 20–25 age group. Within the sample, the highest level of education achieved was master's degree and the lowest level of schooling was high school. Over one-third of respondents (almost 37 per cent) had completed specialised tertiary study, while the remainder were divided evenly between high school education, undergraduate university degrees and master's degrees. None of the respondents had completed doctorates. These figures are far higher than the average and display this sample's unique position in relation to the wider population.

In Table 2.1, I have ranked education numerically from one to five, with one representing the lowest level of education achieved amongst the participants and five being the highest level.

In Table 2.2, these educational rankings are provided for each participant, along with their job description and age. Here it can be seen that of the four high school graduates, two worked as accountants, and two worked in hospitality: one as a restaurant foreperson and one as a bar manager. At the higher end of the education spectrum, of the four master's degree holders, one was the chief representative for an international management consulting firm, one was a consultant with an international human resources firm, one was the vice-director of a Chinese human resource company and one was a senior business manager with an American joint venture telecommunications organisation. Of the four participants with undergraduate degrees, one was the director of a human resources company, one was the product marketer and quality controller for a foreign electrical appliances manufacturing company, one was a teacher and the fourth was a manager in the import-export division of an American

Table 2.1 Educational levels

Education	No. of participants	Average age	%*
(1) Secondary	4	33–4	21.05
(2) Tertiary – undergraduate	4	33	21.05
(3) Tertiary – specialised	7	38–9	36.85
(4) Master's degree	4	38	21.05
(5) Doctorate	–	–	–

*Percentages have been rounded up.

Table 2.2 Interview sample

Respondents	Age	Education level	Position
A	31–40	4	Chief representative with an international management consultancy
B	40+	3	Restaurant manager
C	20–5	2	Director of small shipping company
D	26–30	3	Deputy manager, marketing department of an enterprise development company
E	40+	4	Vice Director of a human resources company
F	40+	1	Accountant at a throat hospital
G	31–40	2	Product marketer and quality controller with an international electrical appliances company
H*	40+	3	Accountant at a state-owned water company
I	31–40	4	Senior business manager with large American joint venture telecommunications company
J	31–40	1	Bar/club manager
K	20–5	1	Restaurant foreperson
L	31–40	4	Consultant with a global human resources firm
M	26–30	3	Responsible for sales & marketing of a beer company
N	40+	3	Accountant
O	26–30	3	Accountant
P	26–30	1	Accountant
Q	26–30	2	Teacher
R	40+	3	Pharmacist in charge
S	40+	2	Manager of the import-export department for a large American automotive parts manufacturer

*State-sector employee

automotive parts manufacturer. Seven of the participants had specialised tertiary qualifications. In this group there were three accountants, a restaurant manager, a deputy manager of an enterprise development company's marketing department, a sales and marketing manager for a beer company and a chief pharmacist.

It is evident from these results that educational level is reflected in career position. A distinction can be made, however, between those working in hospitality and entertainment with those working in the business and commerce sectors. This distinction will be discussed later when I consider the responses to the question of networking and the perceived personal qualities needed to succeed in a particular job. From meeting with women working in bars, nightclubs and restaurants, I have learnt that personality is believed to play a key role in success in these sectors, while education was not seen as so important for a career in the hospitality industry. The ability to network, as well as a certain degree of self-assurance and persistence, appear to have been common traits amongst all the women working in hospitality and entertainment. Networking will be seen to be of vital importance to a woman's success and progress in any career.

The art of *guanxi*

The question of *guanxi* (networking) was raised to ascertain how important the women being interviewed thought connections and personal relationships were to conducting business.[3] In the urban, commercial context of cities such as Shanghai and Beijing, connections are vitally important to conducting business. One can classify an individual's personal resources, such as skill, talent, entrepreneurial ability and access to political power, as cultural 'capital'. As Christopher Buckley notes, drawing on the work of Pierre Bourdieu, 'social connections with people who have access to valuable information, influence and resources are in themselves a kind of "capital" that can be cultivated, sustained and called up in times of need' (Buckley 2000: 219).

Mayfair Mei-hui Yang is one of the few scholars to have analysed the influence of gender on *guanxi* relationships. In her study of social relationships in China, she argues that most women use *guanxi* for 'small things' such as getting on someone's good side or obtaining goods that are not readily available. The more complicated exercises in *guanxi*, which may involve travel or greater interaction with those beyond the immediate circle of family and friends, such as securing employment, are usually left to male relatives (Yang 1994: 79). Yang's finding that women are primarily involved in 'small' *guanxi* is supported by the responses of the interviewees who spoke of maintaining cordial and warm relationships with their workmates and superiors within the workplace as the main way in which they practised networking. Few mentioned *guanxi* in the context of networking with outside businesses and organisations. Participant S, who will be discussed later, backed up Yang's findings that women are uncomfortable exercising *guanxi* outside their workplace.

The theme common to all women in their responses to the use of *guanxi* was the way they used it to navigate relationships in the workplace. The majority of participants responded that networking was important or extremely important. Two of the three participants who worked in the hospitality field noted that networking was an extremely important aspect of their job, the third felt that it was not necessary but still an important aspect. The majority of women identified friendliness and warmth as key factors in achieving cooperative and rewarding working relationships. Being warm and friendly (*youhao*) with staff and superiors was acknowledged as the best way to ensure a harmonious and cooperative working environment. Participant B, who worked for a small restaurant on Huaihai Road in Shanghai, and participant H, an accountant with a state-owned water company in Shanghai, responded that personal relationships were increasingly important and the best way to use networking was to be friendly with others. Participant B explained that in this way, if she had to criticise or correct someone, they would be more inclined to listen to her if there was a friendly (*youhao*) relationship between them. Participant C, the youngest woman in the sample, explained that she was respectful to others, that she gave people gifts on their birthdays, and most importantly, that she would smile and be warm.

Some women also acknowledged that interacting with men could actually be used to a woman's advantage depending on the situation and the favour or assistance being sought. Interviewee D said that it was sometimes easier for women to do business as men could be more forgiving towards women when they made mistakes than they would be with other men. Interviewee E suggested that for unimportant or trivial matters a woman would be able to use her charm to influence a man. However, if it were a serious or important matter that required a deep understanding and knowledge, a woman should instead rely on her brains and ability, allowing men to see that she was intelligent. Participant E is the director of a human resources company based in Pudong and is also a member of the Female Entrepreneurs Association. Her comments on using female charm when dealing with men is reflected in Yang's study, which suggested that women 'can go a long way' using charm and that it can be used in place of material gifts. According to Yang, female 'charm' is not a discreet term for 'sexual services', but rather refers to the ability of women to play on the attraction between the sexes, which in many cases is sufficient reason for a man to assist a woman (Yang 1994: 83). In some cases, men will send their wives to request a favour on their behalf, seeing it as an effective means of gaining a favour. While this method may enable women to expend less in terms of material or financial resources, Yang argues that they actually 'give up more of themselves than men' (Yang 1994: 84). Additionally, as the majority of big or important favours are asked of men, they must 'play up to male expectations' to get the help they want (Yang 1994: 84).

In response to the question of *guanxi*, some of the respondents replied in a way that suggested a more 'professional' approach. By 'professional', I mean a demeanour that was forthright, honest and straightforward rather than being pleasant and friendly (in other words, non-threatening). Respondent B said that she did her best to be frank when communicating with staff and colleagues, discussing her own thoughts, experiences and ideas about ways for doing things. She felt that then she could gain everyone's cooperation in striving for a common goal. Participant D said that while networking was not necessary but still important, the important thing was to resolve difficulties together. Participant E replied that networking was important in the sense that one could use networking by placing trust in others in the belief that they would trust her in return. She also spoke of being upright and succeeding by learning from wisdom. Participant M said that she received others' ideas humbly, put forward her own professional abilities at appropriate times and joined in after-work activities. Participant N responded that she strove to be more active, do more and think more in her daily work.

However, participant H said that one of the negative aspects of *guanxi* was the practice of speaking well to one's superiors (*haohua*). She felt that it was the most negative aspect of her work and that in her position of seniority she was often the receiver of others' insincerity and flattery in an attempt to curry favour with her. While she understood that it was a necessary part of workplace interaction and dynamics, she nevertheless resented the extent to which people spoke against their true feelings. Her interpretation of *haohua* implied that it was something she was impelled to do rather than something she did naturally.

For the women in the survey, using *guanxi* and mixing with a wide variety of people, often men, was not seen as negatively impacting on a woman's reputation. In fact, the ability to get along with people and having good social skills were seen as necessary qualities, particularly in hospitality and trade careers, where working and mixing with a variety of different people was mandatory. Except for the comments on flattery, I did not encounter an overall negative perception of *guanxi* associated with the 'crude instrumentalism and aggressive tactics' indicated in Yang's study. One respondent did, however, explain that when socialising with clients she would not drink or smoke, especially when she was the only representative of her company and the only female present. Participant S was the manager of the import-export division of an American automotive parts manufacturer. She was head-hunted for her valuable local knowledge and experience, travelled for work regularly and often found herself the only woman in large networking gatherings. She felt uncomfortable in these situations that demanded networking with external business contacts. She found the most appropriate behaviour was to not engage in drinking or smoking at any stage in order to avoid any awkward or embarrassing situations. Apart from this comment, the other women made no mention of networking and socialising with strangers as adversely affecting how others perceived them. In fact, as mentioned earlier, the majority of the women in the sample felt that networking was an integral part of their daily work, and the ability to mix with a wide variety of people was seen as a valuable skill. However, the positive comments made on networking relate more to the participants' immediate work context. Respondent B, a restaurant manager, felt that being forthright and candid was an important quality in her line of work. She also thought that it was important to show concern and consideration for her colleagues to secure their cooperation.

Yang argues that *guanxi* as practiced in China is perceived in the West as a female practice because it revolves around obligations and responsibilities, whereas typically masculine, individualistic behaviour more closely represents the individualism of the West. The relational nature of *guanxi* in China marks it as feminine, in opposition to the West's 'separation and independence of the individual' (Yang 1994: 192–3). In China, however, it is clear that *guanxi* is utilised by both men and women, yet there is often a gendered difference in practice. It appears that women use *guanxi* in a careful and non-threatening way, especially when operating in positions of power. In fact, in a number of women's magazine articles profiling female professionals in private enterprises, attention is frequently given to their warm, friendly and caring natures.

In the light of the predictability of these types of representations as well as the qualities identified by the interviewees, I believe that authority and femininity currently form an uneasy alliance in the Chinese setting. As we saw with the stated importance of being *youhao*, women apparently have to apply themselves to softening their authority and appear warm and non-formidable.

The modern woman

The term 'modern woman' (*xiandai nüren*) is referred to frequently in women's publications. How relevant the concept of 'modern womanhood' is to the women who are often the very embodiment of this modernity was examined in order to gauge the reality of such representations. According to the sample, the characteristic that most identified a woman as being modern was independence.

Participant B responded that independent thought and character, as well as having one's own career, job and life, were integral to being a modern woman. Participant C replied that the term 'modern woman' meant making independent decisions at work, being economically independent and engaging in activities that involved communication. Participant D thought that the term meant being both good at work and at living. For participant E, the term referred to quick thinking, innovativeness as well as confidence, strength and self-respect. Strength was a quality also mentioned by participant N. For respondent O, an accountant under 30 years of age, being a modern woman meant having an independent character and thought, being able to deal independently with matters, having a relatively stable and high salary and having high self-expectation. Participant S also identified the term 'modern woman' with independence, stating that for her it meant being more independent in one's professional and personal life. Participant G, a product marketer for an international electrical appliances company, thought that being a modern woman meant one had a fashionable appearance and was relatively open. Participant M, who was under 30 years old and working for a beer company, believed that being a modern woman meant having a stable and suitable job, courageously trying new things, having belief in oneself, being able to handle both work and family and being independent and self-respectful.

Adaptability was also mentioned as an important characteristic of being a modern woman. Respondent H, the state-sector employee, believed that a modern woman was one who could adapt to and keep up with today's changing environment. This notion of keeping up with a changing environment is reflected in an article that looks at the 'challenges of the new century' (Xiao 1999). The author focuses on the growing importance of the 'knowledge economy' and the need for women to pursue education in order to meet these new challenges effectively. Xiao argues that educational differences have historically put women at a disadvantage, and calls on women to look at ways of rectifying these imbalances by pursuing further study or specialised training (Xiao 1999: 26).

Attitudes towards private-sector employment

The majority of respondents identified higher incomes as the most positive aspect of working in the private sector. Additionally, being able to pursue what one was good and skilled at and ultimately having an opportunity to do something enjoyable were also seen as positive aspects of the private sector. Challenge was identified as a positive aspect of working in the private sector, as was freedom. By using the term 'freedom', the respondents meant having the ability to choose one's occupation, job mobility and gaining fulfilment from one's work.

Participant B stressed that the most positive aspect of private-sector employment was that people could do whatever they were skilled at and interested in. This also meant that people were able to develop potential ability and do what they liked doing. Participant C responded that freedom, lack of restraints and working for oneself were positive aspects of working in the private sector. Reluctant to mention any negative aspects, she stated that even the hardships she encountered were worth it. Respondent D also mentioned freedom and no restraints as positives. In addition, she noted that there was room to climb higher in one's career. Participant E also noted the opportunity for career development and the flexibility of the sector as positive elements. Participant N also noted the lack of restriction as a positive aspect as well as being able to work boldly and openly. Being able to develop one's career was also mentioned by participant O. She additionally appreciated that the environment was relatively relaxed and that there was little difference between rankings in her company.

Salaries were an important part of job satisfaction in the private sector. Participant G noted higher salaries as a positive aspect. Participant H, the state-sector employee, felt that in the private sector talent was more highly regarded than one's gender and that it was less traditional than the state sector. This perception was also supported by participant M, who especially liked working in the private sector because of the importance attached to professional ability. She also thought that there was a relatively large opportunity to expand one's career. Respondent S mentioned the high salary as a positive aspect, as well as the challenges and opportunities of her work.

Women also raised negative aspects concerning work in the private sector such as stringent regulations governing work, long working hours, greater job instability and the relative difficulty of juggling family and career. For participant B, policy and investment regulations were negative aspects to the private sector. Participant S also referred to the tough regulations of the private sector and mentioned the inflexible working hours as a negative side to her work. Participant M similarly responded that her work often required overtime, that the hours were fairly long and that the competition was very intense.

Lack of employment stability and a great deal of pressure were given as negative aspects by participant D. Participant E listed lack of certainty about the future as a negative aspect.

Family and support networks

Interviewees suggested that another important factor in women's career success is the role of the extended family.[4] For some of the women interviewed, leaving children in the care of grandparents has allowed them to pursue their educational or career goals. Participant S raised this point, describing how she had relied on both her parents and her husband's parents so that she could take up a scholarship to study abroad when her daughter was just six months old. At that time, both of the child's grandparents encouraged her to make use of this opportunity and together with her husband looked after her daughter for the year that she was away. She explained that this had been a very difficult decision to make but that it was a life-changing experience for her and had enabled her to overcome her shyness and become independent and self-reliant. As her family had suffered during the Cultural Revolution, they encouraged her to study mechanical engineering rather than a political course so that she would be guaranteed a job regardless of the future political climate.

The One Child policy has now distinctly altered the modern Chinese family structure so that grandparents' time is becoming increasingly available for looking after grandchildren (Unger 1993: 42–3). However, the greater demands of the private-sector workplace on a woman's time and energy, particularly with promotion and seniority, exacerbate the 'double burden' issue facing many working women with families. Some women asserted that as successful women in the private sector, life was tougher for them than for their male counterparts because of their dual roles as mothers and workers. Participant B admitted to a heavy family burden, and said that because she was so busy with her own work matters, she had little time for family, especially her child's education and looking after her older relatives. Participant F, a specialist hospital accountant, believed that it was generally harder for women because of the difficulty in balancing the demands of both family and work. Participant G also felt that women in their late thirties and older had to deal with a lot of pressure because of parental and family demands.

Several women interviewed said that women in Shanghai had more support from their husbands in the domestic sphere than women in Beijing. Men in

Beijing were more 'traditional' and therefore, less likely to take part in roles perceived to be 'women's work'. Participant E believed that Beijing women look after the home more than men, stating that the model was generally that men were involved with government and work while women were involved with home duties. However, the participant from Beijing (S) explained that in her case, where housework, cooking and other domestic chores were not shared equally between her and her husband, her spouse assumed responsibility in other areas. She explained that she held an equivalent position to her husband, who also worked for a foreign company. However, she admitted that she had to wake earlier every morning to prepare breakfast for the family and that because her husband was admittedly a 'traditional man', he did not share any of the food shopping, cooking or cleaning. He did, however, take on a greater amount of responsibility for their teenage daughter's schooling and general care. This appeared to make a satisfactory arrangement for this woman. She said that she was aware, however, that a considerable portion of men in Shanghai were reportedly more supportive of their female partners than was her own husband.

Sexual harassment and discrimination

On the whole, the participants declined to offer examples of problems experienced or discrimination associated with working in corporate structures, often male-dominated ones. Many did volunteer the opinion, however, that it was much harder for women than men to succeed. Participant E rejected the notion that women were discriminated against, adding that they were judged on merit and skill. However, she acknowledged that women justifiably recognise a bias against them and therefore strive to be better than men. She believed that because of a traditional preference for male children, many women were forced to be more 'outstanding', more studious and diligent and to try harder than men.

Many of the participants shared this attitude and were reluctant to identify personal problems or gender-specific hurdles, yet spoke of the innate bias against women in Chinese society. The obvious contradiction here draws our attention to a possible reluctance to put forward what seems to be a feminist position.

Having come across many articles in women's publications concerning sexual harassment, I was interested to see what the interviews would uncover in relation to this issue. However, while it is a popular topic in women's publications, the interviewees did not address the issue of sexual harassment. The women's reluctance to talk of personal hardships was no doubt a factor in their lack of discussion of sexual harassment. I asked the participants if they had encountered any problems with male colleagues as a discreet opening to discussion of this issue, but they were either reluctant to discuss it or it was not an issue they had dealt with. Generally, I found that the women did not want to complain about their work at all (unless it was to say that it made juggling time at home difficult) and so this could be another factor contributing to the lack of discussion about harassment.[5] Not to be discounted, and perhaps of the greatest significance, is that sexual misconduct is always and everywhere a sensational topic, especially in the media. Women's journals regularly include such articles, but this may be more for entertainment and titillation rather than a reflection of a common reality for many women.

Internet use

Internet sites are increasingly recognising Chinese women as a specific and important market, and the online community is an additional space within which Chinese feminine identity is being (re)created. In response to this situation a number of women's professional associations and services for professional women have been established, such as various national and provincial female entrepreneurs associations and Internet sites geared primarily to Chinese women.

Available figures indicate that Chinese women's use of the Internet falls well below that of their male counterparts. A survey of 300,000 Chinese people found that the majority of Internet users were single men with tertiary qualifications (BBC News Online 2000). According to Michael Yue (2000: 1), women account for just over one-quarter (4.27 million) of Chinese Internet users. A survey conducted by the Ministry of Information and the Lantian Market Research Co. concludes that 'men are twice as likely to use the Internet as are women' (ChinaOnline 2000: 1). According to Rosemary Brisco, women in Asia make up only 22 per cent of Internet users (see her website http://WomenAsia.com – discussed later). This percentage corresponds with the figure of approximately 25 per cent for women in China mentioned earlier. However, use of the Internet by survey participants was not as low as might be expected from these figures. Twelve women were so-called regular users (accessing the Internet more than once a month) and eight said they used it every day. Roughly one-third of the sample claimed they never use the Internet. These figures are higher than official reports and statistics, no doubt because the women interviewed were generally well educated, have good incomes and enjoy a high level of personal and professional autonomy. For those who did not use the Internet, the reasons given were lack of free time rather than lack of access. These women accessed the Internet mostly from home rather than work, which gives us some insight into their level of personal computer ownership.

Daily users were split fairly evenly between using the Internet at home and at work, and none of the women said they went to Internet cafés. These venues appear to serve mostly a student population, predominantly young men.[6] The majority of women who used the Internet daily were over 30 years of age, and the main reasons they gave for using the Internet, whether at home or at work, were for communicating with others and work purposes.

In Table 2.3, I list the frequency venues and reasons for participants' Internet use. Many of the favourite sites listed were work related. However, the majority of sites listed were the popular search and information sites such as Yahoo, Sohu

Table 2.3 Internet usage

	Use	Place of use	Purpose for use	Favourite sites
A	Daily	Home	Pleasure/work/research/communicating with others	–
B	Don't use	–	–	–
C	Daily	Work	Work	www.homeday.com.cn www.shipping.com.cn
D	Daily	Home/work	Work/communicating with others	–
E	Daily	Home/work	Work/research	www.51job.com/bo/hr.php
F	Daily	Home	Work/communicating with others	–
G	Don't use	–	–	–
H	Don't use	–	–	www.eastday.com.cn
I	Daily	Home/work	Work/research/communicating with others	www.chinese.yahoo.com www.sohu.com www.sina.com.cn
J	Once a month	Home	Pleasure	www.chinese.yahoo.com
K	Once a week	Home	Pleasure	www.ibm.com
L	Daily	Home/work	Pleasure/work/research/communicating with others	www.chinese.yahoo.com www.sina.com.cn www.cnn.com www.cnn.com
M	Once a week	Home/work	Pleasure/communicating with others	www.eastday.com.cn
N	Once a week	Home	Communicating with others	www.sohu.com
O	Once a week	Work	Pleasure	www.eastday.com.cn
P	Don't use	–	–	–
Q	Don't use	–	–	–
R	Don't use	–	–	–
S	Daily	Home/work/hotels (when travelling)	Work/research/communicating with others	www.chinese.yahoo.com www.sina.com.cn www.sohu.com www.globalresources.com [all other auto makers home pages]

and Sina. These sites offer services such as news, email and search engines and are not targeted at women solely. However, they do provide gender-focused pages, advertising and links. Interestingly, none of the interviewees mentioned sites designed for Asian and Chinese female audiences.

Women's websites

The extent to which websites are effective in facilitating networking amongst women and in bridging gender inequality for women in business are important questions. Internet sites tailored to women can play a doubly influential role. First, they can encourage Chinese women to use the Internet and join the ranks of Internet users worldwide, and potentially transform what is perceived as a particularly male space (and this is reflected in the low figures of women using the Internet in China) into a more welcoming environment for women. And second, they can create a forum for Chinese women and businesswomen within which they can achieve a sense of identity and community.

Below I provide an analysis of Internet sites that catered for the professional and business woman in the late 1990s and early 2000s.

www.WomenAsia.com

www.WomenAsia.com was launched in Singapore in 1996 and was designed for professional women throughout Asia and North America. It provided profiles of successful women used as motivational and inspirational role models. Additionally it offered a directory listing its members' businesses. Through this directory, women could access names of contacts by searching by industry and/or country. The women using this site were encouraged to support each other and foster relationships. Stories of successful women in business were also provided.7

www.gaogenxie.com

A more recently developed site is the Chinese language www.gaogenxie.com. The site was launched in mid-April 2000, and the name translates as 'high-heeled shoes'. At the time of writing, however, this site was inaccessible and possibly closed down. When the site was running, the home page featured eye-catching coloured flowers in the top banner. Down the left-hand side of the page were different types of shoes (sandals through to stilettos), marking the various links women could follow, such as health, beauty and even single life. A secondary and less prominent list of links was offered below and these included more specific topics such as make-up, weight loss, music, movies and marriage. Tara Wang Lucas, educated in Beijing, the United States and France, is one of the site's chief creators. She declared that the website is in 'sharp contrast to the historical images of Chinese women with bound feet isolated in a courtyard'. She also claimed that *gaogenxie* 'represents the rapidly changing face of today's hip, young and educated Chinese woman' (Mooney 2000). The site sets out to address issues concerning women that the state media is reluctant to tackle, including the open discussion of sex, via various channels and chat forums. To highlight the site creators' radical agenda, and coinciding with the release of a survey that showed that an estimated 67 per cent of men in Beijing were reluctant to use condoms, press kits containing colourfully packaged condoms were distributed at the launch of the site to local and international journalists.

www.LadiesAsia.com

A Hong Kong based site, www.LadiesAsia.com, was also launched in 2000[8] and likewise targets the burgeoning group identified as modern Asian women. As part of the launch a lingerie show was staged with male models clad in underwear parading amongst the guests. No doubt this served to reinforce the site's objective to put 'the Asian women of today in the spotlight' by catering to women's personal needs and through the provision of services such as pampering with luxury goods and online shopping. LadiesAsia.com has Chinese, English and Japanese language options as well as a variety of links on the left-hand side of its homepage. These include Fashion and Beauty, Heart to Heart, Path of Life and Give us Your Hand. There are also interactive features to this site, listed as Boutique and Auction for online shopping and Discussion for chat rooms.

www.cwow.com

According to www.cwow.com's pre-launch press release (an abbreviation of 'Chinese Women on the Web'), women form a 'hot vertical segment' and are an attractive consumer group for online advertisers and retailers. As stated on the home page, this site is 'greater China's most comprehensive wedding and baby site' and offers articles and advice on relationships, marriage and children. The site was launched in Hong Kong in June 2000 and offers a choice of Taiwanese, Hong Kong or English as language options. It is highly interactive, with women encouraged to join Cwow to access special services such as designing their own wedding web page. Women are also invited to submit photos of their wedding day or baby snaps, which may then be featured on the site. Users can also vote in online polls and members are sent regular emails advertising special events or features on days such as Valentine's Day and Mother's Day. While the site features multicoloured tabs for some of its links, the majority of colours used on this site are light blues and purples, more subdued than the brighter busier colours of *gaogenxie*. There is a distinct similarity between the logos used on the Cwow and LadiesAsia websites. Both feature the Chinese character for woman superimposed onto a sphere.

www.Eliren.com

www.Eliren.com is based in Beijing and is in Chinese with the use of English limited to the company introduction and link buttons. According to the website's introduction, the target audience is women Internet users aged 16–40 (www.eliren.com/about.htm). Founded in 2000, Eliren features a very full home page. The site offers articles on a variety of topics: these include Officescape (*xiezilou*), Pink Lounge (*hongfen keting*), Boudoir (*juese sifang*),

Rose Garden (*meigui huayuan*), Jade Kitchen (*yu shanfang*), Cyber Bar (*wangba*), Beauty Shop (*meili jiayou zhan*), Women's Health, Wedding, Mom & Child (*mama baobao*) and Hocus Pocus (*mofa wu*). The Hocus Pocus link, which is set out in dark purple and green colours, deals with horoscopes, the Chinese zodiac, fortune telling and match making and has a bulletin board for posting messages.

www.Halfworld.com

www.Halfworld.com promotes itself as 'the ultimate online network' to which every Chinese woman wants to belong. It is based in Xian and sees its role as promoting young women's access to information and consumer goods. To this end, the site provides women with the opportunity to shop online. The site also provides chat rooms and bulletin boards for women to communicate with each other and share their ideas and advice (www.halfworld.com/channel/jianjie/aboutus.html). Unlike many of the other Chinese-language sites, Halfworld's home page is very simple, employing a white background and equal use of Chinese and English. Running along the top of the page is a banner featuring a group of glamorous, laughing young women from a variety of ethnic backgrounds. On the right-hand side of the page are links to the site's contents. One link entitled 'Business' contains links to other websites where one can buy clothing and pets. Established in 1999, the site claims to be the biggest Chinese site offering quality business services for women

www.Yesee.com

www.Yesee.com is a Chinese-language website launched in Beijing in January 2000. The site is aimed at professional women aged 23–35 (*China Trade News* 2000: 2). Like Cwow, the site uses shades of blue and purple. The main menu and links are located in the centre of the page. Categories include Mother, Trends, Relationships, People, Travel, Health and Career, and each of these provides articles on relevant topics. According to the website's profile, Yesee aims to help Chinese women realise life, work and emotional skills and become their number one preferred website. It also claims to promote positively an Internet life-style that is 'warm, open and free' as well as promoting fashion, leading trends and bringing a genuine Internet space to the attention of Chinese women (www.yesee.com/misc/aboutus/index.html).

www.Redskirt.com

www.Redskirt.com is another Chinese language website for women, with chat rooms, advice on issues such as fashion, relationships and work.[9]

The websites discussed above provide examples of some of the identities being constructed and promoted for Asian and particularly Chinese women. These newly transnational female spaces have yet to win a large following among Chinese Internet users; however, they do provide some insight into the possibilities of alternative spaces for female interaction and learning.

The establishment of business associations for women is a significant factor in creating greater opportunities for businesswomen in China. Likewise, Internet companies can play a valuable and self-rewarding role in this endeavour, through the creation of an 'online community' for women, creating a sense of shared identity, access to advice and support, mentoring and contacts. The one overwhelming drawback for women looking to Internet sites for this sense of identity, community and support is that they may find certain aspects too narrow and prescriptive. A site such as *gaogenxie* that equates being 'modern' and 'hip' with wearing high-heeled shoes offers a similar model of feminine identity as that of many women's magazines – namely, one based on appearance and set standards of feminine value and appeal (Hooper 1998). As with popular publications, these sites place great importance on displays of femininity, and suggest that women need to be vigilant in protecting and projecting their feminine qualities when operating in the masculine environments of management and private enterprise.

In recent years attention has been paid to the potential role of China's emerging middle class as spaces for independent and critical opinions.[10] It is possible that, with increased penetration of the Internet into the lives of Chinese citizens and particularly for women, that perhaps a social space will begin to be constructed outside of state control. Yet, the numbers of female Internet users and the limited access to online facilities outside of the urban centres means that an independent space is not yet an immediate possibility.

Conclusion

While the outlook for women seeking to pursue a career in China's increasingly attractive and lucrative private sector may seem more promising than ever before, there are still a number of important factors restricting the rise of the Chinese career woman. Employers who believe that pregnancy and subsequent absenteeism make female employees less desirable perceive women as more of a burden. The recruitment of male over female graduates is evidence of this discriminatory view. Women who have succeeded in securing a good job find that they generally have greater responsibility than their male colleagues when it comes to work and family demands. Furthermore, the media is increasingly transmitting a message of domesticity and servitude when depicting women in advertising. An alternative message is that of the 'flower vase', whereby a woman's value is based on her physical beauty, negating her contributions in real terms.

Nonetheless, businesswomen in other Chinese communities are gradually shaping women's concepts of work and femininity on the mainland. Websites such as the now defunct www.WomenAsia.com, provided women with female role models from all over Asia. However, within regions such as Taiwan, Hong Kong and Singapore there is also a great deal of variance and perhaps the Taiwanese model of a softer, stereotypically feminine businesswoman is more appealing than the 'brassy' model associated with Hong Kong (Croll 1995: 175).

The women interviewed shared a contradiction in their views on working in the private sector. On the one hand they associated qualities such as honesty, independence and being forthright with successful businesswomen. Yet they also spoke of the importance of being warm and friendly, using 'charm' when dealing with men and behaving in an appropriately feminine way. These contradictions highlight the degree of discomfort felt by these women when required to move outside the navigated boundaries of their work.

Modern feminine ideals, while often constructed around Westernised office protocols and globalised consumption patterns, are also shaped by traditional notions of the model woman, defined by such qualities as modesty, femininity and beauty. The women interviewed in this study sought to project an appropriately feminine persona, particularly when dealing with unfamiliar people. In popular magazines and Internet sites directed at women one finds widespread acceptance of women's work in the private sector, but there is also a concerted effort to focus on their stereotypically feminine qualities. This includes discussion of women's roles as wives and mothers, their style of dress and their manner when dealing with others. These attempts to reaffirm the femininity of entrepreneurial and managerial women support the argument that the private sector is culturally defined as masculine space and that women within this environment are going against their gendered natures. Interviewees revealed a sense of contradiction in their responses concerning their place in this competitive workforce. Their ambivalence about how to behave in positions of authority highlight the complexity and confusion of this evolving workplace. Many women have responded by mastering a type of gendered *guanxi* that allows them to adopt behaviour appropriate to each situation.

In conclusion, women's participation in China's private sector creates challenges not only to established norms, which help construct female roles and stereotypes, but also for women themselves. While the interviewees mentioned qualities such as honesty, being forthright and strong as important to a woman's career success, they also spoke of maintaining warm and friendly relationships and being kind to those around them. These contradictions highlight the ways in which such women have to balance the demands of traditional notions of womanhood and professional duties. Many women are finding they are able to adopt a form of gendered *guanxi* that enables them to carry out their necessary obligations while maintaining a harmonious and unchallenging relationship with colleagues and business contacts.

Notes

1 Throughout the socialist period in China, domestic tasks primarily fell to women. As Emily Honig has pointed out, even during the Cultural Revolution, a time when the family and other 'traditional' institutions were challenged, women still bore the main burden of childcare. The commune or work unit did not necessarily provide childcare

in all cases and many women had to rely on family members such as grandmothers (Honig 2000: 99–100).

2 The one exception here was a senior state employee whom I took the opportunity to meet, in order that her feedback would provide an informative contrast with the private-sector participants

3 In the interviews, I used the term *guanxi* in the sense of women's specific use of personal contacts and relationships in a professional setting, noting the value placed on connections and how women perceived their options for networking in and around the workplace. There are ranges of definitions of *guanxi* – for instance, the work of Mayfair Mei-hui Yang (2000), Andrew Kipnis (1997) and Yan Yunxiang (1996) all offer varying interpretations. However, I am using *guanxi* here to refer to networking activities and not to refer to 'corrupt' practices.

4 Jacka (1997: 117–19) describes the importance of grandmothers in caring for young children in rural China. See also the discussion of Shanghai households in Davis (2000: esp. 254) and Unger (1993: 42–3).

5 For a different view see William Jankowiak's research in Huhhot in the early 1980s and his conclusion that 'the extent of sexual harassment in Huhhot is startling' (1993: 188). He reported that all of his respondents claimed to have had experienced or witnessed sexual harassment. However, Jankowiak's findings relate to the early reform period and to a very different urban setting from that discussed here. His interviewees, who were mainly state-sector employees, spoke of occurrences of sexual harassment in public as well as private places.

6 This is an observation based on one year spent in Shanghai at both Fudan and Tongji universities where there were a large number of Internet bars and cafés located around the campuses and the majority of clients at these times were male students.

7 However, this site is no longer in operation, having closed its service on 30 December 2000. The founder and CEO, Rosemary Brisco, is now a member of the Digital Divide Task Force of the World Economic Forum and has written a White Paper on the 'Gender Digital Divide in Asia' entitled 'Turning the Analog World into a Digital Work Force'.

8 The launch was held in Hong Kong on 23 May 2000.

9 <http://www.newton.uor.edu/Departments&Programs/AsianStudiesDept/china-culture.html> contains a reference to this site. However, I have not been able to access it.

10 For divergent opinions on the potential for the growth of civil society in China with the rise of a middle class and strong business and private sector, see studies by You Ji (1998), Brødsgaard (1992), Calhoun (1994), Pearson (1997), Cheek (1998) and Guo (2000).

References

BBC News Online, 'Online Boom for China', BBC News: Asia-Pacific, Wednesday, 19 June 2000; <http://www.news.bbc.co.uk/hi/english/world/asia-pacific/newsid 609000/609971.stm> (accessed 01/11/2001).

Brødsgaard, K. E. (1992) 'Civil Society and Democratization in China', in M. Latus Nugent (ed.) *From Leninism to Freedom: The Challenges of Democratization*, Boulder, CO: Westview Press.

Buckley, C. (2000) 'How a Revolution Becomes a Dinner Party: Stratification, Mobility and the New Rich in Urban China', in M. Pinches (ed.) *Culture and Privilege in Capitalist Asia*, London: Routledge.

Buscombe, A. (1997) 'Women Entrepreneurs: Challenges and Opportunities in the 21st Century', *Pan-Pacific & Southeast Asia Women's Association International Bulletin* (fall). Available online at <http://www.ppseawa.org/97F/Entrepreneurs.html>.

Calhoun, C. (1994) *Neither Gods nor Emperor: Students and the Struggle for Democracy in China*, Berkeley: University of California Press.

Chang, J. (1991) *Wild Swans: Three Daughters of China*, New York: Simon & Schuster.

Cheek, T. (1998) 'From Market to Democracy in China: Gaps in the Civil Society Model', in J. D. Lindau and T. Cheek, *Market Economics and Political Change: Comparing China and Mexico*. New York: Rowman & Littlefield Publishers.

China Statistical Yearbook 1999 (2000).

China Trade News (2001) 'China's First Website for Women', *Chinatradenews*, 20 January. Available online at <http://www.chinatradenews.com.cn/20000120/08.htm> (accessed 18 September 2001).

ChinaOnline (2000) 'Study: China Web Use – and Security Fears – Soars', *ChinaOnline*, 7 June. Available online at <http://www.chinaonline.com/issues/internet_policy/NewsArchive/Secure/2000/june/B100060533.asp> (accessed 25 April 2001).

Croll, E. (1995) *Changing Identities of Chinese Women: Rhetoric, Experience, and Self-perception in Twentieth-century China*, New Jersey: Zed Books.

Davis, Deborah S. (2000) 'Reconfiguring Shanghai Households', in B. Entwisle and G. E. Henderson (eds) *Re-drawing Boundaries: Work, Households and Gender in China*, Berkeley: University of California Press.

Davis, D. and Harrell, S. (eds) (1993) *Chinese Families in the Post-Mao Era, Studies on China 17*, Berkeley: University of California Press.

Gates, H. (1991) '"Narrow Hearts" and Petty Capitalism: Small Business Women in Chengdu, China', in A. Littlefield and H. Gates (ed.) *Marxist Approaches in Economic Anthropology*, Lanham: University of America Press.

—— (1999) *Looking for Chengdu: A Woman's Adventures in China*, Ithaca, NY: Cornell University Press.

Guo, S. (2000) *Post-Mao China: From Totalitarianism to Authoritarianism?* Westport, CT: Praeger.

Hilderbrandt, H. W. and Liu J. (1988) 'Chinese Women Managers: A Comparison with their US and Asian Counterparts', *Human Resource Management*, 27, 3, Fall: 291–314.

Honig, E. (2000) 'Iron Girls Revisited: Gender and the Politics of Work in the Cultural Revolution, 1966–76', in B. Entwisle and G. E. Henderson (eds) *Re-drawing Boundaries: Work, Households and Gender in China*, Berkeley, Los Angeles, London: University of California Press.

Hooper, B. (1998) '"Flower Vase and Housewife": Women and Consumerism in post-Mao China', in K. Sen and M. Stivens (eds) *Gender and Power in Affluent Asia*, London: Routledge, 167–93.

Jacka, Tamara (1997) *Women's Work in Rural China: Change and Continuity in an Era of Reform*, Hong Kong: Cambridge University Press.

Jankowiak, W. R. (1993) *Sex, Death and Hierarchy in a Chinese City: An Anthropological Account*, New York: Columbia University Press.

Judd, E. R. (1990) '"Men Are More Able": Rural Chinese Women's Conception of Gender and Agency', *Pacific Affairs* 63: 1, Spring, 40–61.

Kipnis, A. B. (1997) *Producing Guanxi: Sentiment, Self, and Subculture in a North China Village*, Durham, NC: Duke University Press.

Kitching, B. (2001) 'China', in M. Patrickson and P. O'Brien (eds) *Managing Diversity: An Asian and Pacific Focus*, Qld: John Wiley & Sons Australia.

Korabik, K. (1994) 'Managerial Women in the People's Republic of China: The Long March Continues', in N. J. Adler and D. N. Izraeli (eds) *Women in Business: Perspectives on Women Entrepreneurs*, Cambridge: Blackwell, 114–26.

Liu, B. and Sun, R. (1995) 'Moving Towards the Market: Chinese Women in Employment and their Related Rights', in B. Einhorn and E. J. Yeo (eds) *Women and Market Societies: Crisis and Opportunity*, Cambridge: Edward Elgar, 193–204.

Min, A. (1994) *Red Azalea*. New York: Pantheon Books.

Mooney, P. (2000) 'Digital Diva Launches Women Focussed China Portal', *ChinaOnline News*, 25 April. Available online at <http://www.chinaonline.com/issues/internet_policy/currentnews/secure/C00042421.asp> (accessed 27 April 2000).

Pearson, M. (1997) *China's New Business Elite: The Political Consequences of Economic Reform*, Berkeley: University of California Press.

Rofel, L. (1999) *Other Modernities: Gendered Yearnings in China after Socialism*, Berkeley: University of California Press.

Shanghai Evening Post website – no date provided, item on the Shanghai Women Entrepreneurs Association website <http://www.shanghaiwhb.com> (accessed July 2000).

Smith, P. M. (2000) 'People to People Ambassador Programs Women Leaders in Education, Business and Law Delegation to the People's Republic of China', China Trip Outline June 30–July 1 2000; <http://faculty.newc.edu/PSmith/China/china_trip_outline.htm> (accessed 2000).

Unger, J. (1993) 'Urban Families in the Eighties: An Analysis of Chinese Surveys', in D. Davis and S. Harrell (eds) *Chinese Families in the Post-Mao Era, Studies on China 17*, Berkeley: University of California Press, 25–49.

Verdery, K. (1996) *What Was Socialism and What Comes Next?* Princeton, NJ: Princeton University Press.

Wang, Z. (2000) 'Gender Employment and Women's Resistance', in E. J. Perry and M. Seldon (eds) *Chinese Society: Change, Conflict and Resistance*, London: Routledge.

Woo, M. Y. K. (1994) 'Chinese Women Workers: The Delicate Balance between Protection and Equality', in C. K. Gilmartin, G. Hershatter, L. Rofel, T. White (eds) *Engendering China: Women, Culture, and the State*, Cambridge, MA: Harvard University Press, 279–95.

Xiao, W. (1999) 'Nüxing: xin shiji mianlinde jiaoyu tiaozhan' [Women: Educational Challenges Faced in the New Century], *Nüxing yuekan* (Women's Monthly), April, 24–6.

Yan, Y. (1996) *The Flow of Gifts: Reciprocity and Social Networks in a Chinese Village*, Stanford, CA: Stanford University Press.

Yang, M. M. (1994) *Gifts, Favors, and Banquets: The Art of Social Relationships in China*, Ithaca, NY: Cornell University Press.

You, J. (1998) *China's Enterprise Reform: Changing State/Society Relations after Mao*, London: Routledge.

Yue, M. (2000) 'In Virtual China, Women May Be Second-class Netizens', *e21times* (August 28). Available online at <http://www.english1.e21times.com/asp/sacd.asp?r=412&p=1> (accessed 27/8/2001).

3　The maid in China

Opportunities, challenges and the story of becoming modern

Wanning Sun

Since the early 1990s, an increasing number of Chinese rural labour migrants have left home to seek work in the prosperous rural areas and cities of the People's Republic of China (PRC). This trend towards internal migration has continued unabated, with villagers going to the city *(jin cheng)*, domestic maids or sex workers going south *(nan xia)*, and inlanders journeying to the coast – all of them seeking work and income. Among many employment options taken up by rural migrants, becoming a maid, one of the most menial and lowly paid jobs, provides opportunities for many rural women to enter the labour market in urban spaces. She is often referred to as *baomu* ('nanny' or 'the maid'), and her work has diversified to include cleaning, cooking and baby-sitting; she works on either a casual, part-time, full-time or live-in basis. In this chapter, I show that the *baomu*, or domestic workers as they are now officially called, were among the first social groups to leave their village homes to seek work in the city since the start of economic reforms in the late 1970s. In doing so, the *baomu* maids have precipitated the unstoppable nationwide rural-to-urban migration of the 1980s and 1990s.

I will also show that as both the object to be 'civilised' and the subject who aspires to be modern, the maid embodies the contradictory and unequal process of becoming modern. For this reason, I argue that the story of the *baomu* provides effective empirical evidence for us to start problematising and unravelling the complicities between gender, power and the modernisation process in China. My discussion of the *baomu* is, in other words, premised on the assumption that studies of mobility – both social and spatial – in the era of modernisation need to take into account the variegated, unequal and necessarily gendered nature of mobility. Whether she is called *baomu*, *ayi* (aunty), or domestic worker, the maid, humble as she may be, is a threshold figure, negotiating the boundary between the private and the public, and between the state and the market. As such, she is a figure fraught with tension and ambiguity at the intersection of gender, class and geography.

In spite of her enduring capacity to capture the urban imagination (the story of the *baomu* has become an enduring media narrative in popular culture), the *baomu* has not yet received much academic or scholarly attention, unlike her international counterparts – domestic workers from the Philippines, for example

(Constable 1997; Parrenas 2001). A number of reasons may have contributed to this lack, including, most importantly, a tendency in migrant studies projects to privilege patterns and motivations of migration. Consequently, although the movement of *baomu*, and rural and labour migration in China in general, has dramatically altered the cultural landscape of Chinese cities, little work – with a few exceptions (for example, Jacka 2000; Chen *et al.* 2001; Zhang 2001) – has been done to consider how the subjectivity of both migrants and locals has been reworked and transformed as a result of mobility. This chapter is an initial attempt to address this gap, by looking at the experiences of the *baomu* at three levels. I will discuss her life and work at the material level; examine her movements from one place to another and survey her work, living conditions and everyday practices. Integral to this account of her physical movement is a discussion of her experience at a symbolic level through an analysis of the production and consumption of popular images of the *baomu* and of her place of origin. I also consider the experience of the *baomu* at a metaphoric level; that is, the ways in which she 'travels' through successive 'regions' in the (re)formation of her own subjectivity, in response to both the change in her material life and the ways in which she is imagined in popular perceptions.

Baomu and the servants of the revolution

Working as a maid, doing menial household chores such as baby-sitting, washing, cleaning and cooking in someone's house, is perhaps one of the oldest professions in history. It is in fact one of the few options of paid employment available to women in times when most women were home-bound and immobile. As early as the Qing Dynasty, some well-to-do Beijing households were employers of *laomazi* (meaning 'old woman', referring to the maid, who may or may not be old) from Sanhe, a rural area in Hebei Province, which was known as a sending zone for maids to Beijing.[1] By 1920, there were as many as 2,000 women from adjacent areas and regions working as domestic servants in households inside the concession areas in Shanghai (Chi 1999: 7). Nannies and maids are also common to the European experience (for a study of nannies and maids working in affluent English homes in the Victorian era, see McClintock 1995).

In the case of China, the routine and widespread practice of paying domestic servants to do household chores arose during the last two decades. The nationwide trend of rural women becoming domestic servants in the city can be traced back to a group of entrepreneurial women from the villages of Wuwei, Anhui Province.[2] The history of the 'Anhui maid' starts long before the beginning of economic reforms. A rural area northwest of the Yangtze River in central Anhui, a largely rural province in eastern central China, Wuwei was well known in the history of the revolutionary era. A stronghold of the New Fourth Army led by the Chinese Communist Party (CCP) during the War of Resistance against Japan (Zhongguo Renkou 1987: 72), it was also the headquarters of its 7th Division (Zhang 2000: 1). One narrative dates the entry of the Wuwei maids into Beijing to as early as before 1949, when, courtesy of their connections with these CCP revolutionaries, the first Wuwei women left their village homes for Beijing to work as domestic servants (Wang Xinping 1996). Another narrative points to the founding of the People's Republic of China as the beginning of the Wuwei maid phenomenon. According to those holding this view, revolutionary veterans who were native to Wuwei and the surrounding region were rewarded with important government positions in Beijing for their contribution to the new republic. Settled in Beijing yet missing the food, dialect and life-style of their southern hometowns, these high-ranking Party cadres resorted to bringing women from their villages – including both single and married women – to Beijing to provide domestic services for them and their families, cooking, cleaning and baby-sitting (Zhu 2000). The Wuwei *baomu* maids were thus among the earliest migrant women, known in general as *dagongmei* (working sisters). Between the pre-1949 period to the 1970s, there were around 3,000 women from Wuwei working as maids in Beijing, Tianjin and Shanghai and other metropolitan areas (Wang Xinping 1996).

The use of *baomu* in Beijing in the Maoist era was not a widespread phenomenon and was mainly limited to two types of families: the families of high-ranking Party cadres from Wuwei and Anhui who had been relocated to big cities, and the families of senior scholars (*gaoji zhishi fenzi*) who were used to the southern ways of life, and thus, like the Party officials, resorted to importing maids from hometowns in the south. Most of these maids were paid quite small wages, although it was the convention that employers usually took care of the maid and her family by providing regular material assistance. It was not uncommon for a maid to spend many years in the family, to form emotional bonds with the children they nursed, and to end up becoming a *de facto* family member. During the 1960s and 1970s, the decades of political movements and 'class struggle', *baomu* became a signifier of oppression and exploitation of the proletariats by the 'decadent bourgeoise' or 'capitalist roaders'. Having a *baomu* in one's home could be incriminating evidence against cadres and senior scholars during the era of Cultural Revolution, and, as a result, most *baomu* were sent home (Liu 1998). A small number of maids, however, stuck with their employers 'through thick and thin' during times of political turbulence and continued to work for their disgraced employers.

Qie Ruigu, now a 96-year-old, is one such maid. Qie was a native of Hebei Province. Newly widowed, she went to Beijing in 1953 to look after the children of a couple called Qu and Wang, both senior cadres in the Ministry of Engineering. When her employers were transferred, initially to Shenyang and then to Dalian, Qie followed the family in spite of her desire to stay close to her hometown in Hebei. During the Cultural Revolution, the couple, due to their 'murky past' (they had worked undercover for the CCP before liberation) were denounced by the 'proletarian rebels' and sent to a reform camp in a remote farming area. Qie was told by the Red Guards to wake up to the fact that she had been exploited and that she should cut her ties with the couple accused as 'spies'. She defied the pressure and continued to look after the children of the wronged couple. As Qu's health deteriorated due to constant and severe beatings by the Red Guards, Qie took on an additional role as his nurse and carer. Qu and Wang were rehabilitated in 1976, the year in which their maid Qie turned seventy. Qie, now in her nineties, survived her employer Qu. She lives with the three generations of the family, and presides over family affairs as the most respected and loved elder (Wang Shuchun 2001: 9).

Although a product of socialist collectivism, the Wuwei *baomu* embodied some paradoxes that were to continue into the market economy. Like Qie, most maids in the Maoist era were recruited into the families of 'revolutionaries', and, by rendering domestic service to the state officials, they made a contribution to the collective goal of the socialist state. In order to do that, the maids had to be prepared to leave home and perform menial domestic tasks in the homes of 'revolutionary heroes' of the socialist era. To be sure, the desire of the state officials to have a sense of 'home' – including having the comfort of eating food from home and hearing dialects from home – is understandable and well justified; however, the acquisition of their comfort and a feeling of being at home – both material and cultural – is premised upon women of another class leaving their own homes. In other words, the *baomu* can be seen to be an unsung heroine in the grand narrative of socialist construction. Her contribution to the socialist project, however, not surprisingly, went unrecognised. Moreover, during the socialist era, the humble maid became a figure of contention, caught in the cross-fire between political factions within the party-state.

Wuwei maids and the pioneers of rural–urban migration

At the onset of the economic reforms in late 1970s, some Wuwei women, thanks to the historical connections between Wuwei and Beijing, were quick to see a niche employment market. Capitalising on the reputation of the 'Wuwei maid' in the pre-reform era, some Wuwei women left home and went to Beijing. With one Wuwei maid come many followers, and within a couple of years, a number of villages in Wuwei acquired a name as '*baomu* villages'. By 1993, as many as 30,000 Wuwei women were working as *baomu*. Other statistics (Ma and Xiang 1998) indicate that as many as one-third of Beijing's maids come from Anhui. Another survey (Dutton 1998) confirms this finding: among 329 service persons questioned in Beijing, 30.4 per cent of them come from the southern province of Anhui and as many as 71 per cent of these Anhui women come from one village. Interestingly, while Xiaogang Village, Fengyang County in Anhui is well known to have experimented with the 'family land responsibility system' in the late 1970s, which led to the nationwide economic reform in rural areas (Sun 2002a), it is not generally known that it may have been the humble maids from Wuwei who pioneered rural–urban migration at the start of the economic reform period (from 1978). By taking the first step of leaving their village homes and seeking paid employment in the city, these women embarked on a journey to become 'modern', and in doing so, irreversibly if not single-handedly, precipitated the rural migration which changed the landscape of urban China.

The physical mobility of the Wuwei *baomu* often goes hand in hand with her social mobility. Like many other rural migrants in China, once she has made the decision to leave home, she typically embarks on a journey of self-development. It is common for a village woman to come to the city as a *baomu* and then acquire skills and basic literacy. As she becomes better informed about her options and opportunities in the city, she may become self-employed or even an employer herself. Zhao Yuemin is a noted example. In early 1980s, Zhao, born and brought up in a village in Wuwei, followed the footsteps of her mother and grandmother who worked as maids and went to Beijing. However, although initially she worked as a maid, Zhao was determined that the family history of service as a maid would end with her. While cleaning, cooking and looking after the children of her employer, she enrolled in part-time studies and learned modern techniques in raising chickens. When she had accumulated enough capital, she quit her job as a maid and started her own chicken farm outside Beijing. Becoming competent and confident in her business, she finally decided to return to Wuwei, and became a shareholder and manager in the village-run chicken farm, which generated an annual income of 200,000 yuan (Yang and Guan 1999).

Like Zhao, many *baomu*, once dislocated from their village homes, effectively formed employment networks by liaising between their village home and the city, communicating information about market demand and offering tips about money-making and employment opportunities. Zhang Jingcui, once a maid from Wuwei, is one such networker. She went to Beijing in 1980, and following her introductions and recommendations, many people from her own and her relatives' families also came to Beijing. She has since returned to Wuwei to live but travels regularly to Beijing to see her two sons, who run a toy shop and a fast food business respectively, and her daughter, who works in the retail clothing trade (Hu 2001: 9). This 'Wuwei *baomu*' became an exemplary figure for rural women from other provinces. Zhang's success in leaving home, seeking paid employment in the city was an inspiration to rural women in China. Many of them, particularly those from Henan, Sichuan, and Gansu, largely rural and compatively underdeveloped provinces, followed suit, left home and set out for the city (Wang Xinping 1996: 139).

The stories of these two Wuwei women exemplify a few patterns of the *baomu* profession in the 1980s. First, once they have taken the first step of leaving home, the maid becomes a conduit between home and the city, conveying information about the job market, business contacts and ways of making money. She is an initiator and a vital link in the chain of rural–urban migration. Second, unlike her historical predecessors, most maids nowadays do not see it important to be dedicated to their profession or loyal to their employers. Many maids treat the job of *baomu* as only a first step to independence, a temporary way of finding anchorage in the city, and a stepping stone into some more lucrative and autonomous ways of earning a living. Many move from being a maid into other types of work, finding employment in small businesses, grocery and vegetable retail outlets, restaurants, the retail clothing trade and elsewhere. Lastly, the 'humble' maid, or the '*xiao baomu*' as she is often referred to, is indeed a translocal, or a liminal figure, poised between here and there, who with her introductions, liaison and networking, contributes to revitalising the economies and markets of her hometown, the region as well as the city. Finally, her work as a maid in middle-class families in the city helps to meet the growing demand for the most menial yet responsible domestic work.

The 'branding' of the *baomu*

By the 1980s, with the arrival of maids from Wuwei en masse, 'Wuwei *baomu*' became a household term. 'Mention *baomu*, one thinks of Anhui; mention Anhui *baomu*, one thinks of Wuwei', as the saying goes in Beijing.[3] As with any 'brand name', the Wuwei *baomu* is known among Beijing urbanities to have certain qualities: she is known to be competent, efficient, clean and tidy, and good with children. As with any other 'branded' consumer product that acquires a reputation and currency due to a growing visibility and circulation in the market, dealing with competition is a fact of life.

By the mid-1980s, the monopoly of the Wuwei *baomu* in Beijing came under threat with the arrival of rivals: *Sichuan mei* (sisters from Sichuan). Like Wuwei *baomu*, Sichuan *baomu* are also known to be competent, efficient and clean; in addition, they are reputedly hard-working, gentle, soft-spoken and, above all, 'good-looking', with fairer complexion and prettier features than the Wuwei maids. These reputed qualities prove to be a winning combination, as Beijing residents seemed to prefer Sichuan *baomu* when given a choice. The popularity of Sichuan *baomu* is also said to be linked to a traditional local superstition in Beijing, which holds that one's baby may grow to look like the person who cares for them. Since Sichuan *baomu* are known for their good looks and pleasant demeanour, they naturally hold more cachet. Sichuan *baomu* are also known to be shorter than *baomu* from other provinces, but their height clearly does not bother most employers. Beijing's *baomu* market was dominated by Sichuan *baomu* for several years in the 1980s, but disappointingly to Beijing residents, the number of *Sichuan mei* started to dwindle, and by the end of the 1980s, Wuwei *baomu* recaptured the market by sheer force of numbers. Currently in Beijing, the Sichuan *baomu* is still a favourite 'brand', with an estimated population of around 10,000. Nonetheless, in terms of raw numbers, the market is dominated by maids from Anhui and Henan, with maids from Sichuan, and Gansu Provinces in third and fourth place (Liu 1998).

Although the Wuwei *baomu* still dominates the market in Beijing, in comparison with the competition, she is now perceived to have acquired some 'disappointing' traits, the most significant of which is her reputed tendency to spread gossip about her employers. Wuwei *baomu*, according to some Beijing residents, like to 'hang out' together, which, some believe, leads to another 'undesirable' tendency: veteran *baomu* teach novices how to 'cut corners' and manipulate employers. Gradually Wuwei *baomu*s acquired the reputation of being 'slippery' (*hua*, cunning and disingenuous). By mid-1980s, the Wuwei *baomu* realised that they had to reckon with a somewhat tarnished image.

The production and consumption of 'brand-name' maids is sometimes location-specific. In other words, while some brand names such as the Anhui *baomu* seems to have acquired a national reputation thanks to her history and availability, there are some 'brands' that are only known to and favoured by a particular market. Chifeng *baomu* – maids from Chifeng, a poverty-stricken rural mountainous region in Inner Mongolia Autonomous Region, unknown to most people in China – is a favourite 'brand' among residents in Tianjin. Chifeng *baomu* are known to be honest, hard-working and resilient, and are clearly the preferences of many prospective employers. The creation of Chifeng *baomu* started in 1998, when, as part of the nation-wide, state-initiated policy of 'helping the poor', the grass-roots Women's Federation in Chifeng, under the auspice of Tianjin Women's Federation, secured an agreement with Tianjin Domestic Service Introduction Service to supply fifteen young women to Tianjin to work as maids. The success of this initiative paved the way for more maids from Chifeng to Tianjin, enabling maids from this region gradually to acquire a 'brand name' reputation (Meng 1999: 19).

The *baomu* caters not only to the practical and material needs of the consumer, but more importantly, she helps to enhance the social status and identity of the person who employs her. Increasingly, the use of domestic help, together with a big apartment, a passport, or a car, has become a sign of affluence. While many hire part-timers to do housework they cannot easily do themselves, a growing number of middle-class families are hiring maids mainly because they are available and affordable. Zhang, a retired senior journalist in Shanghai, hires a maid to clean her apartment and do some caring for her elderly mother. Single, she spends most of her day dabbling in the share markets. She told me that with the improvement of housing standards, most of her friends have moved to new apartments around 100 square metres in size. With a bigger apartment comes more cleaning. Since maids are available and so cheap, why not get someone to clean the apartment once a day for as little as 3 to 5 yuan an hour?[4] Her story is echoed by Mr Mi, a young university graduate now working in a computer shop. He and his flatmate are both young and single and do not require much help with housework, however, they get someone in once a day, because 'it is so cheap', particularly if they are from Anhui.[5]

There are a number of ways in which the maid is seen to have been clearly objectified through this 'branding' practice. Akin to a consumer product, she is usually described and defined in terms of her origin, not her individuality, although qualities such as 'being hard-working, competent, and being good with children' are arguably related to the maid as an individual rather than to her origin. This is indeed a paradoxical situation. On the one hand, the maid is employed to provide domestic service, and the quality of her work is contingent on her being a caring, professionally competent and socially responsible person. On the other hand, the popular definition of who she is does not in any way take into account her agency nor describe her subjectivity. In this sense, the discursive strategy of naming or 'branding', a crucial exercise of 'sort[ing] persons into the hierarchically arranged categories of a moral order' (Anagnost

1997: 100), is seen to have validity not only with regard to the governance of the state, as Ann Anagnost observes, but also to the operations of the market.

The practice of 'branding' the service provided by the maid by referring to her place of origin is also a powerful reminder of the disparity and stratification between regions and provinces, and the subordination of those 'peripheral places'. In other words, 'Wuwei *baomu*' or '*Sichuan mei*', as they are referred to in Beijing, or 'Chifeng *baomu*' in Tianjin, are more than just an apt description of the maid and her origin; more importantly, these terms connote the subordination of these peripheral places to the metropolitan centre, including Beijing, Shanghai and other what I call 'internal global cities' in China. As I discuss in detail elsewhere, 'Anhui', as part of the elaborate urban myth, is consumed both as a territorial space whose poverty has conditioned the cultural practice of the Anhui maid, and as an imaginary place whose accessibility, marketability and 'authenticity' emerge not in spite of, but because of, the poverty of the region (Sun, forthcoming). The 'Wuwei *baomu*', or '*Sichuan mei*', or 'Chifeng *baomu*' is seen as a metaphor for the gendered, unequal and uneven relationship between Anhui, Sichuan or Inner Mongolia and metropolitan places such as Beijing and Shanghai, and as such she features prominently both in popular cultural representations and popular consciousness. Mobile, abundant and available any time, the *baomu* is not only useful in that she provides material, practical service to urban families; she is also discursively useful, since she embodies the enduring potency of the metaphor of poverty. The '*baomu* from X or Y place' is a brand name, a product, whose cachet, authenticity and desirability is made possible not in spite of, but precisely because of the popular perception that these places are 'poor'. In this sense, the association of these places with poverty operates on a metaphoric level – Anhui or Sichuan is like a maid in the scheme of the national economy – as well as on a metonymic level: the maid stands for Anhui or Sichuan. In other words, the association of the region or province *as* a place with the body of the maid *from* that place in the popular consciousness brings to light the complexity of what Massey refers to as the 'geometry of power'(1993: 59).

Indeed, the Wuwei, Sichuan or Chifeng maid is in constant circulation in the national economy in both a bodily and a symbolic sense. However, this 'consumer item' can only gain its 'currency' through the desire of the consumer – a socially upwardly mobile group that hires the maid – to see these places as fixed and frozen in their poverty, and therefore able to continually supply products that are mobile, cheap and always ready to serve the metropolitan centre. Finally, the 'branding' of the maid serves to differentiate the 'upmarket' products, such as Beijing or Shanghai *baomu*, from 'downmarket' products, such as *baomu* from Anhui and other poor provinces.

Between the state and the market

The start of the flow of the *baomu* from villages in the province to metropolitan cities in the 1970s and early 1980s was a response to, and dictated by, the logic of supply and demand of the market economy. As the story of the Wuwei *baomu* suggests, most *baomu* during this period got their jobs through informal networks, either through the introduction of their previous employers or via the recommendation of other *baomu* to prospective employers. However, the *baomu* market grew rapidly in the 1980s, with both prospective *baomu* arriving in the city en masse looking for work and an increasing number of employers looking for domestic assistance.

This growth created the need for a more direct and institutionalised access to the *baomu* market, whereby both prospective employers and *baomu* could come into contact and 'pick and choose'. Consequently, public places in the city, such as the triangle corner of Chongwen District in Beijing, for instance, have become a 'black market', where prospective employers and maids meet, negotiate and reach an agreement. This mode of recruitment may be a cheap and quick way to those eager to strike a deal, since verbal agreement is all that matters and requires no papers, bureaucratic formalities, or contractual agreements. It also means, however, that neither the employers nor the *baomu* are protected from potential problems. Employers may find, only too late, that they have invited an unwelcome guest into their house. Urban tales abound, for instance, about the maid 'doing a runner', taking valuables and even the baby with her. Inexperienced women may also realise, upon arriving in a new home, that the employers may be unreasonable, exploitative or even abusive. Again the urban press perennially publishes stories of unsuspecting maids being treated inhumanely by employers. Police blamed the existence of these 'black markets' for people trafficking and the recruitment of prostitutes.

By the mid-1980s, the social problems caused by the *baomu* phenomenon became so widespread that the state decided to intervene in the *baomu* market. In 1983, Beijing's Women's Federation set up the 'March 8th' Domestic Service Centre (*sanba jiazheng fuwu gongsi*) in Chaoyang District, which became the first *baomu* introduction agency in the city, if not in the country. The establishment of the centre was considered to be the first step towards the regulation of the *baomu* market. By 1986, the China Women's Federation publicised the successful experiment with the March 8th Introduction services, and within a short period of time, each of the eight districts in Beijing had set up their own District March 8th Domestic Service Centre. From 1996, *baomu* from as many as 130 counties in eighteen provinces have been recruited through this official channel, supplying as many as 900,000 households in Beijing with domestic services, recruiting about 70 per cent of the *baomu* currently working in Beijing. Since the mid-1980s, domestic service introduction agencies have also proliferated at the level of neighbourhood committees in the city, under the supervision and directorship of the Women's Federation (Liu 1998).

In the hope of regulating supply and demand of the *baomu* market, the Beijing's Women's Federation works closely with more than ten provinces, carrying out negotiations with local governments, local women's federations, and departments of labour and employment. Recruitment processes have also become more or less standardised, with prospective *baomu* needing to pass literacy tests and physical check-ups. Upon arriving in Beijing, recruited *baomu* will need to go through interviews before signing the employment contract, enrolling in training courses, and familiarising themselves with the official document, *Handbook for Domestic Service Workers* (*jiazheng fuwu yuan shouce*). Once registered, the *baomu* will become a 'domestic worker' (*jiazheng fuwu yuan*). In 1997, the China Ministry of Labour announced that 'domestic work' is an officially recognised profession (Liu 1998). Compared with other rural migrants trying to make a living in the city by working in the construction industry, in factories, small businesses or in prostitution, the *baomu* migrant group has received more support and assistance from the state and the government.

The involvement of the Women's Federation in the *baomu* market takes the form of collaboration between its headquarters in the city and its county-level branches in the sending zone. Very often, individual maids play a significant role in initiating the link between the Women's Federation at the sending and receiving zones. Jiao Xiumei, a young woman from a village in Quanyang County in central Anhui came back from Beijing after a few years' experience as a domestic worker. Delegated by the Women's Federation in Beijing, Jiao went back home to establish a recruiting and training centre, supplying as many as 1,000 maids to Beijing from 1993 to 1994. Jiao made a handsome amount of money from this enterprise, and she also became a media celebrity upon receiving the title of one of the 'ten rural entrepreneurs of the year' in 1994 (Qiao 1996).

The *baomu* and modernity

The replacement of '*baomu*' by 'domestic worker' in the official idiom was intended to replace the connotation of inequality based on a master–servant relationship, with one of equality marked by a customer–client relationship. It also reflects the diversification of domestic service rendered by these women nowadays, ranging from baby-sitting, shopping, cooking, cleaning, caring for the old and the sick to house-minding. However, in spite of the 'equal' and 'modern' flavour associated with 'domestic worker', it seems that the term '*baomu*', more than anything else, is most capable of capturing the imagination of the public and the media. While *baomu* remains popular as a way of describing the group of people whose job it is to provide domestic help of various kinds, in most cities, they are also referred to as *ayi* (literally, aunty), or *xiao ayi* (young aunty).

Around 90 per cent of maids who went to Beijing in the 1980s were employed to look after children, many of whom lived in the house of the employers. In contrast, the current employment pattern in Beijing shows that around 60 per cent of the *baomu* look after children, 25 per cent are carers of the elderly and the sick, and about 15 per cent do other kinds of domestic chores (Liu 1998). The exact nature of the maid's work, of course, depends on the individual circumstances of the household, and is negotiable between the maid and her employers. Another change in the *baomu*'s employment pattern is that, while it was customary for *baomu* to live in, with food and lodging provided by her employers, some maids nowadays work for their employers during the day but do not, or prefer not to, sleep over. This is particularly the case if the *baomu*'s family is also in the city. This pattern is common in other major cities such as Shanghai and Guangzhou. Increasingly, this seems to be an arrangement favoured by both the *baomu* and their employers, since it allows privacy and convenience for both parties.

Chen Caiyun,[6] a 46-year-old woman from Wuwei, works for Ms Zhu, a Shanghai woman and her Taiwanese businessman husband in their home in Putuo District in Shanghai. Chen and her husband came to Shanghai three years ago. Their son and daughter have grown up and now work as a waiter and kitchen hand, respectively, in Shanghai. Chen had worked as live-in *baomu* in Beijing before, but had decided to go to Shanghai because it was 'closer' to home, although she also said that she had not returned to her home village for three years. Chen, her husband and two children live in a rented flat in Shanghai's Putuo District, paying a rent of around 300 yuan a month, plus around 60 yuan for electricity and water bills. She complained about how expensive accommodation was in Shanghai, as most of her current income would go to the payment of the rent; however, she conceded that this arrangement gave her more personal freedom, and allowed her to live with her own family.

It is difficult to be exact about a maid's wage, since it depends on many variables that are hard to quantify. Some employers, for instance, may set the wage low but complement regular pay with either material reward or a bonus. In addition, the *baomu*'s payment changes from time to time to reflect the level of income of the urban residents. In 1983, for instance, a live-in maid in Beijing could expect to be paid around 20 yuan a month,[7] plus food and accommodation. Throughout the 1980s, a live-in maid expected around 45 yuan a month. In 1994, a live-in maid's monthly wage rose to around 100 yuan in 1994, and by 1995, the Ministry of Labour and Domestic Service Centre recommended an official wage of 150 a month for baby-sitters, with a monthly increase of 10 yuan till it reached the maximum of 260 yuan. Carers for the sick and elderly may start with 220 yuan, since their work was perceived to be more difficult. These are the official guidelines and are usually lower than the actual amount paid to the maid. In practice, a baby-sitter usually gets around 300 to 500 yuan a month. Chen Caiyun, as mentioned before, had worked as a day-time maid for her current employer five to six days a week, mainly cooking and cleaning. Her payment consisted of 450 yuan a month plus a meal during the day. She had just agreed to a new deal proposed by Ms Zhu, who is now pregnant and wanting Chen to work from seven in the morning to seven in the evening for seven days a week, for a salary of 1000 yuan. Chen agreed to the deal, for although it meant long hours; it was a stable job and she would not need to rush from one family to another.

In some cases, it is customary for the employers to give maids practical 'things' (*dongxi*), as part of the payment, or as a reward for their good work. A number of employers I interviewed in Shanghai cited giving the maid food and used clothes as evidence of their good will, generosity or even their willingness to treat maids as equals. One interesting aspect of this 'gift-giving' is that very often, an act intended to show generosity on the part of the giver is not necessarily interpreted in the same vein by the recipient. When I mentioned to Chen Caiyun that her employers sometimes gave her used clothes, her answer is: 'Why should I want their clothes? If I want clothes, I have money to buy my own.' Chen's understanding of generosity is worth considering here: she would like to be treated as an equal by her employers, not as a servant; and being equal may entail declining – rather than being grateful for – charities which are motivated more by the employers' desire to feel good about themselves or to assert superiority rather than by her real needs. In this case, Chen's refusal to relate to her employers on terms imposed on her – after all, it is her employer who decides what clothes to give her and when – can be seen as an expression of a consciousness of citizenship, however incipient it may be. It is also an example of the way in which some maids have adopted a more 'modern' view, preferring money rather than other material forms of exchange.

Chen preferred Beijing employers as she believed them to be more 'generous' (*shuangqi*), whereas Shanghai employers tend to be 'stingy' (*xiaoqi*). She formed this impression from her experience of having worked for five Shanghai families prior to Ms Zhu's family. 'In most houses I have worked in, the family usually has a habit of eating a piece of fruit at the end of the meal. As part of the deal with my employers, I eat a meal with these families on the day I work there, but they seldom offered me a piece of fruit after the meal.' Here, Chen is complaining about not being offered a material handout from her employers, and in so doing, may seem inconsistent with her refusal to accept the gift of used clothes. This, I argue, may not be the case. To be sure, the cost of a piece of fruit would be miniscule, and indeed, she could bring her own if she really wanted to eat a piece of fruit after the meal; nevertheless Chen's sense of being deprived seems genuine and well-justified. She rightly feels that what is denied her is not just a piece of fruit, but more importantly, a right to expect that, in spite of her status as a maid, she will be treated in the same way as everyone in the family. In other words, it is not a matter of material gain or loss, but a matter of principle of decency and respect.

Apart from live-in and day-time *baomu*, it is increasingly common for maids to work as part-timers (*zhong dian gong*), and on flexible time, with many households requiring a maid for one or two hours every day or once a week, mainly cleaning, cooking and washing up. Mr Mi's maid is Chen Shuiying, a 38-year-old woman from Jinde County, in central Anhui. Chen left home six years ago, with her husband and more recently her daughter. Her son is still living at home with her parents. The family live in a rented flat of 14 square metres on the outskirts of Shanghai, for a rental fee of 150 yuan a month.

Chen used to work as a live-in *baomu*, but now she is a part-timer, working for seven employers a day, each for one hour. Chen got her job through the neighbourhood domestic service introduction agency, and is paid from 4 to 5 yuan an hour. She works from morning till late afternoon, hurrying from one job to another. She makes around 800 to 900 yuan a month, half of which is spent on living expenses and accommodation. Although admitting that her work is very hard, Chen still prefers part-time work to being a live-in *baomu*, as it gives her more freedom. 'He [she referred to Mr Mi, her employer] trusts me and gives me the key to his flat, and he is usually not there when I work.'

Chen's desire for autonomy and independence is resonant with quite a few part-time younger cleaners I interviewed in Shanghai. While employers may want their maid to know as little as possible about their private life, so the maid may desire to be free from the scrutiny and judgement of her employers. When I asked Chen to tell me which 'fantasy' job would give her the ultimate freedom and independence, she said, 'I would like to work in a factory, where I clock in and clock out, and the job is secure.' Chen's answer may come as a surprise to many people, for factory work is hardly associated with freedom and autonomy. However, I choose to read Chen Shuiying's wish as an indication of her incipient 'modern' subjectivity. In her imagination the factory represents a more public and impersonal workplace, unlike the job of a *baomu*, which is limited to the family and domestic sphere, and thus subject to surveillance and close scrutiny.

Home and away: *Baomu* in the city

The two domestic maids mentioned earlier say that they do not like Shanghai. 'It is noisy and full of thieves. I never go shopping alone because it is not safe,' said Chen Shuiying. 'I don't like Shanghai because the only thing that matters here is money. We speak a different dialect and people look down on us because we sound different', said Chen Caiyun. To these women, Shanghai represents the ultimate otherness of the modern life: it is an alienating and unfriendly place. On the other hand, both also told me that they would like to work in Shanghai for as long as they can, including settling down, if possible. 'The city is better than the country (*chengli zong bi xiangxia hao*). It's easy to make money here', said Chen Shuiying. Asked if she would settle down in Shanghai, Chen Caiyun replied, 'I don't think it is possible, but if it was, I would.'

While Chen Caiyun seems uncertain about her prospects in Shanghai, she is keen to see that her children have a life in the city. She said that her son wanted to get into one of the three trades: cuisine, mechanical repair and taxi-driving. Her daughter wanted to enrol in computer literacy classes. The city, to her, is a land of opportunities; although she may not find the city to her liking, she intuitively knew that it is the city, not the village back home, which represents the future.

If these migrant women are ambivalent about the city, they are equally ambivalent about home. Both Chen Caiyun and Chen Shuiying have been in Shanghai for a number of years, but both say that eventually they may go back home, for 'after all, home is home' (*jia zong gui shi jia*). Having said that, they also contradicted themselves by implying that home is not where one wanted to be. 'The environment is no good' (*huanjing buhao*), said Chen Caiyun. 'Home is good but there is no money to be made,' said Chen Shuiying. Contrary to Shanghai, 'home' affords them a strong sense of belonging, and such, evokes emotional identification; however, 'home' is also a place to go away from in order to have a better future.

These seemingly contradictory feelings about the city and home are echoed by a number of younger women working as part-time cleaners in Shanghai. These young women talk about their homesickness, but at the same time remember with distaste the ubiquitous muddiness of the village roads back home. The ambivalence that marks the spatial imagination of these women seem to both articulate and embody an irreconcilable tension they come to experience in the process of becoming 'modern'. As objects to be 'civilised' and modernised, and as subjects who aspire to be modern, they articulate a strong yearning for home but at the same time acknowledge the irresistible power and seduction that modernity holds for them. The maid in each case has to negotiate a spatial relationship marked by an essential inequality between the periphery and the centre. Moreover, she is confronted with the (sometimes frightening, sometime exciting) prospect of departing from her familiar space and arriving in unknown territory. Furthermore, the maid is constantly compelled to negotiate the desire and anguish of being simultaneously 'here' and 'there', and the sense of loss brought about by the displacement. As Chen Shuying said simply but eloquently, 'Of course home is good, but I have grown more and more used to the city.'

From translocal to local: New competition in the *baomu* market

The profession of *baomu*, until recently, has always been an implicitly translocal practice, involving women from rural, poor and peripheral regions travelling to metropolitan areas for the prospect of making money or starting a new life in the city. As argued earlier, these journeys of upward social mobility inevitably go hand in hand with spatial dislocation and displacement. For this reason, 'rural women's presence in the city', as Louisa Schein succinctly points out in her discussion of the migrant body, 'can serve as dislocated signifiers of places'. This is because, as she argues, 'places are not only constituted by their location and physical features', but also by the 'specific, often regulated, forms of bodies that inhabit them' (Schein 2002: 9). My own analysis of the representation of the rural female body, on Chinese television and films, also suggests that the body of the female peasant in an urban space is crucial to the narrative of modernity and transnational capitalism, as it functions discursively to make class interests invisible by erecting the familiar tropes of city versus country, tradition versus modernity (Sun 2002b).

Once upon a time, the profession of *baomu* was considered the lowest in the job market, since it was associated with servitude and docility. For many urban residents, to become a *baomu* was to lose face (*mianzi*), and therefore it was usually a last resort when other means of eking out a living were not available. From 1982 to 1995, there were practically no local *baomu* in Beijing. Economic realities, however, proved to be a powerful factor in bringing about the sea change. The monopoly of the *baomu* market by migrant women from poor regions and provinces has recently ended, with the arrival of the local *baomu* in the labour market.

The downsizing of state enterprises, as a result of the nationwide economic and industrial restructuring, resulted in women workers in the city being laid off en masse. These women, mostly in their early and late middle age, suddenly found themselves jobless and with a family to support. Unable to compete with young women on account of their appearance, because a youthful appearance is highly sought after in the retail and hospitality industries, and too old to be retrained and re-skilled for other types of work, many former factory workers, contemplated doing the 'unthinkable' – that is, becoming a maid in spite of the enduring social stigma associated with *baomu*. Though small in number, local *baomu* in Beijing, Shanghai and other cities have became a noted social phenomenon simply because this trend represents a fundamental shift in people's values regarding work, self-worth and money.

In *Professor Tian and his Twenty-eight Baomu*, a well-known television drama series about the life of *baomu* and her relationship to her employers, a professor has a bedridden mother who is in need of constant attention. Professor Tian has at different stages employed twenty-eight maids, but, for various reasons, each of these maids fails to perform satisfactorily. Featuring prominently in the narrative of the recurrent arrival of the new maid and the departure of the old one is the professor's daughter, an unhappy, laid-off factory worker who is portrayed as haughty, snooty and reliably 'picky' with each maid Professor Tian hires. The last episode ends, poignantly if not convincingly, with Tian's own daughter appearing on his door-step, much to the shock of everyone in the family, as the twenty-eighth maid, who, having been embarrassed by her own previous 'status-conscious' behaviour and her downward social mobility, decides to 'turn over a new leaf' and serve her own family while getting paid for it.

Local *baomu* are known to have natural advantages over maids from elsewhere. They have local knowledge and are believed to understand better the local ways of doing things; they are mostly mothers themselves so are considered to be more experienced in household matters and child-care; furthermore, since they are local residents, employers do not need to provide accommodation. Because of these, local *baomu* command a higher wage. In Beijing, a local *baomu* can expect to earn from 500 to 800 yuan, while a *wai lai mei baomu* (a maid from outside the town) can only expect to make around 300 yuan. In Shanghai, a local part-time maid or cleaner can expect to be paid 5 to 6 yuan an hour, whereas her counterpart from Anhui can only expect around 3 to 4 yuan an hour.

Xu, a medical professional working for a foreign pharmaceutical company in Shanghai has a local maid.[8] Most of her friends also have local maids. Xu told me that local maids command a higher price, and they are not as easily available as Anhui maids. According to Xu, there are several reasons for this discrepancy. Local maids are more 'expensive' because they tend to be older, more experienced with household work including childcare, and more 'reliable'. They are also thought to be more capable of running a modern household, such as operating an automatic washing machine or programming a microwave. Another reason for her preference of Shanghai maids is their local origin. Anhui maids come from somewhere else, have no permanent addresses, and can leave without a trace. Xu mentioned stories of maids from outside Shanghai stealing or 'ripping off' employers and then vanishing. In contrast, local maids are bona fide residents and 'easy to track down' (*zhi geng zhi di*, literally meaning that one has 'intimate knowledge of their roots and background').

The emphasis on fixed address in the selection criteria for a reliable and trustworthy maid testifies to the double bind facing the *wai lai mei* maid. The maid from Anhui or Sichuan has to leave home and remain mobile in order to be employable, but she is deemed a less competitive and trustworthy 'product' than local maids because of her (dis)location. In this sense, the Anhui or Sichuan maid – although the Sichuan maid has more currency than the Anhui maid in Beijing – is in a way bearing the brunt of her place of origin being perceived as a pre-modern and backward place, since she has less bargaining power than her Shanghai or Beijing counterpart. The advantage of being local rather than translocal is also evidenced in the fact that most domestic service recruitment agencies with a transnational clientele usually favour local maids over *wai lai mei*.

Maids in Foreigners' Homes, a popular television drama series screened in China recently, for instance, tells the stories of three maids all working for foreigners (including people from Taiwan and Hong Kong) living in an expensive suburb of Shanghai. One of them is a *wai lai mei*, and the other two are local laid-off factory workers. Throughout the story, the *wai lai mei*, a hard-working and honest young woman, is seen to have benefited from her two friends, who patiently teach her 'modern' and 'civilised' ways of behaviour, the key to gaining acceptance in the foreigner's house. She is often told to leave behind her 'unclean' habits and 'coarse' manners of the countryside since she is now in the transnational space of Shanghai.

Conclusion

The experience of leaving her village home and becoming a maid in the city has indeed set the maid on an irreversible journey towards modernity. Again, as an object to be 'civilised' by the modernisation process, and as a subject who aspires to become 'modern', the maid displays a spatial imagination marked by contradiction and ambivalence regarding both 'home' and the 'city'. In addition, although her primary goal of being in the city is to make money, her work and life experience in the city also seem to have the potential of enabling her to take on modern views regarding subjects such as equality, privacy, freedom and individual rights. She is by no means, as many urban residents imagine, merely the object of a civilising process, voiceless, inarticulate and reassuringly pre-modern.

This point having been made, it is also clear that although the *baomu* features prominently as the pioneer of the nationwide rural–urban migration in the grand narrative of economic development and modernisation, the work of the *baomu*, more than many other ways of making a living, is subject to a regime of difference, marked along the lines of gender, class and place. For an increasing number of families in the Chinese city, having a maid – whether part-time or full-time live-in – is either an affordable and necessary way of coping with the duties of a modern household, or a convenient and common way of signifying one's consumption power and social status in a modern society. The professionalisation of the *baomu*, seen in the transformation from *baomu* to the domestic worker, arose with the emergence of globalisation and the Chinese market economy. In this sense, the *baomu* can be seen to have the opportunity to participate in modernity, but her presence and participation in the modernisation process is conditional on her willingness to accept modernity's conditions and consequences.

Notes

1 Legend has it that only married women from Sanhe were allowed to go to Beijing to work as maids. It is believed that Sanhe *laomazi* (old woman) had two motives for becoming maids in Beijing: money and experience. Returned maids were usually perceived to be better housewives since they had the experience of living in rich people's houses. See Liu (1998).
2 For a detailed account of Anhui's economic development and social change see Sun (2002a).
3 'Jingcheng *baomu shu Anhui, Anhui baomu shu Wuwei.*'
4 The interview with Zhang took place in Shanghai in April 2001.
5 The interview with Mr Mi took place in Shanghai in April 2001.
6 I interviewed Chen Caiyun and Chen Shuiying in April 2001 in Shanghai.
7 1 yuan is roughly the equivalent of US$0.12. Or, in reverse 1 US dollar is the equivalent of more than 8 Chinese yuan.
8 I interviewed Xu in Shanghai in April and June 2001.

References

Anagnost, A. (1997) *National Past-Times: Narrative, Representation, and Power in Modern China*, Durham, NC, and London: Duke University Press.
Chen, N., Clark, C. and Gottschang, S. (eds) (2001) *China Urban: Ethnographies of Contemporary China*, Durham, NC: Duke University Press.
Chi, Z. (1999) 'Dagong mei de lishi kaocha' [An historical account of the working sister], *Guangming Daily*, July 9: 7.
Constable, N. (1997) *Maid to Order to Hong Kong*, Ithaca, NY: Cornell University Press.
Dutton, M. (1998) *Streetlife China*, Cambridge: Cambridge University Press.
Hu, X. (2001) 'Beijing libukai Anhui mingong' [Beijing cannot do without Anhui migrant workers], *Xin'an Evening News*, Feb. 8: 9.
Jacka, T. (2000) 'My Life as a Migrant Worker', *Intersections* 4 (Sept.) Online. <http://www.sshe.murdoch.edu.au/intersections/issues4/>.
Liu, X. (1997) 'Space, Mobility, and Flexibility: Chinese Villages and Scholars Negotiate Power at Home and Abroad', in A. Ong and D. Nonini (eds) *Ungrounded Empires: The Cultural Politics of Modern Chinese Transnationalism*, New York: Routledge.

Liu, Y. (1998) *Cangshen Fanjing: Beijing Yan* [Ordinary People Extraordinary Times: The Eye of Beijing], Beijing: Zhongguo Shehui Chubanshe.

Ma, L. and Xiang, B. (1998) 'Native Place, Migration and the Emergence of Peasant Enclaves in Beijing', *The China Quarterly*, 155: 546–81.

McClintock, A. (1995) *Imperial Leather: Race, Gender, and Sexuality in the Colonial Conquest*, New York: Routledge.

Massey, D. (1993) 'Power-geometry and a progressive sense of place', in Jon Bird *et al.* (eds) *Mapping the Futures: Local Cultures, Global Change*, London: Routledge, 59–69.

Meng, X. (1999) 'Chifeng *baomu* chuang Tianjing' [Chifeng's *baomu*'s adventure in Tianjing[, *Zhongwai Funu Wenzai*, 6: 19.

Naficy, H. (1999) 'Between Rocks and Hard Places: The Interstitial Mode of Product in Exilic Cinema,' H. Naficy (ed.) *Home, Exile, Homeland: Film, Media, and the Politics of Place*, New York: Routledge, 125–50.

Parrenas, R. S. (ed.) (2001) *Servants of Globalisation: Women, Migration and Domestic Work*, Stanford, A: Stanford University Press.

Peters, J. D. (1999) 'Exile, Nomadism, and the Diaspora: The Stakes of Mobility in the Western Canon', H. Naficy (ed.) *Home, Exile, Homeland: Film, Media, and the Politics of Place*, New York: Routledge, 17–44.

Qiao, C. (1996) 'Shichang jingji tiaojian xia nongcun funü jiuye huanjing mianmian guan' [Employment Prospects for Rural Women in the Market Economy] F. M. Gao (ed.) *Funü Yu Shehui Fazhan* [Women and Social Development], Hefei: Anhui Renmin Chubanshe (Anhui People's Press).

Schein, L. (2002) 'Negotiating Scale: Miao Women at a Distance', paper presented to Translocal China: Place-Identity and Mobile Subjectivity, 8th China's Provinces in Reform Workshop, 3–5 June, Haikou, China.

Sun, Wanning (2002a) 'Discourse of Poverty: Weakness, Potential and Provincial Identity in Anhui', in J. Fitzgerald (ed.) *Rethinking China's Provinces*, London: Routledge.

—— (2002b) *Leaving China: Media, Migration and Transnational Imagination*, Maryland: Rowman & Littlefield.

—— (forthcoming) 'Anhui *Baomu* in Shanghai: Gender, Class and a Sense of Place', in J. Wang and D. S. G. Goodman (eds) *Locating China: Space, Place and Popular Culture*, London: Routledge.

Wang, S. (2001) 'Banshen *baomu* yisheng qinren sishi tongtang' ['Half a life as a *baomu*, a life-time family member, and four generations under one roof'], *Pearl City Weekend*, Jan. 20: 9

Wang, X. (1996), *Dui Anhui Dagongmei qunti fazhan de toushi*, [An Investigation into the Whole Cohort of Anhui Maids] Anhui Renmin chubanshe.

Yang, X. and Guan, W. (1999) 'Fenghuang Huanchao Chuang Xin Ye' [Phoenix Returns to Nest and Builds New Career], *Anhui Fuyun* [Anhui Women's Movement], 267: 24.

Zhang, L. (2001) *Strangers in the City: Reconfigurations of Space, Power, and Social Networks Within China's Floating Population*, Stanford, CA: Stanford University Press.

Zhang, Y. (2000) 'Renjin qili, Caijin qiyong', *Chaohu Daily*, June 19: 1.

Zhongguo Renkou, (1987) *Anhui Fengce*, [Chinese Population: Volume on Anhui], Beijing: Zhongguo Caizheng Jingji Chubanshe.

Zhu, Q. (2000) 'Yiniang zhenghui shiyi wan' [An annual income of 1.1 billion yuan], *Xin An Evening News*, April 22: 1.

4 Feminist prostitution debates

Are there any sex workers in China?

Elaine Jeffreys

Are there any sex workers in the People's Republic of China (PRC)? At first glance, this question may seem superfluous. After all, it is well known that, following its accession to political power in 1949, the Chinese Communist Party (CCP) embarked upon a series of campaigns designed to eradicate prostitution from mainland China, and its apparent success in realising this goal by the late 1950s was subsequently acclaimed as one of the major achievements of the new regime.[1] This meant that the subject of prostitution effectively disappeared as a serious object of governmental and intellectual concern in the PRC for a period of nearly three decades. Since the mid to late 1980s, however, governmental authorities in the PRC have readily admitted that the phenomenon of prostitution has not only reappeared on the mainland but that it also constitutes a widespread and growing problem (Quanguo renda changweihui 1991: 12–13). In fact, it is now considered that new laws and regulatory measures have proved unable to curb the prostitution business.[2] My opening question is thus purely rhetorical: sellers of sex can be found throughout present-day China.

For anyone interested in the politics of cross-cultural translation and transnational feminism, however, my opening question is far from redundant. Nowadays it is more or less standard academic practice to substitute the words 'prostitute/prostitution' with the terms 'sex work/sex worker' on the grounds that the latter avoid the pejorative moral connotations of the former, by suggesting that the provision of sexual services constitutes a form of labour like any other, and that individuals have the right to realise economic determination and control the use of their own bodies. The popularity of this practice, even though the notion of sex work remains fiercely contested within certain feminist circles, is amply demonstrated by the recent plethora of texts that deploy the terms 'sex work/sex worker' to discuss commercial sexual activities in non-Euramerican settings, for instance, 'Chinese Sex Workers in the Reform Period' by Gail Hershatter (1996: 199–224). While I personally approve efforts to improve the position of women in prostitution, it nonetheless strikes me that many of these texts fail to consider whether the term 'sex work' can be successfully transposed across different cultural and temporal boundaries. To pose the question 'Are there any sex workers in the PRC?' is thus to query the homogenising practice of translating the selling and buying of sex in terms of metropolitan concerns with issues of individual rights and identity politics.

The need to query the transcontextual application of terms such as 'sex work' and 'sex worker' is highlighted by the fact that the Chinese government is currently under pressure to revise its policy of banning prostitution in two conflicting directions. On the one hand, certain international human rights organisations have drawn on extant United Nations (UN) frameworks to criticise the Chinese government for failing to place the prostitution transaction under the jurisdiction of commercial and labour laws, thereby denying women in prostitution the right to control their own bodies and lives (Human Rights in China *et al.*1998). Although central government guidelines in the PRC proscribe public arguments in favour of legalising prostitution, a pro-sex-work position is also variously promoted by members of China's public health, public security, taxation and other governmental authorities, on the grounds that recognising prostitution as work will facilitate the implementation of HIV/AIDS prevention programmes, allow the police to concentrate on the more serious problems of crime and corruption, generate additional funds for local government via the extension of the tax net, and promote the development of China's burgeoning tourism and leisure industry (*Aizibing* 1996; Kwan 1995: 6). In short, while operating on the basis of different rationales – concerns about the lack of individual rights for 'Chinese sex workers' *vis-à-vis* concerns about the more effective management of prostitution businesses and practices – international and domestic interest groups are variously pushing the Chinese government to recognise prostitution as a legitimate form of employment.

On the other hand, if the Chinese government were to abandon its policy of banning prostitution, it would no doubt be taken to task by the All China Women's Federation (ACWF), and potentially by non-governmental organisations (NGOs) associated with the feminist anti-prostitution lobby, for condoning sexual exploitation, and thereby contravening the PRC's laws and extant UN frameworks concerning the human rights of women to physical and mental integrity. Certainly, members of the ACWF have played an instrumental role in formulating the PRC's prostitution laws and laws pertaining to the promotion of women's rights and interests, all of which construct the existence of prostitution as harmful to the rights of 'woman-as-person' (Quanguo renda changweihui 1991; *Zhonghua renmin gongheguo hunyinfa* 1994). As a result, the ACWF is currently pushing the Chinese government to affirm its historical commitment to eradicating the institution of prostitution, by introducing new supportive measures for women and directing the punitive emphasis of China's prostitution controls more strictly towards those who profit from and demand the services of women in prostitution (Ding Juan 1996: 9–10).

In sum, there is something akin to an international and domestic consensus that the Chinese government has to revise its official ban on prostitution, but there is considerable disagreement over how that policy should be altered. Some NGOs and an assorted group of domestic commentators maintain that prostitution in China should be reconfigured as work in order to protect the individual rights of sex workers, facilitate HIV/AIDS prevention strategies, and enable the more effective management of prostitution practices and businesses. However, representatives of the ACWF and other domestic commentators dismiss the views of pro-sex work advocates as 'male' and contend instead that the goal of eradicating prostitution in China should be retained in order to protect and promote the position of Chinese women as a whole (Ding Juan 1996: 9–10). The Chinese government is thus being pressured to address the subject of prostitution in terms that resemble the fierce conflict within the United Nations between the feminist pro-sex work and anti-prostitution lobbies.

The aim of this chapter is, accordingly, threefold. First, I will outline the broad parameters of international prostitution debates by detailing the divergent arguments and strategies advanced by the feminist anti-prostitution and pro-sex work lobbies. Second, I will highlight some of the diverse ways in which the 'selling and buying of sex' has been identified as an object of governmental concern in present-day China. I use the phrase 'selling and buying of sex' here because the Chinese term for prostitution, *maiyin piaochang*, refers simultaneously to the practices of selling sex (*maiyin*) and frequenting prostitutes (*piaochang*), and therefore highlights the relational nature of the prostitution transaction. Finally, I will demonstrate that the problems associated with the PRC's prostitution controls are not amenable to resolution via the imposition of some 'idealised', transnational feminist response, especially one that fails to acknowledge the liberal underpinnings of the concept of 'sex work'.

Feminist prostitution debates and international law

Although questions concerning the appropriate moral and legal status of prostitution have vexed the feminist movement since its inception, feminist prostitution debates are now polarised around two diametrically opposed perspectives. At one extreme of the debate there is the feminist anti-prostitution lobby, which relies heavily on radical feminist theorisations of sexuality. Radical feminists oppose the institution of prostitution on the grounds that it arises from a particular system of political oppression – male supremacy – and denies women their full status as human beings by reducing them to the level of objects (Barry 1995; Jeffreys, S. 1997). In keeping with their ongoing critique of the system of hetero-patriarchy, they also locate prostitution on a continuum with the forms of sexual abuse and inequality that women frequently experience within the traditional family system, and insist that prostitution will continue to exist so long as existing gendered structures of power and desire remain intact.

At the other extreme of the debate there is the pro-sex work lobby, which comprises an assorted group of feminist scholars and prostitute activists who are unified primarily by their opposition to radical feminist theorisations of sexuality. In this respect, Gayle Rubin's 'Thinking Sex: Notes for a Radical Theory of the Politics of Sexuality' has proved seminal, being consistently cited as a key theoretical contribution to the 'sex debates' which have redefined the terrain of contemporary feminisms since the mid-1980s (Rubin 1984; 1993:

3–31). Briefly, Rubin maintains that progressive sexual liberationists should acknowledge that consensual sexual acts, whether cross-generational, sadoma-sochistic or commercial, are not vices to be prohibited and thereby kept marginal and distorted. Achieving the desired feminist goal of sexual liberation demands a 'pro-sex' approach, one that allows people to engage in what are ultimately consensual, if unconventional, sexual practices, whilst continuing to oppose systemic, structural inequalities (Rubin 1984; 1993: 3–31). In doing so, the work of scholars such as Rubin has enabled prostitute rights' activists to promote a celebratory conception of the prostitute subject as being both a sex worker and a transgressive, sexual-political identity, and simultaneously to reject traditional feminist concerns with 'the problem of prostitution' on the grounds that they display an anti-sex/sexual difference position; that is, they are 'sexuality-blind' (Hunter 1992: 109–15).

The perception that orthodox feminist approaches are 'sexuality-blind', and thus 'anti-prostitute', gained increased critical purchase with the establishment of the international movement for prostitutes' rights in 1985. Pro-sex-work activists often cite the development of the International Committee for Prostitutes' Rights (ICPR) as ground-breaking in that it gave birth to a new politics of prostitution, one that claims to be based on the perspectives of prostitutes themselves (Pheterson 1989: 3). This position demands public recognition of prostitutes' rights as an emancipation and labour issue and opposes any construction of prostitution in terms of criminality, immorality or disease. It also challenges radical feminist constructions of prostitution as paradigmatic of women's oppression under capitalism/hetero-patriarchy by insisting that prostitution is predominantly a voluntarily selected occupation which should be treated as equivalent in social status to other forms of waged labour, and that legal restrictions on the practice of prostitution constitute a violation of civil rights regarding the freedom to choose employment and should therefore be repealed.

Complicating the routine equation of the pro-sex-work lobby with the 'voice' of the prostitute subject, however, organisations such as WHISPER (Women Hurt in Systems of Prostitution Engaged in Revolt), which was also founded in 1985, have rejected ICPR's construction of prostitutes as legitimate workers and an oppressed sexual identity. According to WHISPER, the prostitutes' rights movement has constructed a mythology of 'liberal lies' to the effect that prostitution is a 'career choice', that prostitution 'epitomises women's sexual liberation', and that prostitutes 'set the sexual and economic conditions of their interactions with customers' (Giobbe 1990: 67). For members of WHISPER, nothing could be further from the truth. So far as they are concerned, prostitution is 'nothing less than the commercialisation of the sexual abuse and inequality that women suffer in the traditional family and can be nothing more' (Giobbe 1990: 80). And in refutation of ICPR's depiction of prostitution as potentially empowering, or, at the very least, no worse than any ordinary job, WHISPER's Oral History Project, a first-person documentation of the lives of women self-described as having been 'used' in systems of prostitution, is replete with accounts of women physically degraded and emotionally traumatised by their experiences.

In keeping with these competing 'voices', feminist responses to prostitution are now polarised around two opposing strategies. Supporters of the pro-sex-work lobby are currently lobbying organisations within the UN to accept that prostitution is an issue that relates to matters of work, privacy and choice, hence prohibitory prostitution laws constitute a violation of the individual rights of women to realise economic and sexual self-determination. In consequence, they are pushing to have the UN Convention on the Suppression of the Traffic in Persons and of the Exploitation of the Prostitution of Others (1949), still in force, replaced by a new convention, one that recognises the right to self-determination of prostitute women and therefore differentiates between 'forced' prostitution and prostitution that is 'voluntarily' chosen as a form of work.[3] Such pressure has contributed to the introduction of governmental policies in places such as the Netherlands, which decriminalise prostitution practices occurring within the context of licensed commercial premises.

In opposition to 'anti-abolitionist' strategies of this kind, the feminist anti-prostitution lobby is currently pushing organisations within the UN to acknowledge that prostitution is an issue that relates to matters of inequality, exploitation and violence, and, as such, its very existence constitutes a violation of human rights. To realise this goal, the Coalition Against Trafficking in Women (CATW) has drafted a new Convention Against Sexual Exploitation with the support of UNESCO. This Convention maintains that it is a fundamental human right to be free from sexual exploitation in all its forms and contends that the 1949 Convention should be expanded in order to make prostitution and trafficking violations of human rights.[4] Briefly, the draft Convention argues for the introduction of positive programmes in work, education and other economic and supportive structures, so as to diminish the economic necessity for women to engage in prostitution, and includes a clause designed to penalise the male customers of prostitution, while simultaneously demanding the removal of all punitive provisions for women-in-prostitution. In Sweden, abolitionist arguments of this kind have resulted in the implementation of a new prostitution policy, one that criminalises the act of buying but not the act of selling sex (Gould 2001: 437–56).

While the arguments mounted by both sides are rhetorically persuasive, they are also flawed in a number of crucial respects. The understanding of prostitution as violence against women and the understanding of prostitution as an unremarkable configuration of 'private sexuality' similarly function to homogenise prostitution practices by eliding the experiential diversity of sellers and buyers of sex. Moreover, even though the tactical reconfiguration of prostitution as work has given the prostitution transaction an imprimatur of acceptability, it remains the case that the concept of 'sex work' is fraught with problems, not the least of which is the question of what is meant by the terms 'sex' and 'work' and hence the very rendition of prostitution as *sex work* (Prestage and Perkins 1994: 6–21).

Nevertheless, the broad parameters of these debates look set to influence the shape of Chinese legal responses to prostitution for the foreseeable future. I have therefore highlighted the disputatious nature of feminist responses to prostitution in order to situate the following question: 'How well do the respective platforms of the feminist anti-prostitution and pro-sex-work lobby travel to China?'

Debating the Chinese response to prostitution

As noted previously, the Chinese government is currently being pressured by certain international human rights organisations to abandon its policy of banning prostitution. In a recent report on the PRC's implementation of the UN Convention on the Elimination of All Forms of Discrimination Against Women (CEDAW), various NGOs criticise China's governmental authorities for failing, among other things, to tackle the domestic and intra-country trafficking in women for the purposes of 'forced' prostitution and for refusing to recognise 'voluntary' prostitution as a legitimate form of work (Human Rights in China *et al.* 1998). At the same time, the NGO report somewhat erroneously castigates law and government officials in China for targeting only the poorest and most vulnerable of female prostitutes, for penalising women who sell sex while exonerating men who buy sex, for ignoring the ongoing problems of police and governmental complicity in the running of prostitution businesses, and for refusing to acknowledge the problems associated with the policing of the traffic in women. Whilst admitting that the PRC's prostitution laws are designed to penalise those who organise prostitution, rather than participants in the prostitution transaction *per se*, the report concludes that China has failed to meet international human rights standards as stipulated by the UN with regard to the regulation of 'workers in the sex industry'. More specifically, the report concludes that the PRC has failed to recognise sex work as a legitimate form of labour as advocated by a 1998 study of 'the sex sector' in Southeast Asia, sponsored by the International Labour Organisation (ILO).[5]

Contrary to the critical impetus of this particular report, however, the Chinese government does not have legally to reconfigure prostitution as work in order to meet extant UN stipulations. This is because the recommendations outlined in the ILO-sponsored study do not bind state-parties to any course of action and they remain highly contested. In any case, the PRC's prostitution laws are not only in keeping with the abolitionist thrust of the UN Convention for the Suppression of the Traffic in Persons and of the Exploitation of the Prostitution of Others (1949); they also concord with Article 6 of CEDAW, which calls upon signatory nations to suppress all forms of traffic in women and exploitation of prostitution of women.

Indeed, viewed at the abstract level of the law, the PRC's prostitution controls are out-of-step with neither extant UN regulations nor with contemporary feminist strategies. On the contrary, in banning prostitution as a violation of the rights of 'woman-as-person', the PRC's prostitution laws offer an imperfect replica of the abolitionist platform advocated by the feminist anti-prostitution lobby and socialist anti-prostitution campaigners within the Council of Europe. Likewise, by continuing to regulate participants in the prostitution transaction according to the Chinese system of administrative sanctions, as opposed to the criminal code, the PRC's response to prostitution can be technically described as abolitionist, not prohibitionist, in that it aims to penalise those third parties who profit from and promote the institution of prostitution rather than participants in the prostitution transaction *per se* (Shan Guangnai 1995: 592).[6] What China's prostitution laws do not admit are the arguments of the pro-sex work lobby. That is to say, they leave little space for arguments to the effect that prostitution refers to an unremarkable transaction between consenting individuals and that laws against 'consensual, commercial sex acts' constitute a violation of civil rights.

This does not mean that the PRC's prostitution controls are unproblematic and cannot be called into question. The absurdity of making such a claim is highlighted by the fact that mainland Chinese professionals – whether policing and public health officials, sociological-sexologists, women's studies scholars, or researchers for the ACWF – quite readily admit that the official policy of banning prostitution is imperfect. In fact, domestic commentators are highly critical of China's current prostitution controls, with a consistent focus of complaint being the gender-biased and discriminatory nature of such controls, as well as the human rights abuses associated with the practice of fining and/or detaining participants in the prostitution transaction according to the Chinese system of administrative sanctions. Domestic commentators are also divided on the question of whether it would be more appropriate to legalise the 'sex sector' and thus 'sex workers', or whether China's existing prostitution controls should be strengthened in order to halt the exploitation of women in prostitution (*Aizibing* 1996).

Given the general consensus that China's prostitution controls are in need of revision, the pertinent issue at stake is surely which proposed international strategy is most likely to realise immediate improvements in the situation of Chinese women in prostitution. Viewed from this perspective, NGO efforts to see prostitution reconfigured as work in China are potentially misdirected. One way of illustrating this contention is to note that the NGO report itself points to the multiple problems associated with female employment, the lack of independent trade unions, and the limited access of individuals to civil redress *vis-à-vis* occupational health and safety issues, in China. Given these structural and legal limitations, it is difficult to see how legally recognising prostitution as work is supposed to empower Chinese women in the immediate future. In fact, if the arguments of the ACWF are given any credence, it could well lead to the creation of another female job ghetto, whilst simultaneously generating more profits for the predominantly male-run hospitality and tourist industries, as well as generating funds for local governments through the extension of the tax net (Ding Juan 1996: 9–10).

The work of mainland scholars such as Pan Suiming further suggests that the act of recognising prostitution as work may not function to guarantee the rights and interests of Chinese women in prostitution, or even to enable the more effective administration of 'the sex sector' (cited in Zhang Zhiping 2000: 32–3). This is because, as with many other countries, prevailing social mores will continue to militate against sellers of sex being treated as equivalent to any other wage-labourer. For example, surveys conducted in China suggest that clandestine forms of prostitution will continue to proliferate alongside the establishment of legal prostitution businesses, since survey responses indicated that 'virtually no one would like to openly work in a red-light district', and virtually no one would have the temerity to patronise a 'red-light district' (Pan Suiming cited in Zhang Zhiping 2000: 32–3). Bearing these comments in mind, and given the virtual if not total absence of sophisticated and recognised prostitute unions in developed first-world countries,[7] metropolitan human rights activists might be better advised to focus on the kinds of changes that can be rendered both 'thinkable' and 'operable' in China for improving the situation of women in prostitution, rather than attempting to turn the PRC into a replica of our own 'idealised self'.

At any rate, it is somewhat curious that the NGO report draws on the work of mainland Chinese professionals to indict the Chinese government for failing to protect the rights of female 'sex workers', whilst never acknowledging that these same professionals outline a provisional response to prostitution that could garner considerable support both in China and abroad. This response was articulated in the 'Consensus and Recommendations on HIV and Prostitution' (*Aizibing* 1996: 104–6), the outcome of a conference held in Beijing. The 'Consensus Recommendations' veer between implicitly calling for the legalisation of prostitution, in order to facilitate the introduction of improved STD/HIV prevention strategies, and explicitly calling for the continued suppression of prostitution businesses and practices. Specifically, the 'Consensus Recommendations' argue that the punitive emphasis of China's prostitution controls should be directed at those who buy sex and those who organise prostitution, especially government officials and law-enforcement agents. Given that many of the concerns outlined in the 'Consensus and Recommendations' replicate those of the NGO report, even though they do not admit the liberal construction of the prostitute subject as an oppressed sexual minority, a delimited version of the legal response advocated by the feminist anti-prostitution lobby might offer a more effective means to agitate for women's rights in China. That is to say, if the NGOs in question are truly concerned with achieving immediate improvements in the lives of Chinese women in prostitution, they might be better advised to recognise the existing parameters and *domestically acknowledged* limitations of the PRC's prostitution controls, and offer interim support for the domestically generated recommendation that the Chinese government provide supportive programmes for women in prostitution, whilst simultaneously directing official attention towards those who create the demand for and organise prostitution.

Regulating the selling and buying of sex in the PRC

The actual practice of prostitution in the PRC is intricately connected with the new socio-economic hierarchies of the reform period and with an issue of critical importance to China's future – corruption by official cadres. Our knowledge of prostitution in the PRC is largely a product of investigations conducted by or under the auspices of the Chinese police.[8] For, in order to manage 'the problem of prostitution', and hence to render prostitution practices and businesses into a form that can be made open to programmes of corrective intervention, the Chinese police have been obliged to conceptualise the field upon which they are expected to intervene. Police-led campaigns have been accompanied by nationwide 'media blitzes' – blitzes designed to publicise the PRC's laws and regulations, as well as to arouse public awareness of the specific objectives of a given campaign, and thereby induce people to become active citizens by disclosing, reporting, and criticising, the existence of proscribed activities. The general public is thus made aware how China's policing authorities have chosen to conceptualise and categorise 'the problem of prostitution'.

What has emerged from the ongoing campaign process, therefore, is a composite picture of the various forms of prostitution practices and businesses that exist in China today. This 'picture' highlights the heterogenous nature of sellers and buyers of sex in PRC by showing that prostitution practices are characterised by a proliferation of types, venues, prices and labour migration patterns which both reflect and exacerbate the kinds of gendered and socio-economic hierarchies that make up contemporary Chinese society. This 'picture' also undermines the liberal construction of prostitution as a 'private and unremarkable transaction' by exposing the links between certain forms of selling sex and governmental corruption. In doing so, it points to the practical difficulty of unifying the forms of selling and buying sex that exist in present-day China under the rubric of 'sex work'.

To elaborate, on the basis of policing campaigns conducted during the late 1980s and early 1990s, by the mid-1990s the Chinese police had apparently determined that prostitution practices in reform-era China could be categorised according to a descending hierarchy of seven tiers.[9] The first level known as *waishi* or *baoernai* refers to women who act as the 'second-wives' or relatively long-term 'mistresses' of men with money and influential positions, including government officials and bureaucratic entrepreneurs from the mainland, as well as businessmen from Hong Kong, Taiwan, Japan and South Korea. This practice is defined as prostitution, not a genuine love-relationship, on the grounds that the women in question actively solicit men with money and rank – namely, men who can provide them with fixed-term accommodation and a regular allowance. The second tier, *baopo*, a 'hired or packaged wife', refers to women who also solicit men with money and rank, but rather than living in flats provided by male buyers of sex, they accompany their 'clients' for a fixed duration of time, for example, during the course of a business trip, and receive a set payment for doing so.[10]

The third tier, *santing* (the 'three halls': *geting, wuting, shiting*), refers to women who 'accompany' men in karaoke/dance venues, bars, restaurants, and teahouses and so on, and who receive financial recompense in the form of 'tips' from the individual men they accompany, as well as from a share of the profits generated by informal service charges on the use of facilities and the consumption of food and beverages. Although governmental authorities in China do not equate 'hostessing' with prostitution *per se*, 'hostessing' is nonetheless viewed as an activity that encourages prostitution by abetting the practice of 'accompanying first and engaging in prostitutional sex later'. The fourth tier refers to women who are colloquially referred to as 'doorbell girls' *(dingdong xiaojie)*, that is, women who solicit potential buyers of sex by phoning all the rooms in a given hotel, and who subsequently announce their arrival at the room of prospective 'clients' by knocking on the door or ringing the doorbell.[11] The fifth tier, *falangmei*, refers to women who work in places that offer commercial sexual services under the guise of massage or health and beauty treatments; for instance, in health and fitness centres, beauty parlours, hairdressing salons, barber shops, bath-houses and saunas.[12]

Chinese commentators usually differentiate the two lowest tiers of prostitution practices from the aforementioned upper five tiers on the grounds that they are characterised by the more straightforward exchange of sex for financial or material recompense. In other words, they refer to prostitution practices that are neither explicitly linked to governmental corruption, nor directly mediated through China's new commercial recreational business sector. The sixth tier, *jienü*, refers to women who solicit male buyers of sex on the streets, or outside of public places of recreation and entertainment; for example, at the entrance to hotels and cinemas, and in busy public spaces such as railways stations and parks. The seventh and lowest tier, *xiagongpeng* or *zhugongpeng*, refers to women who sell sex to China's new transient labour force of male workers from the rural countryside. That is to say, it refers to women who sell sex predominantly to men (read peasants) from the rural hinterland who have migrated to urban centres in order to work on the construction of primary infrastructure, such as roads and buildings, and who live in temporary work camps or accommodations. Unlike women who sell sex in the first five tiers, the Chinese police maintain that women who sell sex in the lowest two tiers usually do so in return for small sums of money, and women in the lowest tier often do so in exchange for food and shelter.

Although this typology predominantly classifies urban modes of prostitution, and does not exhaust the forms of prostitution businesses and practices that exist in the PRC today, it nonetheless underscores the complexity of the issues that the Chinese police have both identified and subsequently been enjoined to address. For example, two of the most controversial modes of selling and buying sex in present-day China are the practices of keeping a 'second wife' and 'hiring a wife'. These practices have become the focus of heated public debate because they are explicitly linked to government corruption through the embezzlement of public funds and the appropriation of public resources to finance a 'second home' and/or to support a 'short-term mistress' (Hu Qihua 2000: 2). In consequence, many domestic commentators contend that these practices should be made the first and foremost subject of China's prostitution controls because they constitute a concrete expression of 'bourgeois right'. That is to say, the diffident policing of such practices demonstrates that government officials both conceive of themselves and are treated as a privileged class who are somehow 'above the law', whereas ordinary citizens are subjected to the full (moral and penal) brunt of China's prostitution controls (Pan Suiming 1996: 52–7).

Members of the ACWF similarly maintain that the practices of 'keeping a second wife' and 'hiring a short-term mistress' should be made an explicit target of governmental controls, albeit for somewhat different reasons. While concurring that the continued existence of such practices undermines the credibility of the CCP as an exemplary 'vanguard party', the ACWF were actively involved in efforts to see 'concubinage' and 'mistress-related corruption' banned according to the PRC's new Marriage Law of 2001 as practices that violate the emotional and economic surety of the marriage contract. I stress the notion of economic surety here because foreign newspaper correspondents tended to portray the ACWF's efforts as a sign that China is peculiarly 'anti-sex', or, more precisely, opposed to sex in any form other than monogamous marital sex. However, the underlying logic of the revisions put forward by the ACWF is not so easily dismissed, even though those revisions reinforce the institution of the family. According to members of the ACWF, many divorces stem from infidelity on the part of men and the PRC's lack of comprehensive legislation regarding the provision of maintenance places women in the undesirable position of having to accept marital infidelity or face economic hardship (Liu Yinglang 1997: 4). Put crudely, therefore, the ACWF's condemnation of practices such as keeping a 'second wife' and hiring a 'short-term mistress' is premised on the understanding that if men want to 'have their cake and eat it', then, they will have to pay for the consequences of doing so.

Adding to such pressure, women's groups in Hong Kong and Taiwan also called on the Chinese government to ban such practices, on the grounds that businessmen from Hong Kong and Taiwan who work in the PRC often maintain a 'second wife' or a series of 'mistresses' on the mainland (Kuo 1999; Lander 2000: 4; McGivering 1998: 8). These concerns not only fuelled the controversy surrounding the promulgation of the PRC's 2001 Marriage Law, they have also resulted in the formulation of various other legal stipulations designed to address the practices of keeping or hiring a 'second wife'. The 1997 Communist Party Discipline Regulations, for instance, contain specific provisions to the effect that party members will be stripped of their posts for using their position and/or public funds to keep a 'second wife', a 'hired wife', and to buy sexual services ('Communist Party Discipline Regulations' 1997). Nonetheless, the Chinese police have been consistently accused of refusing to police such phenomena actively, with commentators claiming that they endorse and partake of the privileges that accrue to China's governmental and entrepreneurial elite, or China's *nouveaux riche* (Pan Suiming 1996: 52–7).

But, if the Chinese public security forces have so far proved unable to police prostitution practices in the form of keeping a 'second wife' or hiring a 'short-term mistress', it is equally clear that the changes engendered by the process of economic reform have effectively robbed them of the capacity to do so. After all, despite trenchant condemnation of 'concubinage' and 'mistress-related corruption', the growing public acceptance of pre-marital and extra-marital affairs has meant that the Chinese police are now professionally constrained not to intrude on people's personal relationships in an overt or coercive manner. As a result, they are more or less obliged to *know* that the particular relationship in question is 'bigamous' or 'prostitution-like' before they can take appropriate action (Jiang Rongsheng 1992: 34). Previously, such knowledge often came from an aggrieved spouse on the understanding that it would result in the 'other woman' being detained by the Chinese public security forces, whereas no serious action would be taken against the man in question. However, given that government employees convicted of engaging in such practices now stand to lose their livelihood and public standing (that is, the legal weight of such sanctions is now also located on the male side of demand), this particular source of information is presumably not so forthcoming.

In a similar vein, the ability of the Chinese police to control 'mistress-related corruption', particularly in the form of hiring a female seller of sex for the duration of a business trip, is limited by the fact that such women are usually presented to hotel personnel as personal secretaries, public relations officers, lovers and so forth. In consequence, the capacity of local security organisations to police this form of prostitution is reduced to the tactic of enforcing laws forbidding the hiring of hotel rooms to couples of the opposite sex who cannot produce a valid marriage certificate, and, subsequently, by raiding rooms where relevant personnel have informed them that members of the opposite sex are 'keeping company after normal hours'. Not surprisingly, this tactic has proved to be extremely unpopular with the general public and overseas tourists alike. Moreover, it has simply encouraged women who sell sex in hotels to ply their 'trade' during the day instead of during the evening. In fact, although the practice of selling sex by telephoning hotel rooms is now banned as comprising a form of sexual harassment, presumably due to complaints by affronted (male) hotel guests,[13] the Chinese police are still obliged to rely on hotel security personnel to apprise them of the existence of suspected prostitution offenders. And, for a wide variety of reasons – including indifference on the part of hotel personnel, the fact that hotel staff may be receiving 'kickbacks' from sellers and buyers of sex, and a general unwillingness on the part of those in charge to tarnish the 'clean' record of a given venue and thereby bring themselves to the attention of Chinese public security organs – this information is often not forthcoming.

Likewise, apart from conducting regular patrols of public spaces, and hence attempting to use a strong (and costly) police presence as a deterrent, the ability of Chinese policing authorities to apprehend sellers and buyers of sex in the two lowest tiers of China's prostitution hierarchy is heavily dependent on the 'eyes and ears' of members of auxiliary mass-line organisations. In consequence, sellers and buyers of sex who meet on the streets have adopted a wide range of tactics designed to avoid apprehension, such as buying a valid train ticket that can be subsequently (re)sold, and therefore having a legitimate reason for 'hanging around' a busy train station and engaging in 'idle conversation' with various people. Concomitantly, prospective sellers and buyers of sex may simply establish, often via a 'go-between', that they have a mutual interest in participating in the prostitution transaction, and then arrange to meet at a later hour or day, and in a different place, both in order to reduce the initial negotiation time, and also to avoid attracting unwanted attention by leaving together. Indeed, scholars of Chinese policing often aver that the spatial mobility which is afforded to the 'prostitution-offender population' by virtue of modern communications systems, such as mobile phones and electronic pagers, and by modern forms of transportation, such as taxis and private cars, has severely reduced their ability to determine exactly who is engaged in acts of solicitation and who constitutes a legitimate suspect (Ouyang Tao 1994: 15–18).

Unlike street sellers of sex, who utilise spatial tactics to evade the 'eyes and ears' of localised mass-line security organisations, women who sell sex to migrant workers feature in 'apprehension statistics' precisely because of the 'floating' nature of the transient population. By this I mean that women in the lowest tier of China's 'prostitution hierarchy' are far more likely to be apprehended as an indirect result of the system of establishing checks over the transient labour force and migrant-related accommodations than as a direct consequence of the implementation of 'draconian' anti-prostitution campaigns. For although such women feature in the previously mentioned hierarchy of prostitution practices, they feature less heavily in campaign-related evaluations than women who sell sex in recreational business enterprises (Beijing dongcheng gongan fenju 1993: 14–17).

This latter consideration brings into question the standard feminist criticism that the PRC's prostitution controls, as with 'prohibitory' approaches everywhere, are targeted primarily at the lowest levels of the prostitution hierarchy. Women who sell sex to migrant workers are indubitably vulnerable to police apprehension by virtue of their low socio-economic position and due to the problematic nature of existing controls over the transient labour force. But this vulnerability is not the result of a deliberate attempt on the part of the Chinese public security forces to target the most downtrodden of female prostitutes. It is a side-effect of various mass-line policing efforts – often conducted under the auspices of non-professional, localised crime prevention teams – to ensure that male members of the 'floating population', in particular, possess appropriate work-cards and temporary residency permits, so as to contain the perceived high levels of criminality associated with this new sector of China's urban population.[14]

In consequence, the primary target of the PRC's prostitution controls in practice is China's burgeoning hospitality and entertainment industry. Recreational venues were made an increasing focus of new regulatory measures and policing campaigns throughout the 1990s, culminating in the 'strike hard' campaigns of late 1999 and 2000 to enforce the 1999 Regulations Concerning the Management of Public Places of Entertainment (hereafter the Entertainment Regulations) (Zhonghua renmin gongheguo guowuyuan 1999). This sector of the economy has become an explicit target of combined campaigns against illegality, prostitution and corruption, because campaigns conducted during the late 1980s and early 1990s, particularly in southern China's new Special Economic Zones or open coastal cities, had demonstrated that recreational business enterprises frequently operate as 'fronts' for the crime of organising prostitution, as well as what is now described as the crime of hiring or keeping women to engage in 'obscene' activities with other people. These preliminary investigations had also revealed that recreational business operations are directly linked to governmental corruption, in the form of local government involvement or collusion in the running of such enterprises, and in the more indirect form of the widespread abuse of public funds to finance consumption within such venues.

In the early 1990s, for instance, the National Bureau of Statistics estimated that between 60 and 70 per cent of the income accruing to high-grade hotels, guesthouses, restaurants and karaoke/dance venues came from consumers spending public funds, at an estimated annual cost to the public of around 800 billion yuan (Wang Tie 1993: 35; Zhang Ping 1993: 25; Zhao Jianmei 1994: 35). Given that these consumers are predominantly (male) government employees, it is generally accepted that their conduct has to be corrected. Hence practices such as spending public funds within commercial recreational venues, using public funds to hire the company of 'short-term hostesses-cum-mistresses', and local government complicity in the running of illicit businesses, including those that provide commercial sexual services, were constructed as problems in need of urgent remedial attention. During the mid to late 1990s, therefore, China's relevant authorities introduced a whole host of regulations designed to ban members of the public security forces, and other kinds of government employees, both from running recreational and entertainment venues and from protecting illegal business operations in this connection ('Army Banned from Business' 1998). Concomitantly, numerous regulations were introduced in order to curb the spending of public funds within such venues. These measures are now being policed, not strictly on the basis of police-led campaigns and information derived from public informants, but on the basis of disciplinary procedures that are integral to the reform era itself – namely, via the practice established in 1998 of auditing government officials, and thereby combining the forces of the CCP's disciplinary committees with those of the State Auditing Administration (Bruel and Wu 2000: 36).

However, if campaigns conducted during the late 1980s and early 1990s helped to expose the complex links between governmental corruption and commercial sexual activities, the process of economic development itself has effectively ensured that the task of 'cleaning up' China's burgeoning hospitality and recreational business sector has only recently been presented as a task for *national* government. To offer one of many possible examples, reports by policing authorities in Beijing suggest that they were not aware of any commercial enterprises offering recreational, as opposed, to medical massage services in the capital until late 1992. By the end of 1993, the Beijing police had either registered, or were aware of, 21 such business enterprises; and this number expanded to 77 businesses in 1994, and to more than 300 by the end of 1995. Hence, at the start of 1996, policing authorities estimated that the city of Beijing alone contained 142 business enterprises offering massage-related services within the confines of high-grade hotels, and therefore operating on the basis of high capital overheads, and 180 business enterprises offering massage-related services within more localised venues such as health centres, hairdressing salons and beauty parlours, and therefore operating on the basis of a lower capital outlay (Xin Ran 1996: 14–20).

In short, by the start of the new millennium a whole host of disparate concerns had converged to ensure that China's burgeoning hospitality and service industry was posited as a necessary target of 'macro political' intervention. I say 'necessary' in the sense that, if the late 1999 'strike hard' campaign to enforce the Entertainment Regulations was designed to control illicit business operations and the activities of 'hostesses-cum-sexual service providers', the follow-up campaign of 2000 further aimed to address public and governmental concerns over the continued link between the provision of commercial sexual services and governmental corruption. In consequence, the Ministry of Public Security and the Ministry of Culture were urged by the National People's Congress to organise a major crackdown on 'accompaniment-style services' within China's recreational venues, irrespective of the cost to relevant departments, and irrespective of local government fears concerning the potentially deleterious short-term economic effects on local tourism and service industries of doing so. The response was a nationwide campaign to reduce drastically the number of recreational business operations in the PRC, both in order to control the heavy competition amongst them, which is deemed to encourage prostitution and illegality, and also to curb the excessive establishment of luxury nightclubs and 'private' or 'covert' venues – namely, business enterprises that are not patronised routinely or openly by the general public, and therefore may be profiting from the abuse of public funds, the provision of proscribed activities, and on the basis of local government and police protection (Zhang Zhiping 2000: 33).

Accordingly, during the latter half of 2000, China's public security forces, in conjunction with numerous other government departments, closed down nearly 1 million recreational business operations of miscellaneous forms ('Million Bars Closed' 2001: 22), including hotels, karaoke/dance venues, bars, 'massage parlours', saunas, bath-houses, health and fitness centres, beauty salons, hairdressing salons, teahouses, video arcades and Internet cafes, the overwhelming majority of which were closed for not possessing relevant business licences and standard fire and safety equipment. The tactics used to achieve the temporary and possibly permanent closure of such business operations merit attention, not because they underscore the 'arbitrary powers' of the Chinese police, but rather because they reveal an underlying desire to bring all commercial enterprises into the domain of governmental administration, by obliging them to 're-register' with the relevant authorities and thereby obliging them to comply further with existing regulations, including extant labour and commercial laws. Likewise, the very diversity of venues that were closed down by the Chinese police demonstrates that this campaign did not target prostitution alone. It targeted a whole host of 'ungoverned', as in illicit, irregular, and/or unlicensed, business operations.

The very diversity of venues and people that were targeted by the late 2000 'strike-hard' campaign undermines recent claims by foreign newspaper correspondents to the effect that it was strictly a moral campaign against prostitution, one that inadvertently exposed the entrenched size and economic significance of 'the sex industry' in China, hence the political futility of attempting to ban it. According to one business report, for instance, bank deposits in Guangdong Province alone dropped by 36 million yuan as a result of the decision to launch this campaign, with prostitutes withdrawing their savings and returning to their native places of origin until the campaign was over, after which it would soon be 'back to business as usual' ('Banking, the Oldest Profession' 2000: 11). In a similar vein, another report maintains that China's 'new left' economist, Yang Fan, estimated that, following the implementation of the 1999 Entertainment Regulations, the Chinese Gross Domestic Product (GDP) slumped by 1 per cent, due to the lack of consumption on the part of female prostitutes (Zhong Wei 2000). As this latter report concludes, it is thus not 'moonshine to talk about the economic importance of the "sex industry"', since it may well move the Chinese economy along 'with an annual level of consumption of 1 trillion' yuan (Zhong Wei 2000).

What these economistic arguments elide, even as they offer implicit support for liberal arguments concerning the need to legally recognise 'the sex sector', is that their estimated figures with regard to bank deposits and the Chinese GDP are not indicative of the supposedly high earnings of female prostitutes. These estimated figures refer to the 'untaxable' profit derived from a whole host of 'ungoverned' business operations and to a related rate of consumption that is fuelled in no small part by bribery and corruption. Given that the monies derived from unlicensed and illicit business operations are subject to fines and even confiscation by the Chinese government, the aforementioned 36 million yuan does not demonstrate the lucrative nature of prostitution for female sellers of sex. It points to the profits to be gained by those who run illicit or unlicensed business enterprises with low capital overheads for a delimited period of time; namely, in the less risky 'non-campaign' period.

At first glance, this latter consideration would appear to support the popular construction of Chinese policing campaigns as punitive crackdowns that, once concluded, are promptly followed by the restoration of 'business as usual'. Such a conclusion is flatly countered by recent reports to the effect that prostitution activities have been severely curtailed in site-specific business operations such as karaoke/dance venues and hairdressing salons, even as new and non-site-specific forms of commercial sex, such as 'telephone sex', have begun to emerge in China (Kwang 2000). In short, campaigns against prostitution businesses and practices may have failed to eradicate prostitution *in toto*, but the conclusion of each and every campaign has not exactly been accompanied by a return to the status quo. On the contrary, the productive nature of regulatory measures to turn China's recreational venues into 'open and healthy' public spaces is demonstrated by the fact that, even though campaign-related investigations have resulted in expanded legal definitions of what counts as a prostitution-related offence, they have simultaneously helped to create a legitimate female service worker with the right to refuse to engage in practices that do not conform with the 'valid labour contract', as well as the right to be free from sexual harassment in the work-place. At the same time, such measures have not only demonstrated that 'sex sellers' do not form an homogeneous group of 'wage-labourers', they have also done much to draw attention to the varied nature of what, in the absence of any agreed terminology, might be loosely called 'sex-sector consumers' and 'sex-sector capitalists'.

Conclusion

The ongoing struggle of China's governmental authorities to turn the commercial hospitality and service industry into a standardised and regulated sector of the economy calls into question the recent feminist insistence that the international community should oblige national governments to legally recognise 'the sex sector' and hence 'sex workers'. While not disputing the validity of concerns about prostitutes' rights, a consideration of the Chinese case suggests that such concerns are not only underpinned by liberal conceptions of the sexual-political subject, they also presume that the organisation of modern societies is to all extents and purposes identical. To put the matter bluntly, arguments concerning the perceived benefits that will accrue to sex workers, flowing from a legal recognition of 'the sex sector', effectively assume that all nations possess an established commercial business sector, with equitable and enforceable labour laws, into which the 'prostitute-as-(rightful) worker' can somehow be slotted.

An examination of the Chinese case further questions the tendency of pro-sex work activists to homogenise all female sellers of sex as 'sex workers' and to treat male buyers of sex as 'private consumers'. Given the controversy that currently surrounds the first two tiers of China's 'prostitution hierarchy' (namely, the practices of 'keeping a second wife' and 'hiring a short-term mistress'), the act of legally recognising prostitution, if such an option were socially acceptable and politically feasible in the PRC, would oblige the Chinese government to determine which particular forms of 'selling sex' could be legitimately defined as 'work' and which could not. Likewise, the tendency of the pro-sex work lobby to elide the male side of demand, on the grounds that male buyers of sex are individual citizens participating in an unremarkable, 'private' transaction, is seriously challenged in the context of China by the demonstrated link between the demand for prostitution and the expropriation of public funds.

An examination of the Chinese case thus brings into focus the constant reliance of pro-sex work activists upon a meta-discourse bounded by Western liberal conceptions of 'the individual', 'the state', 'the law', and ultimately 'the UN', in order to resolve a series of historically and culturally specific problems with moral dimensions. For all of the aforementioned reasons, we need to resist the popular association of the concept of 'sex work' with theoretical and political 'correctness'. Even more importantly, we have to question the recent tendency of metropolitan commentators to mobilise the concept of 'sex work' as a means to demonstrate the assumed (as in 'already known') inadequacy of the PRC's response to prostitution. Exponents of this approach claim all the kudos that accrues to those who speak with moral indignity against the Chinese government, and on behalf of the 'downtrodden, subaltern prostitute subject', without the accompanying ethical burden of investigating whether the strategy they want adopted can be operationalised in different cultural contexts in a way that is unambiguously better than the strategy which they want replaced.

As a corollary, therefore, we need to be wary of dismissing the platform of the feminist anti-prostitution lobby out of hand. Radical feminist theorisations of sexuality may be institutionally outmoded, but this does not mean that the strategy advocated by the feminist anti-prostitution lobby possesses no practical utility. There can be little doubt that the 'learned' cultural memory of the CCP's successful eradication of brothel prostitution in the 1950s, combined with growing international concerns over transnational crime and women's human rights, has meant that the PRC's prostitution laws bear a *surface* resemblance to the strategy advocated by the feminist anti-prostitution lobby. This commonality could offer feminist activists on both sides of the 'prostitution/sex-work divide' a means to agitate for improvements in the PRC's prostitution controls, not by demanding the socially and politically 'unthinkable', but rather by following the ACWF's tactic of exploiting the interstices created by the historical and legal indeterminacy of the prostitution transaction in China as neither a 'crime' nor an 'accepted social practice', and also by encouraging the recent shift of China's governmental authorities towards problematising the male side of demand. Concomitantly, an examination of the diverse ways in which China's governmental authorities have sought to transform the ethical milieus of recreational business ventures could open the theoretical space for inventing other possible practicable alternatives to the governance of prostitution.

In sum, the professed aim of metropolitan human rights activists *vis-à-vis* the governance of prostitution – namely, to stop the exploitation of women in prostitution – might be better advanced by examining the complex governmental landscape in which sexual-political subjects such as 'sellers and buyers of sex' have been both created and positioned in China, rather than measuring the apparent imperfections of the PRC's prostitution controls with reference to an 'idealised' transnational response. The adoption of such a reading tactic would allow for different kinds of questions to be asked and different local responses to the governance of prostitution businesses and practices to be envisaged. In doing so, it would enable us to analyse and politically engage with the operation of government in present-day China without assuming that sexual-political, legal categories such as 'sex worker' refer to universal 'givens' and subsequently resorting to the prescriptive dead-ends of morally impelled criticism.

List of terms

ACWF   All China Women's Federation
CATW   Coalition Against Trafficking in Women

CCP   Chinese Communist Party
CEDAW   Convention on the Elimination of All Forms of Discrimination
             Against Women
GAATW   Global Alliance Against Trafficking in Women
ICPR   International Committee for Prostitutes' Rights
ILO   International Labour Organisation
NGO   Non-governmental organisation
WHISPER   Women Hurt in Systems of Prostitution Engaged in Revolt

Notes

1 From the very founding of the People's Republic, the work of eradicating prostitution
   – a feat that had not been accomplished in capitalist countries – was heralded as a task
   of great historical significance and an important measure towards realising the
   liberation of all women. See 'Duanping jiefang jinü' (1949). The subsequent
   construction of the CCP's eradication of prostitution in the 1950s as a sign of the
   political capacity of the new regime, and the concomitant primacy of Chinese
   Marxism, is evidenced by the fact that this feat continues to be lauded despite the
   transparent revival of prostitution in China today. See chapter 1 of a Chinese
   government white paper entitled 'Historic Liberation of Chinese Women' (2000),
   which cites the CCP's eradication of prostitution in the 1950s as effecting an 'earth-
   shaking historic change in the social status and condition of women'.
2 In a report to the National People's Congress Standing Committee on 28 February
   2000, the Chinese Cultural Minister, Sun Jiazhen, is cited as stating that 'the problem
   of prostitution' in the PRC is virtually out of control, see Kwan (2000).
3 For arguments in favour of abandoning the 1949 Convention see the website of the
   Global Alliance Against Trafficking in Women (GAATW).
4 See Coalition Against Trafficking in Women, 'Proposed United Nations Convention
   Against Sexual Exploitation'.
5 The study in question is Lim (1998).
6 According to the Chinese system of administrative sanctions, citizens who are
   classified as sellers and buyers of sex may be physically detained for varying periods of
   time, and may also be obliged to undergo reform through rehabilitative education and
   labour. However, the practice of detaining such people cannot be viewed as equivalent
   to penal incarceration as in the West. This is because detention for rehabilitative
   education and labour is defined as the maximum administrative punishment that can be
   imposed upon those who have committed illegal acts, but whose criminal liability is
   not deemed sufficient to bring them before the courts. In theory, therefore, the
   activities of those who participate in the prostitution transaction are not criminalised in
   China. Rather, such activities are viewed as undesirable forms of social behaviour that
   can be opened to governmental programmes of corrective intervention.
7 This is not to deny the existence of prostitute collectives and organisations. It is
   simply to point out that, unlike trade unions, these organisations are not based on a
   group of workers – identified and unified by a shared or similar form of occupation –
   who collectively agitate within their workplaces, and with union members from other
   workplaces, to improve their conditions of employment. In fact, attempts to unionise
   sex workers in Australia and elsewhere have proved unsuccessful to date, largely
   because the majority of women who work in 'the sex sector' do not want to be
   formally identified and thereby represented as 'sex workers'.
8 The work of China's 'new social scientists' on prostitution, for instance, is often
   conducted in conjunction with the Chinese public security forces, and popular

Chinese-language texts on prostitution generally consist of a sensationalised reworking of cases investigated by the Chinese police.

9 For reports that attribute this typology of prostitution practices to the Chinese police, see 'China Makes Headway in Fight against Prostitution, Gambling' (1999); and O'Neill (1999). See also 'Sex Work in China' (2000) and Pan Suiming (1996: 52–7).

10 For accounts in the popular press of bureaucratic entrepreneurs being arrested for hiring women to accompany them on business trips, see Liu Fanqi (1993: 24–6) and Zhang Yanshang (1993: 12–19).

11 For a fictional account of this practice see Li Yongshan (1995: 13–17).

12 For policing and other accounts of massage services within a diverse array of venues, see 'Jingcheng qudi yixing anmo' (1996); Wang Huanju (1995: 44–9); and Xin Ran (1996). For accounts in the popular press of women who work in 'hairdressing salons', see Huang Chen and Huan Yan (1993: 34–5); Huang Min (1994: 32–5); and Li Juqing (1993: 40–1).

13 For a brief discussion of the act of soliciting by female prostitutes, as well as the activities of women attempting to attract customers for businesses such as restaurants, constituting a form of sexual harassment, see Pan Suiming (1992: 39, trans. Rosen [1994: 37–8]).

14 For a discussion of some of the problems surrounding efforts to police the transient workforce, see Zhao Shukai (2000: 101–10).

References

Aizibing: shehui, lunli he falü wenti zhuanjia yantaohui (1996) [Report of the Expert Workshop on HIV and Prostitution: Social, Ethical and Legal Issues], Beijing: Chinese Academy of Social Sciences, 29–31 Oct.

'Army Banned from Business'. Available online at <http://www.202.96.63.1/bjreview/98Aug/bj98-33-4.html> (accessed 21 September 1998).

'Banking, the Oldest Profession' (2000) *ABIX – Australasian Business Intelligence Asiaweek (abstracts)*, 6 Oct.: 11.

Barry, K. (1995) *The Prostitution of Sexuality*, New York: New York University Press.

Beijing dongcheng gongan fenju (1993) [The Dongcheng District Division of the Public Security Bureau in Beijing], 'Dui erbailiushi ge maiyin piaochang renyuan de fenxi' [An Analysis of 260 Participants in the Prostitution Transaction], *Fanzui yu gaizao yanjiu*, 10: 14–17.

Bell, S. (1994) *Reading, Writing and Rewriting the Prostitute Body*, Bloomington: Indiana University Press.

Bruel, S. and Wu Y. (2000) 'Misuse of Over 96 Billion Yuan since 1998: Auditors', *China News Digest* (Global News, No. GL00–133), 30 Oct.: 36.

'China Makes Headway in Fight against Prostitution, Gambling' (1999) *Xinhua News Agency Bulletin*, 12 Oct.

Coalition against Trafficking in Women, 'Proposed United Nations Convention against Sexual Exploitation'. Available online at <http://www.catwinternational.org/about/Unconv.html> (accessed 24 January 2003).

'Communist Party Discipline Regulations' (1997) Xinhua News Agency, Beijing, 10 April, trans. *Selected World Broadcasts – China*, 14 April 1997, FE/2892 S2/1–18.

'Consensus and Recommendations on HIV and Prostitution' (1996), in *Aizibing: shehui, lunli he falü wenti zhuanjia yantaohui* [Report of the Expert Workshop on HIV and Prostitution: Social, Ethical and Legal Issues], Beijing: Chinese Academy of Social Sciences, 29–31 Oct.: 104–6.

Ding, J. (1996) 'Guanyu jinü, xingboxue, baoli de gean yanjiu' [A Case Study on Female Prostitutes, Sexual Exploitation and Violence], in *Aizibing: shehui, lunli he falü wenti zhuanjia yantaohui* [Report of the Expert Workshop on HIV and Prostitution: Social, Ethical and Legal Issues], Beijing: Chinese Academy of Social Sciences, 29–31 Oct.: 9–10.

'Duanping jiefang jinü'(1949) [A Brief Commentary on the Liberation of Female Prostitutes], *Renmin ribao*, 22 Nov.: 1.

Giobbe, E. (1990) 'Confronting the Liberal Lies about Prostitution', in Dorchen Leidholdt and Janice G. Raymond (eds) *The Sexual Liberals and the Attack on Feminism*, New York: Pergamon Press: 67–81.

Global Alliance against Trafficking in Women (GAATW). Available online at <http://www.inet.co.th/org/gaatw/about.html> (accessed 24 January 2003).

Gould, A. (2001) 'The Criminalisation of Buying Sex: The Politics of Prostitution in Sweden', *Journal of Social Policy*, 30, 3: 437 56.

Hershatter, G. (1996) 'Chinese Sex Workers in the Reform Period', in Elizabeth J. Perry (ed.) *Putting Class in its Place: Worker Identities in East Asia*, Berkeley: Institute of East Asian Studies, University of California, Center for Chinese Studies: 199–224.

'Historic Liberation of Chinese Women', chap. 1 of a Chinese government white paper on the position of Chinese women. Available online at <http://www.peopledaily. com.cn/english/whitepaper/8(1).html> (accessed 10 April 2000).

Hu, Q. (2000) 'Amendments to Oust Mistresses', *China Daily*, New York, 24 Oct.: 2.

Huang, C. and Huan, Y. (1993) 'Tequ falangnü de qinggan shijie' [The Emotional World of Women who Work in Hairdressing Salons in the Special Economic Zones], *Xiandai funnü*, Feb., 73: 34–5.

Huang Min (1994) 'Ai, haikou falangmei' [The Women who Work in Seaport Hairdressing Salons], *Jizhe xie tianxia*, 1: 32–5.

Human Rights in China, Asia Monitor Resource Centre, China Labour Bulletin and the Hong Kong Christian Industrial Committee (1998) 'Report on Implementation of CEDAW (Committee on the Elimination of all forms of Discrimination Against Women) in the People's Republic of China'. Available online at <http://www.iso. hrichina.org/old_site/reports/cedaw.html> (accessed 24 Jan. 2003).

Hunter, A. (1992) 'The Development of Theoretical Approaches to Sex-Work in Australian Sex-Worker Rights Groups', in Sally-Anne Gerrull and Boronia Halstead (eds) *Sex Industry and Public Policy: Proceedings of a Conference held 6–8 May 1991*, Canberra, ACT: Australian Institute of Criminology: 109–15.

Jeffreys, S. (1997) *The Idea of Prostitution*, Melbourne: Spinifex Press.

Jiang, R. (1992) 'Maiyin piaochang xingwei de rending' [Identifying Prostitution], *Renmin gongan*, 6: 34.

'Jingcheng qudi yixing anmo' [Beijing Bans Opposite-Sex Massage] (1996) *Minzhu fazhi*, June 1996, 225: 4.

Kuo, D. (1999) 'Taiwan Men Prosecuted for Bogus Marriages to Mainland Women', *Asian Intelligence Wire*, 24 May, Central News Agency (Taiwan), Chamber World Network International Ltd.

Kwan, D. (1995) 'Speaker Berates Cadres' Liberal View of Prostitution', *South China Morning Post*, 11 March: 6.

—— (2000) 'Minister Decries Vice Levels', *South China Morning Post*, 29 Feb.

Kwang, M. (2000) 'Undercover Dealings in Flesh Trade', *Straits Times*, Singapore Press Holdings Ltd, 8 Nov.

Lander, M. (2000) 'Dongguan Journal: For Hong Kong Men, Mistresses on the Mainland', *New York Times*, 14 Aug., A4.

Li, J. (1993) 'Wuguang-shise de "falangnü" [The Many Kinds of Women who Work in Hairdressing Salons]', *Qingnian yu shehui*, Sept.: 40–1.

Li, Y. (1995) 'Xuelei maiyin lu' [Tears of Blood: The Path of Prostitution], *Jindun*, 9: 13–17.

Lim, L. L. (ed.) (1998) *The Sex Sector: The Economic and Social Bases of Prostitution in Southeast Asia*, Geneva: International Labour Office.

Liu, F. (1993) 'Dangbuzhu de youhou?' [A Hidden but Unceasing Attraction?], *Fayuan*, 152, 12: 24–6.

Liu, Y. (1997) 'Experts Push for Amendments to Marriage Law', *China Daily*, New York, 26 April: 4.

McGivering, J. (1998) 'Two-timers to Do Time', *Australian*, 17 Dec.: 8.

'Million Bars Closed'(2001) *Advertiser* (Adelaide), 30 Jan.: 22.

O'Neill, M. (1999) 'Vice-like Grip on Oldest Profession Loosened', *South China Morning Post*, 28 Sept.

Ouyang, T. (1994) 'Dangjin woguo maiyin piaochang fanzui de zhuangshi tedian ji duice' [Prostitution Offences in Contemporary China: Characteristics and Countermeasures], *Fanzui yu gaizao yanjiu*, 10: 15–18.

Pan, S. (1992) 'Nanren, ye zai bei xing saorao' [Men, Too, Are Sexually Harassed], *Funü yanjiu*, 4: 39 (trans. Stanley Rosen in *Chinese Education and Society*, 4: 37–8).

—— (1996) 'San tan "dixia xingchanye"' [The 'Underground Sex Industry': No. 3], in *Aizibing: shehui, lunli he falü wenti zhuanjia yantaohui* [Report of the Expert Workshop on HIV and Prostitution: Social, Ethical and Legal Issues], Beijing: Chinese Academy of Social Sciences, 29–31 Oct.: 52–7.

Pheterson, G. (ed.) (1989) *A Vindication of the Rights of Whores*, Seattle, WA: Seal Press.

Prestage, G. and Perkins, R. (1994) 'Introduction', in Roberta Perkins, Garrett Prestage, Rachel Sharp and Frances Lovejoy (eds), *Sex Work, Sex Workers in Australia* Sydney: UNSW Press: 6–21.

Quanguo renda changweihui, xingfashi bianzhe, fazhi gongzuo weiyuanhui (1991) [Criminal Law Office and the Legal Council of the Standing Committee of the National People's Congress], *'Guanyu yanjin maiyin piaochang de jueding' he 'guanyu yancheng guaimai bangjiafunü, ertong de fanzui fenzi de jueding' shiyi* [An Explanation of the Decision on Strictly Forbidding the Selling and Buying of Sex and the Decision on the Severe Punishment of Criminals who Abduct and Traffic in or Kidnap Women and Children], Beijing: Zhongguo jiancha chubanshe.

Raymond, J. G. (1995) 'Report to the Special Rapporteur on Violence against Women: The United Nations, Geneva, Switzerland' (P.O. Box 9338, N. Amherst, MA 01059 USA, fax (413) 367-9262).

—— (2000) 'Legitimating Prostitution as Work: UN Labor Organization (ILO) Calls for Recognition of the Sex Industry'. Available online at <http://www.hartford-hwp.com/archives/26/119.html> (accessed 23 Jan. 2003).

Rubin, G. S. (1984, repr. 1993) 'Thinking Sex: Notes for a Radical Theory of the Politics of Sexuality', in C. Vance (ed.) (1984) *Pleasure and Danger: Exploring Female Sexuality*, Boston: Routledge & Kegan Paul; reprinted in H. Abelove, M. Aina Barale and D. M. Halperin (eds) (1993) *The Lesbian and Gay Studies Reader*, New York; London: Routledge: 3–31.

'Sex Work in China'. Available online at <http://www.amrc.org.hk/Arch/3303.htm> (accessed 24 Jan. 2003).

'Sex Workers of the World Unite!' (2001) *Feminist Review*, 67: 151–3.

Shan, G. (1995) *Zhongguo changji – guoqu he xianzai* [Chinese Prostitution – Past and Present], Beijing: Falü chubanshe.

United Nations (1949) Convention for the Suppression of the Traffic in Persons and of the Exploitation of the Prostitution of Others, approved by General Assembly resolution 317 (IV) of 2 December 1949, entry into force 25 July 1951, in accordance with Article 24. Available online at <http://www.hri.ca/uninfo/treaties/33.shtml> (accessed 24 Jan. 2003).

—— (1980) Convention on the Elimination of All Forms of Discrimination against Women, General Assembly Resolution 34/180, UN Doc. A/Res/34/180. Available online at <http:www.aiusa.org/cedaw/index.html> (accessed 24 Jan. 2003).

Wang, H. (1995) 'Yixing Anmo' [Opposite-sex Massage], *Renmin jingcha*, Jan., 430: 44–9.

Wang, T. (1993) 'Gongzhi renyuan dc fubai duzhi yanjiu' [Research on Corruption and the Neglect of Work by Public Employees], *Shehuixue yanjiu*, 3: 35.

Xin Ran (1996) 'Jingcheng yixing anmoye tan wei' [An Inquiry into the Opposite-Sex Massage Industry in Beijing], *Renmin jingcha*, 8: 14–20.

Zhang, P. (1993) 'Dangjin Zhongguo shehui bing' [Social Problems in Contemporary China], *Shehui yanjiu*, 3: 25–9.

Zhang, Y. (1993) 'Piaochangzhe xintai lu' [A Series of Psychological Profiles of Prostitute Clients], *Jindun*, 12: 12–19.

Zhang, Z. (2000) 'Does China Need a Red-light District?' *Beijing Review*, 12 June: 32–3.

Zhao, J. (1994) 'Manhua "chi he wan le quan baoxiao"' [An Informal Discussion: 'Eat, Drink, Play, and Ask for Complete Reimbursement'], *Dashidai*, 6: 35.

Zhao, S. (2000) 'Criminality and the Policing of Migrant Workers', trans. Andrew Kipnis, *China Journal*, Jan., 43: 101–10.

Zhong, W. (2000) 'A Close Look at China's "Sex Industry"', *Lianhe zaobao* (Singapore), 2 Oct. Available online at <http://www.usembassy-china.org.cn/english/sandt/sex-industry.html> (accessed 24 Jan. 2003).

Zhonghua renmin gongheguo guowuyuan [State Council of the PRC] (1999) *Yule changsuo guanli tiaoli* [Regulations Concerning the Management of Public Places of Entertainment], Wenhua chubanshe.

Zhonghua renmin gongheguo hunyinfa, Zhonghua renmin gongheguo funü quanyi baozhangfa (1994) [The Marriage Law of the People's Republic of China and the Law of the People's Republic of China on the Protection of Women's Rights and Interests], Beijing: Zhongguo fazhi chubanshe.

Part II
Women in the professions

5 Constraining women's political work with 'women's work'

The Chinese Communist Party and women's participation in politics

Louise Edwards

One of the key markers used to identify the relative status of women internationally is a comparison of the percentage of women working as politicians. This marker has come into common use over the course of the century and derives from the 'ladder of progress' narrative established by the women's suffrage activists from the late nineteenth and early twentieth centuries. The suffrage activists accurately predicted that the level of women's engagement with formal politics would be a key measure of a country's level of 'civilization'. At the close of the twentieth century, league tables of progress are commonplace features of United Nations statistics charts and Women's Studies readers (Neft and Levine 1997). The assumption behind these ratings charts is that women's engagement in formal politics indicates women's access to formal political power – women's ability to influence legislative changes that would represent women's interests. Within this logic, women politicians would work for women's social and economic interests through their access to formal political power.

Over the course of the twentieth century, this apparently unproblematic conception – women politicians working to enhance women's interests – has been cast into doubt. Women politicians are far from a homogeneous group. The political identity of women working in the political arena is framed by a myriad other markers – class, residential status, ethnic origin and level of career ambition. Similarly, the women citizens these women politicians aim to represent are likely to have diverse economic and social needs and aspirations. The identification of a discrete, unified constituency – women – temporarily disclosed these other differences. Women working in politics have proved to be as varied in their political interests and agenda as men politicians.

Over the course of the last 100 years, powerful political interests have made good use of women's desires to work in government to buttress or consolidate causes that have little interest in feminism *per se*. Simplistic calculations about the numbers of women working in politics often reveal little about women's status but a lot about well-entrenched political inequities in a given society. For example, Mina Roces has explained how the election of women Presidents in the Philippines is connected directly to kinship politics – where the women represent particular family and clan groups – rather than a feminist ascendency (Roces 1998). In China during the 1970s the numbers of women working in top central political bodies was high by international standards. However, in the case of the membership of the Politburo, these women were wives of high-level men and their gender was a product of heterosexual marriage customs rather than evidence of an improvement in women's status. Thus, the questions about the connection between feminist intent and women's work in politics are legion and entirely specific to a historical moment.

In China during the twentieth century women aspirants to political work and women politicians have faced a unique set of challenges. Initially, some of China's feminists embraced the women's suffrage campaign that united women around the globe in their fight for formal recognition as equal political citizens to men. In the years between 1911 and 1913 several groups vied to persuade an intensely conservative all-male political class of the value of women's political participation. This goal was achieved in piecemeal fashion during the early 1920s at the provincial level in Guangdong (1921), Hunan (1921), Zhejiang (1921) and Sichuan (1923) and at the national level in 1936 (Edwards 2000a). However, these gains were largely theoretical, because the country was embroiled in a war of national defense against the Japanese and a civil war between the Chinese Communist Party (CCP) and the Nationalist Party. Women's political participation at a formal level involved engagement with various wartime governments, a political leadership in crisis, and calls for demonstrations of their loyalty to national salvation or party salvation.

With the defeat of the Nationalist Party in 1949 and the rise of the 'dictatorship of the proletariat' within the People's Republic of China (PRC), political work in China changed irrevocably for both men and women. In the PRC women aspiring to employment in politics function within a political system dominated by one party – the Chinese Communist Party. In 2001 the Vice President of China's Mayors' Association, Wang Yinpeng, described the unitary Chinese political state as follows: 'China's system of political parties is a system of cooperation between multiple political parties under the leadership of the Communist Party' (Wang Yinpeng 2001: 4).

The leadership of the CCP is unquestionable within this 'system of political parties'. Thus, formal 'political work' and 'party work' have become almost synonymous over the course of the second half of the twentieth century. In contrast, the early twentieth century women aspirants to political office saw themselves as members of numerous contesting parties whose role was independent and critical. They did not perceive of women's work in politics as being the subordination of women activists to party discipline. The extent of the shift in perceptions of women's involvement in politics is clear when we examine the different meanings attributed to the term '*funü canzheng*' (women's participation in politics) over the period in question. For the first half of the twentieth century this was understood to mean 'women's suffrage', whereas for the second half of the century it connoted 'women's participation in politics'. Moreover, when commentators from the PRC talk about the problems of falling rates of 'women's participation in politics', they are referring to low rates of women's engagement with CCP politics.

Over the course of the past 100 years another important change occurred in perceptions of women's connection to formal politics. From the early 1920s on, women's political engagement became conceptualized increasingly around the notion of 'women's work' (*funü gongzuo*). That is, women's political aspirations were legitimized and institutionalized within a concept of 'women's work' within the party structures of both the dominating political parties – the Nationalists and the CCP. Civil liberties were limited in both the PRC and the Republic of China (ROC) on Taiwan (the Nationalist Party fled to this island on their defeat in the civil war in 1949). One consequence was the curtailing of feminist political action beyond the authorized 'women's work' of the parties' policy platform. The function of women party members was thus constructed as 'women's work'. Their task was primarily to mobilize and politicize the mass of women in China to participate in party activities and implement party policy. Antagonistic action against patriarchal power and privilege – which informed the early feminist campaigns of the 1900s and 1910s – has been neutralized by the binding of 'women's work' to 'party work'. This trend was evident within both the Nationalist Party and the CCP but has reached its full power within the PRC and its consolidated one-party rule since 1949. 'Women's work' is positioned in a domesticated marital relationship with party work (real work, men's work) and China's women politicians became wives of the party machine.

As this chapter will demonstrate, a number of problems for women's work in formal politics emerged as a result of the hegemony of 'women's work'. These emerged from as early as the formation of the idea of 'women's work' in the 1920s and many continue to plague women working in PRC politics today. Throughout the twentieth century, women activists record tensions between party work and feminist work. Records of this period reflect the resentment of women politicians that their energies are isolated in the low-status political arena of 'women's work'. The reification of 'legitimate' political action by women within the 'women's work' rubric requires careful examination. This chapter focuses primarily on women's political participation in the PRC but draws examples from the Nationalist Party history where comparisons are informative.

Women's work, party restructuring and the left wing

In the 1920s, China's political landscape for the remainder of the twentieth century was being shaped by the emergence of the two main political parties – the CCP and the Nationalist Party. The Soviet Union, through its Comintern wing for international outreach, provided a template of party structure for the revitalizing Nationalist Party from 1923. In addition, the Comintern provided support for the CCP, which emerged in Shanghai in 1921 (Li 1956: 442). Following Comintern advice and in the spirit of left-wing solidarity, individual CCP members joined the larger Nationalist Party. From within this uneasy alliance 'women's work' developed its major features and concomitant problems.

'Women's work' was the prime task of the Party's Women's Department. In this management structure, women's concerns were regarded as having a unique place. This privileged status – there was no Men's Department – provided recognition of women's particular oppression within Chinese culture but simultaneously isolated women's issues from central party concerns. At each Nationalist and Communist Party branch, a Women's Department was supposed to be established and women cadres charged with the task of engaging in 'women's work'. The ideological imperative for a special women's department developed at this time within conceptions of 'women' as a disenfranchised constituency worthy of mobilising. Other constituencies were also identified – 'workers', 'youth', 'merchants' and 'peasants' – each became targets of special party programs. The Nationalist Party established a special bureau or department for each of these groups in order to promote targeted propaganda campaigns (Fitzgerald 1996: 276). The goal for Women's Department activists was to harness the energies and networks of the existing women's organizations – which were explicitly feminist in their anti-patriarchal agenda – and draw these women into the party's campaign for nation-building while promoting women's liberation. Gilmartin describes the project as follows: 'The explicit aim of this intense effort of mass mobilisation was to bring women into the political process, usually for the first time, and make them feel like an integral part of the new political order that was being created' (Gilmartin 1994: 198).

The formal structure of a Women's Department grew directly from the model provided by the Comintern. In 1919 the Bolshevik Party in the Soviet Union had formed the Women's Section, Zhenotdel, to mobilize the work of women for the cause of the revolution. By 1921 Alexandra Kollantai, the main advocate for the establishment of the Women's Section of the party, also became the secretary of the International Women's Secretariat of the Comintern. China's left-wing parties adopted her structure along with the financial and moral support they received from the Soviet Union. Nonetheless, as Christina Gilmartin has pointed out, the Chinese Women's Departments also emerged as a result of the sympathy for women's liberation held among the reformist intellectual class politicized during the decade of the May Fourth and New Culture Movements (1915–25). 'The cause of women's emancipation influenced many political activists of both the Nationalist and Communist parties and predisposed them to support the development of a large-scale women's mobilization campaign.' (Gilmartin 1994: 199). During these years of 'China's Enlightenment', the increasingly public role of women in all spheres of life aided in this reformulation (Wang Zheng 1999). Thus, the combination of Soviet structural modeling and the sympathy of Chinese reformist intellectuals for women's rights resulted in the establishment of special sections of party structure devoted to 'women's work'.

For a large part of the 1920s, the Women's Department of the Nationalist Party incorporated the energies of women leaders from both the CCP and the Nationalist Party. Together CCP women members and Nationalist Party women members cooperated in carrying out 'women's work'. Veteran political activist He Xiangning (1878–1972) led the Central Women's Department for the Nationalist Party from 1924 with the formalization of party structures in that year (Gilmartin 1995: 223). Other prominent women political leaders led

Women's Departments in other metropolitan centres or regions. For example, the communist martyr Xiang Jingyu was a driving force in the Shanghai Women's Department (Lin Jiling 2001: 192). This spirit of cooperation ended in 1927 with the expulsion of the CCP members from the Nationalist Party. From this point women's work was divided along party lines – but it was nonetheless still constructed as a discrete and separate section of political mobilization within both party structures.

The commitment to segregated women's bureaux within the Chinese political scene has continued through to the present. Women's Departments operate in both the PRC and the ROC. In the PRC the women's-work organization is called the All China Federation of Women (ACFW – *Quanguo funü lianhe hui*) – and on Taiwan it goes by the name of the Women's Bureau (*Funü bu*). The Nationalist Party also has a Central Women's Work Directorate (*Zhongyang funü gongzuo zhidao huiyi*), which reports directly to the Central Committee (*Zhongyang weiyuanhui*). Taiwan's Democratic Progressive Party (*Minjin dang*) similarly has established a women's desk, called the Women's Development Bureau (*Funü fazhan bu*).

Why encourage women to work in politics?

The continued support for Women's Departments, staffed by women and aimed at mobilizing women, over an eighty-year period, suggests strong encouragement by both political parties for women's participation in formal and informal politics. However, as is clear below, the support for Women's Departments and the women working within these Departments has a far broader range of functions within the various systems of governance during this period than simple support for women's employment in politics.

From the outset, within both political machines, women's work was aimed at harnessing the energies of ordinary women for party building and implementing party policy among women. The parties' needs were paramount and the Women's Departments, as creatures of the party structures, were called upon to serve the parties' needs. Women's rights were instrumental but not the prime focus. Women's liberation was sought but it was not the ultimate goal of the Women's Departments. Women were encouraged to work in politics through 'women's work' in order to assist in strengthening the CCP or the Nationalist Party.

From the point of view of the early CCP leadership, women's liberation from patriarchal oppression was seen as an important reason for encouraging women to work in politics. But this feminist sentiment was not sufficient in itself. It is clear that communist leaders saw women as potentially useful in the campaign to build the strength of the fragile CCP. To this end, women of all classes were a distinct constituency that could be converted to the CCP cause within the rubric of women's liberation (Goodman 2000). Bourgeois women's groups could be harnessed to the communist; they would bring with them a wealth of organizational knowledge and networks that would potentially benefit the CCP cause as well. Women peasants could be mobilized to support the military campaigns by relieving their husbands of farm work and facilitating the menfolk enlisting in the army. Moreover, women had become accepted and widely understood symbols of 'oppression' and the 'potential for liberation' as a result of the May Fourth Movement – so the CCP consciously used the 'symbolic woman' to mobilize men to the CCP cause as well. Nicola Spakowski has argued that women featured prominently in recruitment drives for the People's Liberation Army – the military wing of the CCP – primarily because the image of women soldiers on the posters would shame men into enlisting. The goal was not to recruit women soldiers (Spakowksi 2002).

Women's liberation was not the sole focus of the work, rather the intent of these various Women's Departments was to harness women to enhance the national revolution and later the communist revolution. The twin focuses of the Women's Departments in the Nationalist Party is also clear from the resolution emerging from the second national congress of the Party on January 16 1926: 'While leading women in joining the national revolution, the Party should pay special attention to women's own emancipation' (Min 1995: 503–4). At the same time, the CCP in particular was keen to avoid alienating men, who were little interested in women's liberation – in part because they were directly addressing a wider cross-section of the Chinese population than the Nationalists by targeting peasants and not only the modernized urbanities. The establishment of a separate department could create the impression that women's business would remain contained as women's business and not spill over into the broader social and political scene.

Once the CCP's control over China had stabilized, women were no longer required for their potential to build the Party. Rather, we see a role for women politicians emerging as disseminators of party policies on women and social change. In New China, women's work was the mobilization of women for CCP social and economic agenda. This resulted in the fluctuation of policies on women as the overall thrust of CCP policies for China changed. In the 1950s women were encouraged to work in paid employment external to the home, but by the early 1980s women were encouraged to leave the workforce and go 'back to the wok' (Jacka 1990). Population planning has similarly shifted from being pro-natalist in the 1950s to being anti-natalist, culminating in the One-Child Family Policy instituted in the late 1970s (White 1994). Women politicians in the PRC have presided over each of these policy shifts as political wives to the male party machine.

In the twenty-first century, a new imperative for women's political work has emerged. Women's political engagement performs vital rhetorical functions within the justification and legitimization of socialism as the underpinning political economy of the nation-state. This view espouses the notion that women's engagement in politics is a prerequisite to a socialist society and one of a socialist society's founding principles. Women's participation in politics is central to the Maoist notion that 'women hold up half the sky' (Ye Zhonghai 2000: 208). Moreover, women's continued work in politics in the PRC is presented as demonstrating the superiority of this national political structure. In 2000, Ye Zhonghai, researcher on women in leadership in China, argued that in a socialist society women are able to participate in politics in a more complete sense than women constrained by private property and class in non-socialist societies (Ye Zhonghai 2000: 208). Thus, women's work is still valuable to the party in the twenty-first century – it serves to demonstrate the superiority of the current political and economic order – and for these reasons continues to win Party support.

In addition, recent advocates of enhanced women's political participation have pointed out that leadership processes will be improved and Party functioning made more effective if women are included in the leadership structure. Sun Changzhi argued that women's political participation ensured that the Party maintains close relations with the masses – since women make up half of the population (Sun Chengzhi 1989). The logic of this argument is that women politicians bring a female perspective to leadership that would enable the CCP to connect with the bulk of women citizens. The CCP's interest in not being isolated from the population it leads is paramount in this argument.

The PRC government is also keen to adhere to international standards in relation to women's engagement with politics as part of the effort to enhance China's international reputation and integrate the PRC into the global political economy. Ye Zhonghai pointed out that developing strong numbers of women in politics would serve to build China's international reputation on women's rights. Ye noted that, because the numbers of women in politics are used as the most importance international benchmarks for women's status, China should be concerned to improve its record (Ye Zhonghai 2000: 208).

In 1995, as part of its preparation for the Fourth World Conference on Women to be held in Beijing, the State Council – the supreme level of the National People's Congress – developed the *Program for the Development of Chinese Women (1995–2000)*. It highlighted the importance of expanding women's participation in the decision-making and management of state and social affairs. Its first target was a two-pronged attack on low rates of women's participation in leadership.

- The participation of women in the decision-making and management of state and social affairs.
- Actively work to take into account the role of women at all levels of government leadership and to raise the percentage of the women leaders in government departments.
- Among the members of the leadership of the sectors, departments and enterprises and firms where women workers are concentrated there should be more female leaders (State Council 1995).

In 2001, a ten-year plan for women's development was released and promoted internationally with similar 'semi-specific' targets for women's participation.

1   To enhance women's participation in administration, management and decision-making in state and social affairs.
2   To raise the proportion of women in the administration. To make efforts to ensure that there is more than one woman in the leading bodies of governments at all levels and that women are represented in the leading bodies of more than half of the ministries and commissions under the State Council and in the leading bodies of more than half of the government departments at the provincial and prefecture levels. To introduce measures to ensure a significant increase in the number of women holding principal office or posts of major importance.
3   To work to ensure a gradual increase in the percentage of women cadres among the total cadre force.
4   To make efforts to ensure that the percentage of women in the management of the professions and sectors where women predominate is in proportion to their percentage therein.
5   To aim at ensuring an appropriate percentage of women among the members of villagers committees and residents' committees.
6   To expand channels for and enhance women's democratic participation (State Council 2001).

Rates of women's participation in politics, it appears, now serve as tools to legitimize the continuation of socialism in China and to enhance China's international reputation. Women's participation in politics is still useful to the CCP – but in quite different ways from the 1920s. Indeed, I have argued elsewhere that recent interest by PRC scholars to incorporate the women's suffrage movement in CCP history serves to create a teleological line connecting the CCP of the 1920s with the democratizing CCP of the 1990s and 2000s (Edwards 2002). Nonetheless, as is shown clearly in the tables accompanying this chapter outlining women's political participation in a range of state and Party bodies, the situation is not improving for women even though the general levels of democratization in the country are improving.

Not all arguments mobilized for increasing the numbers of women working in politics are framed within the interests of the state or Party. There are assertions that improving women's participation in politics is important because of the benefits that women politicians could garner for women citizens. As Chen Muhua, China's top woman politician of the early reform period, noted in a speech to the ACFW (which she led), 'Women must become involved in politics. Or else nobody will speak on your behalf' (Jiang Tiantian 1990: 4). Similarly, Ye Zhonghai noted that women's participation in politics is part of the path to a more complete liberation based on the four principles of 'self-respect, self-belief, self-reliance and self-improvement' (*zizun, zixin, zili, ziqiang*). The ACFW has promoted these 'Four Selfs' among women since the 1990s in line with the dismantling of state support and protection for women (Edwards 2000: 67). Ye's argument is that women's engagement with politics provides women with the space within which they can exercise their rights as citizens.

At each point in the evolution of the rationale for women's engagement with politics, the CCP asserts the importance of women's liberation for its own sake. However, women's liberation has always been constrained within the overarching political needs of the CCP – be they strategic, military, economic or moral. Antagonistic, anti-patriarchal feminism is curtailed within these notions of women's political work by assertions of CCP interest and national benefit.

Problems of 'women's work' for women working in politics

The highly unified and homogeneous nature of formal politics for women within the PRC has resulted in numerous problems for women's political representation and in career limitations for women working in the political arena. These current problems have their origin in the conceptualization and institutionalization of 'women's work' over the course of the first half of the twentieth century. However, as was made clear in the section above, broad and evolving contemporary political needs are being met by the structures of 'women's work' that prevent improvements being made. What are the major problems?

The presentation of 'women's work' as the only legitimate avenue for women's participation in politics has resulted in the silencing of women's feminist activism. The cooption of the women's associations into Party organs as early as the 1920s ultimately saw the women's associations being neutralized by Party discipline and Party patriarchy. In this context, activists involved in 'women's work' ultimately were addressing questions of women's mobilization. The problem of women's oppression by men was perceived by many in the Nationalist Party as likely to be solved as a direct consequence of the success of the national revolution to unify the country and control the warlords. In the CCP, a clear line was drawn between 'women's work' that would benefit all Chinese, and 'selfish', bourgeois feminism, which would benefit only a particular class of women. It is in these distinctions that 'women's work in politics' was tamed. Women's political activism was legitimized and constrained by both the CCP and the Nationalist Party within the overarching notion that national interests should prevail over a gender division. Today in China a feminist movement independent of the 'women's work bureaucracy' is difficult to find. A typical CCP perspective on the ACWF–CCP relationship and the role of independent feminist activity is as follows:

> The Party is a representative and guardian of women's interests ... the Chinese Communist Party has always been the leader of the Chinese women's movement ... women's organisations are highly unified. Although there are women's national, regional and industrial organisations ... they are mostly affiliates of the All-China Women's Federation. ... The Chinese Communist Party and the people's government exercise leadership over the women's movement via ACWF which acts as the spokesperson for all women in China. No other women's organisation in the country can substitute for the ACWF.
>
> (Min 1995: 533–4).

While the CCP asserts its sole right to speak on behalf of the women of China, it has a long history of accepting that 'women's work' is low-status work. From the 1920s it was clear that women cadres charged with mobilization of the women found that their work was not regarded as being particularly prestigious. Delia Davin noted that women's work was 'somewhat despised' (1978: 24) within sections of the Party and this aspect of Party activities was always relegated to women Party members. Women Party members sometimes appear to have felt isolated in 'women's work' even though prominent leaders like Xiang Jingyu strove to mobilize women workers into a unity of the working classes under CCP leadership. McElderry describes the Party's attitude as follows: 'Although resolutions from the Second, Third and Fourth Congresses all contain a statement on women, it appears that the women's movement was essentially a side-show kept alive to a large extent by the work of Xiang and other women in the Party' (1986: 111). Gilmartin explained the situation as 'Women Communists had little opportunity in the first years of the Communist organization to assume important decision-making positions in the power structures of the party except in the Women's Bureau' (1995: 203). Moreover, reflecting the low status of women's work in the Nationalist Party, Gilmartin has shown how difficult it was for He Xiangning to be allocated a budget for the Bureau. Eventually He Xiangning appealed to the Soviet adviser, Mikhail Borodin, through his wife, Tanya, for financial support (Gilmartin 1994: 208).

In the 1950s and 1960s women political activists were almost exclusively found within the ACFW. From their positions in the Federation they would be elected to positions higher up in the county or province and at national levels. At the local level, the ACFW followed the structure of the newly established commune system, whereby a women's congress was convened at each level – 'basic-level congress of women', brigade and production team – where women cadres were elected from among the women. Their tasks were to serve as full-time cadres with the special function of paying attention to 'special problems pertaining to women' (Zhang Junzuo 1992: 44). In fact, Zhang argues that these cadres were primarily top-down organisers. They continued the pre-1949 tradition of serving to mobilize women for Party policy and initiative rather than acting as a voice for women (Zhang Junzuo 1992: 45). Equality between the sexes was seen as being embedded within the process of socialist transformation of the society.

The low prestige associated with 'women's work' and the corralling of women politicians in women's work continue to the present. In his study of women in the PRC political arena, Stanley Rosen noted that 'the majority of women holding political positions are restricted to doing women's work' and 'that there are few women not doing such work who are important enough to merit appointment to the Central Committee' (Rosen 1995: 320). He reports a 1987 survey of women cadres in Hunan Province where '89.8 per cent felt that their efforts were not appreciated or understood; 54.7 per cent said that women's work is not taken seriously by the township leadership and is not supported' (Rosen 1995: 339). Moreover, in the State Council's *Program for the Development of Chinese*

Women (1995–2000), introduced above, the second main target for increasing women's involvement in politics specifically states that it is desirable to have women appointed to leadership positions *in areas where women workers and staff are concentrated* (State Council 1995) (my italics). This reiterates the notion of separate spheres of political work for women. On this view, women leaders should most appropriately dominate in sectors where women are more numerous than men.

In the 1995 *Program*'s successor document, the 2001 *Program for the Development of Chinese Women (2001–2010)*, the strategies identified for increasing women's participation in Administration and Management (*xingzheng guanli*) reinforce the view that women's political leadership is most appropriate in areas relating to women. Three of the five strategies stress the importance of women leaders managing women's issues – primarily through the ACFW – and serving as conduits between the government and the broad masses of women. The program makes the following recommendations that the government

1   Make efforts to fully ensure the right of women to participate in administration, management and decision-making. In state and social affairs, guide women to participate, according to law, in the management of economic, cultural and social affairs, and enhance the proportion of women and their participation in politics.
2   Improve the mechanism of equal competition, the management of civil servants, and the mechanism of supervision and monitoring during the reform of the personnel system; seek to create equal competition opportunities for women to participate in decision-making and management; among the candidates who have the same qualifications, give priority to women from in the selection of cadres.
3   Solicit opinions and suggestions from women deputies to people's congresses and to people's political consultative conferences at all levels, from the broad masses of women and from women's organizations, in the formulation of principles and policies concerning women's fundamental interests.
4   Bring into full play the role of women's federations at all levels in democratic participation and democratic supervision, and ensure that they are enabled to play their role as a bridge to link the masses of women, and as a major channel to convey women's opinions and suggestions.
5   Give great importance to the opinions and suggestions of women's federations about the training and selection of cadres from among women, and about women's political participation and political discussions (State Council 2001).

Where two of the strategies argue for the increased involvement of women in general – and indeed suggest that an affirmative action policy will be implemented – it remains to be seen whether women politicians outside of the 'women's women' rubric achieve entry into formal politics in greater numbers.

Women politicians are overwhelmingly concentrated in the social welfare aspects of government. For example, in 2001, of the 463 women mayors serving China's 668 city governments, 56.2 per cent drew their expertise from culture, education and health. Only 9.5 per cent had a financial and economic background, 2.8 per cent had expertise from industry and agriculture and 4.4 per cent identified their background experience as urban construction (Wang Yinpeng 2001: 14). Wang identifies as a major obstacle to the promotion of women's participation the fact that 'Women make up a relatively small proportion in high-ranking decision-making bodies ... on economic management' (Wang Yinpeng 2001: 16). Moreover, Rosen has noted that the close identification of women with the 'soft' aspects of government has reduced their appeal at the county elections. Cadres engaged in industry or agriculture can produce "tangible" results visible to all. For those in "softer" jobs like culture and education, it is more difficult to "quantify" their achievements. Voters doubted such cadres had strong enough decision- and policy-making abilities' (Rosen 1995: 327).

Academic commentators have expressed grave concern about the rates of women's participation in politics, which have declined as a result of the liberalization of the Chinese political scene since the start of the 1980s. Shi Tianjian describes how the electoral system has changed over the years since 1979. In that year limited-choice elections were held within some enterprises and the National People's Congress introduced new electoral laws for the Local People's Congresses that 'required each precinct to offer voters a choice of one and a half to two times the number of deputies to be elected' (Shi Tianjian 1999: 1116). Further liberalization followed in 1982 with the abolition of the People's Communes and their replacement with Village Committees. In 1987 it was decreed that all members of these committees should be directly elected (Shi Tianjian 1999: 1117). Although there are still problems with the validity and operation of these ballots, there has been a marked increase in freedom of choice since 1980. However, women CCP members could no longer be guaranteed a place in the Local People's Congress by dint of their Party membership.

Moreover, the liberalization weakened some of the previously protective measures – such as special quotas and targets for women. Jacka explains how there was a relaxation in the system of 'targets and quotas' for women delegates in the villages and counties as a direct result of the electoral changes of the reform period. Over the course of the 1980s there was great variation in whether quotas or targets were applied or aspired to around the country (Jacka 1997: 88 and 228). As a result of this shift, there was grave concern that the numbers of women elected to political office would decline. As this chapter will reveal, a decade since the start of the reforms the situation appears to be slightly more complicated than a simple decline in numbers resulting from the decline in protective measures. (See the accompanying tables for an overview of women's participation in both Party and state bodies.)

In the state structure – as opposed to the CCP structure – it appears that a maximum limit for women may have been established. Numbers of women delegates to the NPC have been stable at 21 per cent since 1978, despite the removal of quotas and targets (see Table 5.1). Moreover, women have represented about 22 per cent of the deputies at the local and provincial level in the last two elections as well (averaging variations for specific provincial and county conditions) (see Table 5.4). It appears that the targets and quotas have become unofficial maximum limits. The 'quota/limit' in numbers permitted into the political scene is accompanied by a 'glass ceiling' that serves to stop women progressing to the upper echelons of NPC decision-making structures. The numbers of women in the higher levels of NPC – that is, at the State Council and Standing Committee levels – remain low for the entire post-1980s reform period (see Tables 5.2 and 5.3). The peak in numbers for these higher echelon positions that occurred during the Cultural Revolution in 1975 and 1978 has not received a positive appraisal in recent years. This is because the discrediting of the Cultural Revolution as a whole denies this particular aspect of 'success' as being regarded as anything other than an aberration – indeed it has been described as having led the women's movement along an 'unhealthy path' (Ye Zhonghai 2000: 222). Lin Jiling describes it as a period when equality between the sexes went so far as to diminish any distinctions between the sexes – clothing, work divisions and aesthetics (2001: 256).

At the broader political level, women have a marginal place within China. In 1993 women represented only 17 per cent of the Leading Cadres of the China's Mass Organizations, one of which is the ACFW, so much of this 17 per cent would be involved solely in 'women's work'. Mass Organizations serve to link specific groups within society and integrate them with national and local political affairs. They are also charged with defending the legitimate rights and interests of their constituency, but in effect, these organizations are CCP organs. The Communist Youth League of China, and the All China Federation of Trade Unions are two other examples of Mass Organizations. Similarly, women

Table 5.1 Number and gender composition of deputies to the National People's Congress

NPC and year of election	Female delegates (no. of persons)	Male delegates (no. of persons)	Proportion female (%)
1st NPC, 1954	147	1,079	12.0
2nd NPC, 1959	150	1,076	12.2
3rd NPC, 1964	542	2,492	17.8
4th NPC, 1975	653	2,232	22.6
5th NPC, 1978	742	2,755	21.2
6th NPC, 1983	632	2,346	21.2
7th NPC, 1988	634	2,344	21.3
8th NPC, 1993	626	2,352	21.0
9th NPC, 1998	650	2,329	21.8

Source: Adapted from Wang Yinpeng (2001), p. 6.

Table 5.2 Number and gender composition of deputies to the Standing Committee of the National People's Congress

NPC and year of election	Female Standing Committee members (no. of persons)	Male Standing Committee members (no. of persons)	Proportion female (%)
1st NPC, 1954	3	73	4.0
2nd NPC, 1959	4	58	6.5
3rd NPC, 1964	17	79	17.4
4th NPC, 1975	39	105	27.1
5th NPC, 1978	35	148	19.1
6th NPC, 1983	13	125	9.4
7th NPC, 1988	16	121	11.7
8th NPC, 1993	17	121	12.3
9th NPC, 1998	16	118	12.0

Source: Adapted from Wang Yinpeng (2001), p. 6.

Table 5.3 Number and gender composition of Chairs and Vice Chairs to the National People's Congress

NPC and year of election	Female Chairs & Vice Chairs (no. of persons)	Male Chairs & Vice Chairs (no. of persons)	Proportion female (%)
1st NPC, 1954	1	14	7.1
2nd NPC, 1959	1	16	6.2
3rd NPC, 1964	1	18	5.5
4th NPC, 1975	4	20	20
5th NPC, 1978	4	26	15.3
6th NPC, 1983	1	21	4.7
7th NPC, 1988	2	18	11
8th NPC, 1993	2	18	11
9th NPC, 1998	2	17	11.7

Source: Adapted from Wang Yinpeng (2001), p. 6.

represent only 10 per cent of the full-time Leading Cadres in enterprises and only 8 per cent of Leading Cadres in state organs. Ye Zhonghai describes these data as revealing that, 'While women hold up half the sky in society in general, they only hold up a little bit [of the sky] within the ranks of the leadership' (2000: 231).

In the Chinese Communist Party, whose members comprise the vast majority of members of the higher echelons of state power (that is, NPC) as well, the situation for women is similar (see Tables 5.5, 5.6 and 5.7). Women are congregated at the lower levels of Party organizational structures – and moreover,

Table 5.4 Number and gender composition of deputies to the 8th 1993–1998 Local
People's Congresses and their standing committees

Sector level	Female deputies (no. of persons)	Male deputies (no. of persons)	Proportion female (%)	Female Standing Committee members (no. of persons)	Male Standing Committee members (no. of persons)	Proportion female (%)
Provincial	4,524	16,464	21.56	206	1,525	11.90
County	144,367	506,944	22.17	9,079	41,333	18.01

Source: Adapted from Wang Yinpeng (2001), p. 7.

Table 5.5 Female members of the Political Bureau of the CCP in post-1949 China

Central Committee (year selected)	Total members (no. of persons)	Female members (no. of persons)	Proportion female (%)
8th (1956)	17	0	0
9th (1969)	19	2	10.5
10th (1973)	21	1	4.8
11th (1977)	26	0	0
12th (1982)	25	1	4
13th (1987)	14	0	0
14th (1992)	20	0	0
15th (1997)	22	0	0
16th (2002)	24	1	4.1

Sources: Adapted from Rosen (1995), p. 318; China Internet Information (2002); People's Daily
Online (2002).

the CCP compares badly with other communist parties around the world on this
ranking, according to Kuang Shiying (1992: 238). Stanley Rosen noted in
1995:

> Since the founding of the CCP in 1921, only three women have been full
> members of the party's Politburo, while two others have been alternate
> members. No woman has ever made it to the innermost circle of power, the
> standing committee of the Politburo.
>
> (Rosen 1995: 317).

In 2002 Wu Yi, an expert in foreign trade and the petroleum industry, was
elected to the Politburo, she is the first to have been elected to this committee
who has not had marital connections to top men. Of the three women members
of the Politburo prior to her recent election, each was wife to a politically
powerful man: Jiang Qing was the wife of CCP Chairman Mao Zedong, Ye Qun

Table 5.6 Female members of the Party Central Committee in post-1949 China (full
members)

Central Committee (year selected)	Total full members (no. of persons)	Female full members (no. of persons)	Proportion female (%)
8th (1956)	97	4	4.1
9th (1969)	170	13	7.6
10th (1973)	195	20	10.3
11th (1977)	201	14	7.0
12th (1982)	210	11	5.2
13th (1987)	175	10	5.7
14th (1992)	189	12	6.4
15th (1997)	193	8	4.1
16th (2002)	198	5	2.5

Sources: Adapted from Rosen (1995), p. 319; China Internet Information (2002); People's Daily
Online (2002).

Table 5.7 Female members of the Party Central Committee in post-1949 China (alternate
members)

Central Committee (year selected)	Total alternate members (no. of persons)	Female alternate members (no. of persons)	Proportion female (%)
8th (1956)	73	4	5.5
9th (1969)	109	10	9.2
10th (1973)	124	21	16.9
11th (1977)	132	24	18.2
12th (1982)	138	13	9.4
13th (1987)	110	12	10.9
14th (1992)	130	12	9.2
15th (1997)	151	17	11.2
16th (2002)	158	22	13.9

Sources: Adapted from Rosen (1995), p. 319; China Internet Information (2002); People's Daily
Online (2002).

was the wife of Lin Biao, and Deng Yingchao was the wife of Premier Zhou
Enlai. Wu Yi was elected as an alternate member of the Politburo in the
15th Party Congress elected in 1997 (China Internet Information Centre 2002;
Xie Fenghua and Liu Minhua 1999: 334–42) and progressed in 2002 to full
membership at the 16th Party Congress. In the reform period only one other
woman has reached the status of Alternate Member to the Politburo. Chen Muhua
served in this role between 1977 and 1987, undertaking roles in Family Planning
and Foreign Trade and from 1988 to 1998 Chen led the ACFW.

Of the total CCP membership of 66.3 million in June 2002, 11.5 million are women (17.3 per cent) (China Internet Information Centre 2002). Examined in this light, the dearth of women in the top ranks of the CCP leadership is alarming. In 2000 women comprised 18.5 per cent of construction workers, 38 per cent of agricultural workers, 43 per cent of manufacturing workers, 45 per cent of retail and wholesale workers, 57 per cent of catering workers, 57 per cent of health and welfare workers, 44.5 per cent of education workers and 33 per cent of workers in the scientific research sector but only 21.5 per cent of employees in Party Agencies and only 24 per cent of those in Government Agencies (NBSC 2001: 126–7). As I noted in a previous study, 'it is clear that despite the government's rhetoric about gender equality the party and government sector of the workforce remains one of the most difficult for women to enter' (Edwards 2000: 72). Moreover, given that the real political power in China is held by the CCP and not the NPC, the comparatively high rates of women's representation in the latter body (around 21 per cent) are less impressive than a superficial appraisal would suggest. Policy-formation power resides with the CCP and the dearth of women in top leadership positions within the Party exposes the relative weakness of women's political clout in post-reform China.

In addition to the low numbers of women in key political positions, Ye Zhonghai also expressed concern that women politicians congregate in lower levels of the political hierarchy and that women cadres are not regarded as serious politicians by men. She explains these factors as resulting from the resilience of sexual inequality in society; that is, women's specific functions in society are regarded as being of less value than those of men. Moreover, traditional notions of women's inferiority continue to promote the idea that 'a strong woman is not as good as a strong man'. Finally, she argues that the double burden faced by women politicians – home duties and employment duties – limits their career advancement (Ye Zhonghai 2000: 230–3). Lu Yin reiterated the problems of the 'double burden' by repeating a common saying: women cadres must work three times harder than men cadres, have to marshal five times more courage than men, should have seven times the stamina of men and face twelve times more hardship than men (Lu Yin 1989: 18).

One structural problem for women aspiring to enter the PRC's formal political sector is the system of indirect elections beyond the level of the county. Individual citizens – both men and women above the age of 18 – vote directly for candidates to their Local People's Congress in secret ballots. But the People's Congresses above the county level, including the National People's Congress and its executive committee, the State Council, are election by People's Congresses at a lower level. The proportion of women voting decreases dramatically with each step away from the grass-roots. Wang Yinpeng wrote in 2001 that, while there are no extensive statistical data on the division of voters by sex, NPC data suggest that women's involvement in 'grass-roots' elections (direct elections) has stood at above 95 per cent since 1984. In elections above the county level, the proportion of female voters has been 20 per cent or so because the elections are made indirectly and the proportions are determined by the proportions of women deputies in people's congresses at various levels. Within this system, it becomes increasingly difficult for any 'women's vote' to emerge because women represent a rapidly diminishing proportion of the voters as the level of government rises.

However, M. Kent Jennings' data gathered in 1990 suggest that there is a wide disparity between men and women in both participatory and spectator engagement in politics within the rural and semi-rural areas of Anhui, Hebei, Hunan and Tianjin. NPC data appear more generous in their assessment of women's participation in politics than those of Jennings. Jennings suggests a number of possible reasons for the gender gap that study identified – specifically, the absence of a second (non-farming) occupation among women, less advantageous social opportunities for girls (for example, in educational opportunity), low rates of CCP membership among women and a socialization process that discourages girls and women from an interest in politics. Jennings summarizes rural women's low level of interest and participation in politics, saying, 'Despite having undergone vast changes in the past five decades, rural China still possesses visible remnants of a patrilineal, patriarchal and, virilocal society' (Jennings 1998: 971).

Ellen Judd has explained the lower rates of CCP membership among women as partly deriving from the virilocal marriage customs (women marrying into the home of the groom) that are prevalent in rural China. Party membership follows a period of scrutiny by existing Party members, and when women shift villages on marriage this can extend the period of 'scrutiny' as they must insert themselves as strangers into the well-established social network of their husband's village (Judd 1994: 229). In contrast, Shi Tianjin has noted that Beijing women participate in elections at a higher rate than Beijing men (Shi 1997: 169). Shi suggests that this reflects in part the recognition by urban women of the direct personal benefits they have garnered as a result of CCP policy (Shi 1997: 175). In addition, it is possible that urban women are more likely to be mobilized to vote because their work conditions and gender-specific entitlements are more directly influenced by government policy than those women working on the land.

The difference between rural and urban women's participation remains difficult to gauge but a 1993 study revealed a close correlation between level of education and interest in politics and residential location and interest in politics. Rural women recorded a lower 'quality of political consciousness and social responsibility' than urban women. But across all categories (levels of education, residential location and age), men expressed more confidence about their political abilities and knowledge than women (*Zhongguo funü* 1993: 134–7).

Importantly, this study coincided with an increase in the calls for an improvement in the quality of women politicians and not just an increase in their quantity. Indeed, some commentators greeted the removal of quotas for women on the basis that it will result in a higher quality of politicians. In a 1992 article, CCP member Liu Ning blamed the quota system for poor-quality contributions by women. Liu argued that artificial props to women's political engagement simply allowed a lower quality of politics to emerge. Women's enhanced participation in politics would require an improvement in education and political training and not the reinstatement of quotas (Liu Ning 1992: 93). In 1992, Li Weisha noted that one major problem for women politicians was that they were considered as ornaments (*dianzhuipin*) to the political stage rather than an integral part of the process of governance. Li pointed out that the belittling of women's contributions partly stemmed from the low quality of their participation. In particular, those women who were appointed as part of the quota system during the Cultural Revolution made very poor contributions and therefore lost their positions during the reform process (Li Weisha 1992: 37). The discrediting of Cultural Revolution policies in general over the last twenty-five years has not helped the cause of improving women's position in the political arena since pro-woman policies carry some stigma from being associated with this 'ten-year period of chaos'. The rates of participation of women, as is clear from the tables, peaked at every level during the Cultural Revolution – many of these women would have been drawn from the worker and peasant classes.

Current debates about the 'quality' of the contribution of women politicians suggest the return of the intellectual class to political power within the CCP leadership. Higher levels of education it is presumed will lead to more sophisticated and a higher quality of political participation. One can also presume that rural women will become increasingly disenfranchised by this shift towards intellectual-politicians.

The reform period has therefore resulted in a number of changes to women's employment in politics. Most significantly, there has been a decline in women's leadership in the main font of political power – the CCP higher echelons – whereby women now only represent 2.5 per cent of Central Committee members in 2002, down from 5.7 per cent in 1987. This is tempered by the addition of a female member to the Politburo in 2002, the first woman to be elected to this top body since 1987. In the state structure, it appears that women are contained at around the 20 per cent mark up to the NPC level and remain poorly represented in the select standing committees drawn from the NPC. The question of quality and quantity that has emerged over the 1990s appears to empower urban women intellectuals and marginalize women rural dwellers – a factor that requires considerable attention given that most of China's women live outside the major cities.

Conclusion

The concept of 'women's work' as the site for 'legitimate political work for women' in China has both benefited and hindered the progress of women's political engagement. The identification of 'women' as a discrete constituency ensured that women have been represented at higher levels than in most other nations around the world and for a longer period of time. However, the compartmentalization of women within the political structure appears to limit women's participation in politics beyond those questions directly relating to women. Moreover, it also appears to limit women's progress to the higher levels of government, especially in the CCP structure where real political power rests. China's aspiring women politicians are not only constrained by the predominance of CCP power, but also by the subordinate, domesticated relationship that women's political work has performed within the CCP and state structures for nearly eight decades. For a new development in women's political work to emerge, further political liberalization must occur – liberalization that permits the emergence of an independent, anti-patriarchal feminist political voice.

References

China Internet Information Centre (2002) 'Sixteenth National Congress of the Communist Party of China 2002'. Available online at <http://www.china.org.cn/english/features/44519.htm> (accessed 12 November 2002).

Davin, D. (1978) *Woman-Work: Women and the Party in Revolutionary China*, Oxford: Oxford University Press.

Edwards, L. (2000) 'Women in the People's Republic of China: New Challenges to the Grand Gender Narrative', in L. Edwards and M. Roces (eds) *Women in Asia: Tradition, Modernity and Globalisation*, Sydney: Allen & Unwin, 59–84.

—— (2000a) 'Women's Suffrage in China: Challenging Scholarly Conventions', *Pacific Historical Review*, 69, 4: 617–38.

—— (2002) 'Coopting the Chinese Women's Suffrage Movement for the Fifth Modernisation – Democracy', *Asian Studies Review*, 26, 3 (Sept.): 285–307.

Fitzgerald, J. (1996) *Awakening China: Politics, Culture and Class in the Nationalist Revolution*, Stanford, CA: Stanford University Press.

Gilmartin, C. (1994) 'Gender, Political Culture and Women's Mobilisation in the Chinese Nationalist Revolution, 1924–1927', in C. Gilmartin *et al. Engendering China: Women, Culture and the State*, Cambridge, MA: Harvard University Press.

—— (1995) *Engendering the Chinese Revolution: Radical Women, Communist Politics and Mass Movements in the 1920s*, Berkeley: University of California Press.

Goodman, D. S. G. (2000) 'Revolutionary Women and Women in the Revolution: The Chinese Communist Party and Women in the War of Resistance to Japan, 1937–1945', *The China Quarterly*, 164: 915–42.

Jacka, T. (1990) 'Back to the Wok: Women and Employment in Chinese Industry in the 1980s', *Australian Journal of Chinese Affairs*, 24: 1–24.

—— (1997) *Women's Work in Rural China: Change and Continuity in an Era of Reform*, Cambridge: Cambridge University Press.

Jennings, M. K. (1998) 'Gender and Political Participation in the Chinese Countryside', *The Journal of Politics*, 60, 4 (Nov.): 954–73.

Jiang, T. (1990) 'Funü canzheng: Zhongguo nüjie de remen huati' [Women's political participation: A hot topic for Chinese women], *Hainan kaifa bao*, Nov. 16: 4.

Judd, E. (1994) *Gender and Power in Rural North China*, Stanford, CA: Stanford University Press.

Kuang, S. *et al.* (1992) *Dangdai Zhonguo funü diwei* [The status of women in contemporary China], Chengdu: Xinan caijing daxue chubanshe.

Li, C. (1956) *The Political History of China, 1840–1928*, trans. by S. Y. Teng and J. Ingalls, Princeton, NJ: D. Van Nostrand.

Li, W. (1992) 'Nüxing canzheng de kunjing yu chulu' [Problems and opportunities for women's participation in politics], *Shehui kexue* (Hu), 4: 37–40.

Lin, J. (2001) *Ershi shiji Zhongguo nüxing fazhanshi lun* [A discussion of the history of the development of Chinese women in the twentieth century], Jinan: Shangdong renmin chubanshe.

Liu, N. (1992) 'Nüxing canzheng suzhi tigao de qianti tiaojian yu nüxing canzheng' [Preconditions for improving the quality of women's participation in politics and women's participation in politics], *Neimenggu she hui ke xue: jingji shehuiban*, 1: 93–6.

Lu, Y. (1989) 'Zhongguo funü canzheng de xianzhuang yu wenti' [The present situation and problems for women's participation in politics] *Zhongguo jianshe* (Jing), 9: 15–18.

McElderry, A. (1986) 'Woman Revolutionary: Xiang Jingyu', *The China Quarterly*, 105 (March): 95–122.

Min, J. (1995) *The Chalice and the Blade in Chinese Culture: Gender Relations and Social Models*, Beijing: China Social Sciences Publishing House.

NBSC-Zhonghua renmin gonghe guojia tongji ju [National Bureau of Statistics of China] (2001) *Zhongguo tongji nianjian 2001* [China Statistical Yearbook 2001] Beijing: Zhonghua tongji chubanshe.

Neft, N. and Levine, A. (1997) *Where Women Stand: An International Report on the Status of Women in 140 Countries*, New York: Random House.

People's Daily Online 2002, 'Hu Jintao introduced his colleagues'. Available online at <http://www.english.peopledaily.com.cn/200211/15/eng20021115_106863.shtml> (accessed 15 Nov. 2002).

Roces, M. (1998), *Women, Power and Kinship Politics: Female Power in Post-war Philippines*, Westport, CT: Praeger.

Rosen, S. (1995) 'Women and Political Participation in China', *Pacific Affairs* 68: 3 (Fall): 315–41.

Shi, T. (1997) *Political Participation in Beijing*, Cambridge, MA: Harvard University Press.

—— (1999) 'Voting and Non-voting in China: Voting Behaviour in Plebiscitary and Limited-Choice Elections', *The Journal of Politics*, 61, 4 (Nov.): 1115–39.

Spakowksi, N. (2002) 'Women's Military Participation in the Communist Revolution of the 1930s and 40s: Patterns of Inclusion and Exclusion', Paper presented to the Women in Republican China Conference, Freie Universität Berlin, 7–11 Oct.

State Council of China (1995) *Zhongguo funü fazhen gangyao* [The Program for the Development of Chinese Women: 1995–2000]. Available online at <http://www.unescap.org/pop/database/law_china/ch_record016.htm> (accessed 8 Nov. 2002).

—— (2001) *Zhongguo funü fazhen gangyao* [The Program for the Development of Chinese Women: 2001–2010]. Available online at <http://www.womenofchina.com.cn/chinese/program/women.htm> (accessed 8 Nov. 2002).

Sun, C. (1989) 'Guanyu xian jiduan funü canzheng wenti' [On the problems of women's political participation in the current period], *Heihe xuekan* [Hei], 3: 36–40.

Wang, Y. (2001) 'Report on the State of Women in Urban Local Government, People's Republic of China. United Nations Economic and Social Commission for Asia and the Pacific. Available online at <http://www.unescap.org/huset/women/reports/index.htm> (accessed Nov. 4 2002).

Wang, Z. (1999) *Women in the Chinese Enlightenment: Oral and Textual Histories*, Berkeley: University of California Press.

White, T. (1994) 'The origins of China's birth planning policy', in Christina K. Gilmartin *et al.* (eds) *Engendering China: Women, Culture and the State*, Cambridge, MA: Harvard University Press.

Xie, F. and Liu, M. (1999) *Zhongguo zhengtai nüxing dadao zong* [The footsteps of China's top women political leaders], Huhehaote: Neimenggu renmin chubanshe.

Ye, Z. (ed.) (2000) Zhongguo funü lingdao rencai chengzhang he kaifa yanjiu [Research on the maturing and development of talent among China's women leaders] Shanghai: Kexue jishu wenxian chubanshe.

Zhang, J. (1992) 'Gender and Political Participation in Rural China', in Shirin Rai, Hilary Pilkington and Annie Phizacklea (eds) *Women in the Face of Change*, London: Routledge.

Zhongguo funü shehui diwei diaochai congshu editorial board (1993) *Zhongguo funü shehui diwei gaiguan* [General survey of the status of Chinese women in society] Beijing: Zhongguo funü chubanshe.

6 Women and technology in the teaching profession

Multi-literacy and curriculum impact

*Stephanie Hemelryk Donald**

Education (*jiaoyu*) is the basis of the socialist modernization drive, and the State (*guojia*) ensures priority to the development of educational undertakings. The entire society should show concern for and give support to the development of educational undertakings. The entire society should respect teachers (*jiaoshi*).

(*Education Law of the People's Republic of China* (article 4) 1995)

This chapter discusses the experience of modernisation for China's population of primary, secondary and tertiary teachers. In particular, the suggestion is made that the teaching profession, although statistically gender-neutral, has a somewhat higher proportion of women teachers at primary levels, and that this has served to feminise the state's policy to promote nine years of compulsory education. I further argue that this may be to good effect, as modernisation and education are understood in China to be utterly commensurate and co-dependent projects. If education reform is an indication of modernisation in China, then women are at the forefront of those efforts as they play out in the primary schools, where the largest proportion of children are enrolled nationwide.

Education reform is itself symptomatic of the need to move away from the chaotic radicalism of the late 1960s and early 1970s (Pepper 1996: 381), and to modernise China's economy. Modernisation is of course thematic in a book dealing with the labour of women in transitional times. I will assume therefore that the state's commitment to a modernised economy, as well as the uneven and fragmented social processes that follow that commitment, is a contextual given in the discussion that follows. The educational responses to economic change have been discussed in important studies and scholarly collections (Hayhoe 1992a, 1992b; Pepper 1996; Rosen 1992), and continue to be debated in the light of curriculum development and the intensification of the modernising process.

*This research was greatly assisted by the wisdom of Fan Wenfang, and the research assistance of Wang Qian and Zou Luwei, all of Tsinghua University.

The focus on women teachers as opposed to women as students arises from the author's work with children and media technologies (Donald and Richardson 2002), and with her research adviser, Fan Wenfang of Tsinghua University, who has developed and implemented China-wide teaching strategies for learning the English language. It is clear in both these fields that the teachers themselves devise responses to curriculum objectives in their own practice and in their own skills base, so as to meet the challenges of literacy in an uneven educational environment, and the position of children in national development.

Women in education have also been documented, but generally from the perspective of access and achievement or expectations (Rosen 1992, 1995). My focus on women arises from conversations with teachers in mainly urban schools, most of whom tend to be women, and who seem to fall into two groups: those who feel pressured by the technological aspects of reform in the classroom, and those who are highly competent innovators in multi-modal teaching methods.

In this chapter then, modernisation is understood through its mobilisation in classroom technology, the professionalisation (or re-professionalisation) of the teaching community, the interdependence of the nine-year plan with the development of China's socialist market, and the impact of English as a medium of communication in some schools. I approach the conceptualisation of teachers as subjective factors in the modernisation process from three perspectives: the status of the teacher in China since 1949, the emergence of the professional teacher in the reform period, and the technologisation of the workplace in the late 1990s and 2000s.

I am suggesting, perhaps optimistically, that the impact of technology on the Chinese classroom may prove to be a step forward for female status in the PRC, which is in other areas under attack from the inherent gender bias of capital in a developing economy. However, I also accept that there is a measure of in-built 'female' failure for older teachers as they struggle to come to terms with new standards of training and expectations of new competencies. In-built, that is, in the sense that women's work in the classroom is not necessarily measured by the skills which they habitually deploy in the management and care of the young. I also note that there are significant discrepancies in opportunity for teachers based in rural and remote locations in respect to those based in expanding metropolitan centres such as Beijing, Shanghai and Shenzhen.

Visual communications and the multi-modal teacher

In the emergence of the professional, technologically literate Chinese teacher, the notions of 'visual communication' and 'multi-modal literacy' are of foremost importance and will be briefly elaborated here (for general studies, see Anstey and Bull 2000; Garton 1997; Durrant and Green 2000). Visual communications is a broad concept, encompassing all media communications with a visual component, and has been usefully identified by the journal of the same name as 'the use of visual languages and technologies in ... multi-modal genres, texts and communicative events'.[1] Communicative events range from the personal text message embroidered with smiles and scare quotes, to the announcement of policy changes in *The People's Daily*. They are less often associated with the practice of education as embodied in teacher–student communications, but it is this everyday practice that I wish to identify as a chain of communicative events, fundamental to the formation of young people's engagement with the institutions of state and society. The classroom is the locus for the key communicative event in children's daily lives. It is with that understanding that I seek to describe teachers as important cultural figures in reform China.

The use of the descriptor 'multi-modal' is also helpful in acknowledging the teacher's role as a communicator with technologies beyond chalk and talk at her disposal. Metaphorically, it also indicates the teacher's role as an educator with a remit to support the development of the state, 'leave not one child behind'[2] on the road to modernisation, but also to respond to a greater or lesser degree to the talents of a group of particular children in a particular place and time. The teacher must also negotiate across modalities of location identity (urban, rural, metropolitan, minority), age, access to equipment and training, and socio-economic conditions. Multi-modality here engages with the teacher-as-located and specific mediator in a period of change, reform and re-conceptualisation of education (*jiaoyu*) in a modernising society.

Multi-literacy has been variously interpreted in the arts and social sciences, and has been taken up to particularly good effect in education research in Britain and elsewhere (Lankshear *et al.* 1997; Amory *et al.* 1999; Light and Littleton 1999; Cope and Kalantzis 2000). The term requires a multi-modal understanding of language, whereby communication practices take up variously mediated information resources, horizontally connected voices and 'hot-linked' inter-pretations[3] and sources of meaning. Multi-literacy is truly suited to describing digital texts and the relations across them and between them and their users, creators and references. However, it can also be used to describe competency in more familiar technologies of the classroom: from the CDROM game to the textbook to the use of building blocks and tessellated shapes (these learning models introduced into education by pioneers such as Maria Montessori (1870–1952), whose ideas reached China in 1915). Multi-literacy is a concept that both acknowledges and enables differential approaches to the development and constitution of the educated subject. I deploy it in the context of women teachers in the PRC so as to leave an open ending to our very preliminary discussions. Were, for example, the 20 per cent of Urumqi teachers (women under 45/men under 48) who failed a literacy and numeracy test for primary educators,[4] functionally illiterate, or did they possess knowledge and facility in modes of communications that allowed them to work successfully with children in their schools despite their low levels of measurable attainment?

The local and political context in which learning takes place is also of critical importance. Edie Garvie argued in her 1976 book *Breakthrough to Fluency*, 'If the packages of language and experience are carefully matched and put together they offer truly valuable learning material' (Garvie 1996: 111). Garvie was interested in the multi-modal delivery of language training. Her contention reminds us more broadly, however, of the need for a teacher's social and political and visual literacies to be strongly based in local sites of learning in order to 'package' information in a socially coherent and visually meaningful way. The package invariably will include the teacher herself, her skills and her local knowledge. As a creature of radical reform in the late 1960s the teacher needed to embody conflict, but her role now is more an embodiment of stability in a fragmented, and highly uneven, national experience of enrichment.

In the Chinese context, then, these local sites have *regional* but in the past more specifically *political* literacy at their core. Regional location is very important in film education, where locally relevant socialisation projects are tied to wider aesthetic and narrative practices of appreciation. Politics as a topical theme has been more centralised and is less easy to administer in a period of localisation. Teachers in 2002 are still trained in political communications and in ideology, but whereas in the 1949–78 period this role informed the modality of transmission and reception of most of the curriculum, now there is a sense that politics are harder to embed in the literacies of modern China. Teachers say (off the record) that the history of revolution, taught as grounding for contemporary socialisation, has less and less currency with the young. The contradictions between modernised aspirations and pressures and the controlled development of a socialist economy is too stark and incomprehensible. Multi-literacy in the revolutionary/post-Liberation classroom consisted of texts, posters, campaigns and modelled social behaviours. These do continue – for instance, in educational campaigns on the environment (Sayers and Sternfeld 2001) – but in a spirit of accelerated learning: the socialist mentor of past years is under review.

The status of the revolutionary teacher

The importance of education to Confucian Chinese society is well documented (Zhu 1992). So too, is the position of the teacher as a guide and mentor to the student. The *laoshi/jiaoshi* [both terms mean 'teacher'] title enshrines both a descriptive title 'teacher' but also an expectation of moral integrity, and a sense of continuity in culture and social behaviours. The assumption of this role by the teacher is important as in revolutionary culture more generally, leadership was a role generally ascribed to men.

Esther Yau made this point very convincingly in her doctoral thesis (1990), showing how – in cinematic explorations of new post-1949 China – women learned from inspiring male models, rather than the other way round. There were inspiring cinematic women too (and roles taken by the actresses Tian Hua and Yu Lan are the best examples), but they tended to look up to male counterparts and thereby model the modelling process for the audience. The model citizens held up as examples to adults and children were men and women, but it was the men – especially of course Lei Feng (1990) – who benchmarked the moral order of a revolutionary society. Yet the status of the teacher is also clear in films spanning the period 1949–80, where children's or family films in particular concentrated far more on the idealised teacher than on the parent–child relationship. Furthermore, the teacher in question is quite often a female. The narrative typically introduces children with an inspirational educator who has some kind of personal problem (an illness), and whom the children assist, thus demonstrating the successful application of moral guidance learnt initially from the *laoshi*.[5] Masculinised versions of the genre also deal with sporting excellence; these focus on the leadership and – again – the inspirational quality of sports coaches (*Woman Basketball Player no 5, nulan wuhao*, 1957, Director Xie Jin). In the 1950s and 1960s such generic adaptations tended to emphasise the teacher as at the forefront of Chinese determination to succeed on a national, and ideally an international, sporting stage. Their role was to endure hardships and to encourage their team to do the same. Victory was the only possible denouement.

However, the place of women as teachers and students has been uncertain over the centuries. As Stanley Rosen (1992) and Shi Jinghuan (1995: 140) have argued, Chinese cultural tradition, 'a slaughterhouse for women's intelligence' (Shi: 140), has not tended to prioritise women in the educational pecking order. Rather, outside influences, including missionary and colonial interventions, have been instrumental in destabilising the assumption of the inappropriateness of female learning. Arguably, of course, initiatives from within, and the instatement of the CCP in 1949 is a case in point,[6] are much more effective in producing long-term change than impositions and incursions from outside the national cultural imaginary. Between 1898 and 1907 Shanghai authorities began to implement regulations for the education of women who wished to teach (especially at kindergarten level). In 1908 Hu Shi (1891–1962) published a volume suggesting that first, women (mothers) were fundamental to national education, which must begin at home, and that second, girls should therefore be schooled, otherwise the home would not be an adequate educational incubator for Chinese modernisation (*Bainian zhongguo ertong* 2001: 87, 39). Educating girls for motherhood is perhaps a familiar compromise from progressive males wishing to support women's intelligence without being overwhelmed by its more ambitious potential.

From 1949 such initiatives were attached to the stated aim of equality between the sexes in revolutionary China, and women's participation in education increased rapidly (Shi 1995: 141). The progress in women's educational attainments has been monitored and is clearly successful if not complete. The most commonly cited statistic concerns the extension of female literacy. In the late 1940s over 90 per cent of Chinese women were illiterate. By 1998, only three western provinces/autonomous regions (Tibet, Gansu and Qinghai) had levels of illiteracy over 26 per cent. In all provinces, however, a significant proportion (70 per cent) of those semi-literate or illiterate were women.[7] There is also a continuing problem of female retention rates. Although some children manage to complete nine years of compulsory schooling, many of the (conservative estimate) 1 million who drop out annually are female, and of those who do graduate junior school, many do not proceed into further training at high school and at tertiary colleges. This is partly due to levels of personal expectation, and partly due to active discrimination. This was so marked in the 1970s and 1980s that Shi contends that males were admitted to teaching (Normal) universities with lower grades than were the women (Shi 1995: 145).

The statistics are therefore both good and disappointing. Cultural predictors of female achievement levels remain biased – and are probably worsening in some areas as underemployment leads cultural bias back into the equation of whose education matters most in a modern economy with significant unemployment.

Nonetheless, I can contend that the post-1949 teacher has been a figure of – generally female – power in the discourse of revolutionary and liberated China. This revolutionary teacher has also been multi-modal in a sense rather different from that understood in contemporary educational debates. Her roles have been diverse and have required a subjective assumption of a variety of social roles and responsibilities. She was (and arguably still is) in the vanguard of change through her work in political socialisation of the young (most dramatically articulated in the Little Red Schools of the Cultural Revolution period, but more consistently in the instatement of national curricula and the distribution of national textbooks). Prior to the modernisation efforts of reform, she carried some of the responsibility for producing an educated mass able to contribute to a partial modernisation of China, from a society based on privilege to one organised through national priorities and development plans.

As Pepper argues, this responsibility was not achievable in the exam-based, urban-focused educational system of pre-1965 (Pepper 1996: 365 and *passim*). Nonetheless, she more or less successfully taught literacy and numeracy skills to many children, which would serve them and the nation whatever political (factional) group was in the ascendancy. When young people were encouraged to turn against bad class elements in the mid-1960s and re-invent continuing revolution, the attack on teachers was then both inevitable and tragic. They did indeed embody the communication of state policy to young people, and even though not all were engaged in political instruction and monitoring, nonetheless it was impossible to be a teacher without wearing the mantle of the state in the eyes of teenagers and younger children. This period was the nadir of teaching as a class position in modern China. As I argue below, it was followed by an era of modernisation which lifted teachers from class-bound idols and sometime villains into a professional class of educators.

Professionalisation

Modernisation requires a high standard of education in all spheres of employment and deployment, starting with the educators themselves.[8] Professional educators in China have a distinguished history, but their training and status have had to be re-visited in the past two decades of reform. In 1977, the national examination system for entry to tertiary education was restored, having been replaced in the late 1960s by a recommendation process, which proved corrupt (Ma 1995:

293–4). Projects to support the development of the western regions (high on the national economic agenda in the 1990s and today) rely on increased access and retention rates at school (Yang 2000a, 2000b).

Teacher education has been a feature of Chinese tertiary systems since 1949,[9] but its public face is now much more apparent than its previous incarnation as respect based upon political rectitude. Teachers fell from favour in the 1960s arguably because they were perceived to be elite political agents and actors of state authority. Now they are bearers of qualifications, which fit them to direct the socialisation of China's youth towards a principled and appropriate readiness for change. Without figures on overall gender breakdown of recent graduating cohorts one can only surmise from observations and from statistics on teachers in general, that a large number of women are entering training for primary school with only secondary education behind them. Their professionalisation is enhanced by programmes of continuing education, many of which deal with ethics and ideological training, but which also include courses on modern educational technology. The training in itself enhances their prospects for achieving respect in the system, but perhaps their skills in modern technologies will be most likely to filter out to parents and to bolster their status in a society charged with a modernising ethos. The programme of compulsory continuing education for teachers is significant in understanding the shift in how the teacher figures in contemporary China, as an ongoing subject of improvement rather than a static symbol of state power and leadership.

> The overall targets [of continuing education] are to establish a [training] network ... with full use of means of modern information technology and all kinds of education resources ... to develop a modern system of curriculum design and textbook compilation (etc).
>
> (China Education and Research Network, 2000)

The professional educator is not without detractors, however, and the fears associated with modernisation are played out in films questioning the right of a moral leader to a career structure. These films are not vastly dissimilar to the earlier films where teachers are the locus for political allegiance and socialisation (see, for example, *Four Buddies, sige xiao huoban*, 1981, Director Qiqing Gaowa, and a much earlier version *Flowers of the Motherland, zuguo de huaduo*, 1955, Director Yan Gong). In both these films – made at either end of an era – individualistic children are trying to skirt the small duties of socialism. As a result they have failed to become 'Red Flowers' (as in the 1981 film), or to gain membership (and the red scarves) of the Young Pioneers (as in the 1955 prototype). Guidance from teachers and classmates helps them to overcome their aversion to self-discipline. However, the continuities in these narratives (the teacher as moral guide) are matched by differences in newer films (redness tends to be associated with the national flag rather than directly with Party iconography), indicating where society is de-investing in the rhetoric of politics and re-investing in strategic statements of national achievement.

The move away from this version of the classroom teacher is evident in a genre shift in the children's film industry. *Baseball Boy* (2002, Director Qi Jian) won the Golden Calf award for a children's feature in 2002. The film begins with a tussle over real estate, as a baseball pitch on a sporting field is re-developed as a soccer ground to please local property owners. The film ends with a heroic stance by a wounded boy, and the last shot pulls out on an image of him standing on the reclaimed pitch. This same shot also sports an extra-diegetic national flag, which covers the entire sports field and a text rolls over the credits describing the film's young heroes as future Olympic champions in 2008. There is a teacher figure in the film: the young baseball coach, trapped between the need to make a living for himself in adult sports, and his commitment to the boys' baseball team, which he has created from scratch. He is pitted against one boy's entrepreneurial father, who demands that his son quit baseball and take up soccer. These several moral strands running through the film intersect on a vanishing point of selflessness and national priorities. The coach must forego his professional career, and apparently marriage prospects, if he is to support the aspirations of his young team.

The development of the team is predicated on the development of a good relationship between a boy and his father, the latter epitomising modern capital and real estate interests. For our purposes here it is noticeable that the shift from political socialisation to national socialisation through sport (gaining a red scarf, becoming a 'red flower') is matched by a shift from the gentle leadership of a female teacher to the angst-driven leadership of a male coach. There is also a shift from the teacher–student pairing to the father–child relationship. At the end of the film the boy and his father are very much together, and the sports coach is working to build a compromise career with his professional charges. The sports-coach genre is not entirely new, but its prominence in recent film could suggest that the first, the coach is himself less of a final mentor than in earlier films, and second that the class teacher in China's schools is no longer the obvious character in a genre that relies on amateur enthusiasm and selfless dedication. The female teacher in China now is a professional whose qualifications count most for her school's reputation.

Technologies of teaching: 'learn to know, learn to do and learn to develop themselves'

Teacher quality (and skilled teacher shortages) are pressing problems, which threaten the implementation of the nine-year education policy, and the desire to create a 'scientific and humanistic spirit' (Gu 2001) based on the all-round moral education of all children. The teacher in the PRC is trained and deployed by the Ministry of Education and then becomes a formal employee of the state, deployed to an area of need. Teachers trained at national institutions (the most prestigious) may be asked to travel anywhere in the country. In practice, teachers tend to train and work near home. The distribution of teachers across primary, secondary and tertiary schools is perhaps related to this practice. In 1995, the total number of workers in education was 11,863,000, of whom 4,835,000 (42 per cent) were women. The proportion falls to 37 per cent for higher education, 35 per cent for secondary schooling, and then rises to 44 per cent for primary education.

Twenty years of reform has produced a competitive, outcome-driven society, with a focus on the new. A commensurate shift in pedagogic thinking has also occurred, and changes to the curriculum and to teaching styles are underway. Surprisingly, however, while there is a strong demand for vocational 'post WTO' training, many of the advocates of change advise a soft approach to teaching, that emphasises technology but which also makes the knowledge canon more relevant to the interests of students. Proposals also criticise the difficulty of the 1990s curriculum, which, it is argued, has changed only slightly from the 1960s model, and which favours only the cleverest students (Gu 2001: 21–3).

The most far-reaching proposal is to introduce comprehensive (practical, academic and contextual learning) education in areas, which may appeal to the gifted students, but also to the larger majority of average-ability learners. These subject areas include information technology, community services, social research, fieldwork and general technology. Starting in 2001, elementary and secondary schools were strongly encouraged to initiate courses in IT, and to teach students using Internet technology. The aim was to get all schools networked by 2003 (Gu 2001: 22). Experimental schools were set up in the mid-1990s to accommodate these priorities, and their promotional literature looks mainly at teacher qualifications, 'scientific management' (*kexue de guanli*), resources and multimedia equipment.

The technologies of teaching are most apparent in language learning. The curriculum reform requires language tuition to start younger than in previous years. In major cities (Beijing, Shanghai, Guangzhou), students start at Grade One. More usually, they begin in Grade Three. To support these guidelines, new textbooks have been produced at Tsinghua University and trial-tested across twenty-two provinces. The textbooks were designed by a young illustrator, and written by a professor of education.[10] The aim of the books is to professionalise the teaching of English through carefully graduated modules, which will eventually stretch from Grade One up to Grade Nine. The series also makes language learning fun and meaningful for urban and rural students, by drawing on easily (TV) accessed contemporary youth culture to support the experience of 'English' in the classroom. Therefore the design of the books is funky, animé themed and loosely aligned to the fairy-tale world of Japanese cartoons on children's TV and Disney stories on commercial English learning VCD series. The textbook programme feeds into a broader set of initiatives. Current proposals at Ministry of Education level seek to establish bases in institutes of higher education to train masters of foreign language education.[11] The training culminates in an examination process and a one-year placement.

Ministry of Education guidelines also set out the expectation that universities prepare language laboratories and multimedia facilities able to 'meet the needs' of their students. The number of classes conducted in the language lab should amount to at least 30 per cent of language teaching overall, and it is also expected that the on-campus Intranet be fully used to support out-of-class learning

Given that postgraduate study is still fairly limited in Chinese universities in contrast to the numbers entering undergraduate programmes,[12] the specific focus on training and technology for language serves to underline the explicit link between education policy and modernisation, between modernisation and communication, and between communication and citizen development. Citizenship in the Chinese context is a debated term (Keane 2001), but it does gesture towards a subjective norm in the personal quality (*suzhi*) necessary for embodied modernity. The modern education subject thus combines scientific enquiry with a spirit of humanism. The educational theorist Gu Mingyuan has summed this up explicitly – 'The essence of education is to improve the quality of the citizen' (Gu 2001: 23) – and uses the slogan to underline a core concern with education of the whole citizen. The quality (*suzhi*) of the citizen encompasses skills of communication that feed directly into China's immediate and long-term needs in regard to trade and commercial performance. Foreign language learning is therefore a desirable aspect of 'quality', and highly prioritised policy-driven pursuit in contemporary education. However, Gu worries that these priorities can easily be misdirected into pure functionalism, taking vocational training for some and strategic subject choices for others to a point where the moral discipline of *jiaoyu* is utterly bypassed in a rush for domestic jobs and cosmopolitan experience: 'if you master mathematics, physics and chemistry, you can travel the world'.

In this regulatory context, at universities, and at some middle and high schools, traditional language laboratories are still in use. Teachers use them for listening and oral repetition in language classes. Increasingly, however, teachers also access the computers in language labs to prepare other teaching aids for other subjects: PowerPoint presentations and flash files are especially helpful for classes of up to 40 students. Increasingly, too, and in accord with Ministry guidelines, large campuses at well-funded high schools and at university level use the Intranet for class teaching, and to assist students in the assignments. Online learning draws on teachers' tips, assignment details and source materials, as well as discussion forums where students can seek extra help and exchange ideas on the subject topics. None of this is unfamiliar to tertiary teachers elsewhere, the online subject site located on a university server is now a common phenomenon. So too is the debate on the usefulness of such sites, the extent to which they facilitate learning or simply reproduce paper technologies in digital format.

I do not want to engage in those debates here, but would like to suggest that the extension of the teacher's modality through the use of, say, after-class communications, is a significant factor in the modernisation of the teacher's role in the PRC. There has long been an assertion of the teacher as both in-class figure of authority and out-of-class mentor and political-social guide. Now, the teacher's access to technology produces her as a technologically skilled communicator, who is also charged with the 'out-of-classroom' care of the students. This embodiment of the modern is where I stake our optimism regarding the status of the female teacher in the coming years. The outlook is especially positive if read in relation to other modalities of pedagogy, which suggest regional relevance and multi-literacy in teaching modes.

Gulliver's Travels

In 2002 an international conference on Film Courses for Chinese Primary Schools was held in Zibo, Shandong Province. The film course was set up in association with Wang Liuyi[13] (from Blue Cat Productions), the China Children's Film Association and the project team on students' film education at the National Audio-visual Teaching Aid Centre under the auspices of the Ministry of Education in Beijing. The ambition of the project was to increase film literacy in the classroom across the country, with a strong emphasis on films as conveyors of international and historical information, and films as sources of pleasure in learning for young people. First suggested in a discussion paper in 1999, discussed in *The People's Daily* (*renmin ribao*) and then implemented in 2001–2002, the programme works from the following stated motivations:

1   To increase understanding of national differences worldwide, and thus enlarge students, horizons,
2   To develop a 'world outlook' in students,
3   To use film to provide comprehensive approaches to knowledge gathering – for example, *Around the World in 80 Days* can be worked into course materials on 'literature, geography, history, biology, art, music, and sports',
4   To promote happiness in the classroom, and thereby to develop visual sophistication in students.

The plan is to conduct experiments for two years and then extend the programme via the mechanism of the national curriculum, and its emphasis on 'comprehensive teaching'. Student 'quality' is addressed in terms of course comprehension and skilling, but also in relation to the subjectivity of the student as 'all round'. 'All round' includes their vision of a wider world, which may be already quite accessible and familiar to middle-class urban children but will not be so to children in rural schools. It also includes an expectation that happiness is predicated on learning in an environment conducive to learning and that the latter is characterised by multi-literacy, both visual and moral, in the classroom. The motivations underlying this set of objectives flesh out what is meant by a technological classroom and a 'comprehensive curriculum'. The modernisation process is accompanied by education objectives that position the teacher as an embodiment of new technologies, and as a mediator of external realities in the wider world. They also, still, take on responsibility for incorporating the political boundaries of state and Party in their management of the information that they convey – through film, language and other subjects.

Furthermore, the presentation of results at the Zibo Conference leads us to make two observations relevant to our argument here. First, all the presenters, bar one mainland and Hong Kong participant, were female, either representative senior teachers, or teachers who had themselves managed the classroom teaching of the project. There was therefore a strong sense of female competency associated with the event, which was enhanced by the presence of Yu Lan as guest of honour. As in all international meetings, some teachers were initially nervous – or the equipment failed them – but overall the impression was one of commitment, differentiated and inventive teaching and learning, and talent finding a niche.

Schools were offered 216 packages in testing the film course. They were either thematic, edited collections of films (about dogs, monks,[14] witches, Pearl Harbor, space, pirates) or collections of films which have several versions: *Around the World in Eighty Days*, *Six Warring States* (*Zhanguo*), *Cinderella* (five of the available 77 versions were selected for the course), *Tarzan* (twelve films), *Robinson Crusoe* and *Gulliver's Travels*. Many of the films seem rather antiquated to the eyes of a Western educator, but it must be remembered that the course intends to give students a context in which to place their film spectatorship generally. It is the modality of the teaching that makes this experiment interesting. There is a rather proscriptive system of film selection for the trial and presumably for the curriculum once it is in place. Films are required to be 'classical' and to aid 'psychological development' within an overall curricula remit to socialise the young. Nevertheless, at classroom level this programme is implemented by a large cohort of mainly female primary teachers, who mobilise this course for locally differentiated outcomes. I will outline two examples from very different schools to exemplify this.

In a primary school in Jiangxi, Grade Three and Grade Four students (8–10-year-olds) studied the story of Robinson Crusoe in several film versions over an entire semester. The aim of the course was to build a comprehensive understanding of survival and to build physical endurance among students. The teacher in charge argued that, although the catchment of the school was of low to average economic standing, many children in her year groups were single children, and many were somewhat spoilt as a result. She felt that visual appreciation, fun (happiness) and technological training could combine to support a moral agenda. She and her team utilised fieldwork in the surrounding countryside to help the children recreate the Robinson Crusoe story as a collective enterprise. They 'survived' the field trips and made their own film to tell the story and comment on what they had learnt.

The teacher told the story of the project to the conference delegates, and relayed the film through a PowerPoint using video and flash. The exercise combined the up-skilling associated with modernisation with the management of the self in a collective society, that is an ongoing feature of moral education (*jiaoyu*) and socialisation in Chinese schools. It was facilitated by a demonstrably competent woman who manipulated technology in ways that accomplished comprehensive learning in a specific social environment according to state-approved and pragmatic moral standards of self-sufficiency, environmental awareness and collective endeavour.

In Shenzhen, the Nanshan foreign languages school provides (almost) bilingual education to children of wealthy parents. The film project at Nanshan looked at *Gulliver's Travels* and used the semester to emphasise advanced literacy in English. Despite the 'subject' rather than 'comprehensive' focus (and potentially vocational focus of the work given the association of English with work opportunities), the project did promise a multi-modal delivery of the text. Classes were organised around six activities and facilitated by various media (word cards, VCR, VCD, microphone, micro-recorder, paper, video-camera). The activities took the students through the story sequence by sequence, and encouraged them to memorise the text through analysis, imitation, acting and dubbing. The last activity was filmed so that the children again produced their own version of the film. The teachers also published a short booklet beautifully illustrated with drawings by children (mostly in *manga* style), and still images from a cartoon version. The project booklet promised that there would be social as well as subject outcomes to the learning process: 'Students are very interested in acting. They'll feel themselves important through participation, they will gain confidence, and learn more from peers through cooperation.'

The relationship between specialised schools, regional schools and a national curriculum pilot has to be understood in context; only the better schools are chosen for pilot schemes such as the Film Course. Nevertheless, as examples of professional best practice, these (and there were several more) case studies underline the emergence of women as specialised teachers of multi-literacy and multi-modality in the service of the social *and* the modern imperatives. Further, whilst the initiatives do not truly challenge the highly systematic organisation underlying professionalism in Chinese schools, they do suggest a willingness to allow children to work with a visual 'package' in a local context.

Conclusions

There are men and women working in Chinese schools. Nevertheless, as those of us living in developed economies know only too well, teaching is a feminised profession, with low wages, low social value and high levels of stress, and minimal career prospects for most workers. Technology in the classroom does not necessarily militate against this situation. However, the advent of multi-literacy as an articulated concept in the mediated classroom may work to technologise teaching in useful ways. Technologisation can simply conform to skill-based development in teaching outcomes, but it can also deepen the modality of the teacher herself, embedding her and her professional status in more broadly understood social experiences of modernisation. Much has to change and to continue to change for the multi-modal teacher to become a recognised figure on the modern landscape of Chinese society. Just as filmic versions of the teacher become 'professionalised' in films for children and families, so the teacher in the classroom needs to have her negotiations with modernisation recognised in a world beyond the primary school gates.

Notes

1   This handy and nicely discriminated definition comes from the promotional materials for the journal of the same title, *Visual Communications*, <http://www.sagepub.co.uk/frame.html?http://www.sagepub.co.uk/journals/details/j0359.html> (accessed 14 Sept. 2002).
2   This idea has been somewhat lampooned by the Zhang Yimou film *Not One Less* (Yige ye bu shao, 1999), where a very young and distinctly amateur teacher searches for a lost pupil so as not to forfeit her wages.
3   'Hot-linked' refers to the ability to move through digitally created, stored and accessed planes of information and resources.
4   Extracted from *The People's Daily*, 4 April, 2001, by China Education News Archive, 19 Sept. 2002.
5   Teachers are actually termed *jiaoshi* in schools, although *laoshi* is used to denote the special inherent merits of the postholder. They are subdivided into senior teachers (*gaoji jiaoshi*) and first grade teachers (*yiji jiaoshi*). There are also awards for skilful teachers awarded at municipal and provincial levels.
6   Notwithstanding the well-taken claim that a double burden of work and house chores have been the strongest outcome for women in CCP China, a condition that worsens as short-term strategies of modernisation 'rationalise' labour and send women back to the kitchen.
7   *China Statistical Yearbook* 1998; *Unesco World Education Report*, 1998.
8   From the 1980s to 1999 there have been six major education laws promulgated: Regulations on degrees (1980), Compulsory Education Law (1986), Teacher's Law (1993), Education Law (1995), Vocational Educational law (1996) and Higher Education Law (1998). The teacher's law with its requirements for continuous monitoring and in-service training is the key to the professionalisation drive.
9   In 1998, there were 229 Normal training schools (*shihda*), 875 secondary training schools – both of which prepare teachers for *zhongxue* and *gaoxue* (and graduate about 300,000 students). There were also 190 educational institutes and over 2,000 in-service teacher training schools. Teachers for kindergarten and primary schools have only graduated from junior high schools.
10 Fan Wengang.
11 For 'foreign language' in these proposals, read 'English'.
12 Three years or four years.
13 Wang Liuyi – Wang 6/1 has a name that records his birthday on Children's Day, 1 June. His work in children's media seems therefore entirely appropriate!
14 I was gratified to see a class on the Shanghai Animation Studio film *Three Monks*, *Sange heshang* demonstrated at the conference – as it is a film we have used in focus group work among Chinese Australians in Western Australia (Donald 2001).

References

Amory, A., Naicker, K. *et al.* (1999) 'The use of computer games as an educational tool: identification of appropriate games types and game elements', *British Journal of Educational Technology* 30, 4.

Anstey, M. and Bull, G. (2000). *Reading the Visual*, NSW: Harcourt.

Bainian ertong [Chinese Children in the 20th Century] (2000) Xinshiji chubanshe, Guangzhou.

China Education Network: www.tc.columbia.edu/centers/coce

Cope, B. and Kalantzis, M. (2000) *Multiliteracies: Literacy Learning and the Design of Social Futures*, Victoria: Macmillan.

Donald, S. H. (2001) '"History, Entertainment, Education and Jiaoyu": A Western Australian Perspective on Australian Children's Media, and Some Chinese Alternatives', *International Journal of Cultural Studies* 4: 3, 279–99.

—— (forthcoming – 2004) *Little Friends: Children and Media in the People's Republic of China*, Lanham: Rowman & Littlefield.

Donald, S. H. and Richardson, I. (2002) 'The English project: Function and culture in new media research', *Inter/Sections: The Journal of Global Communications and Culture* (forthcoming).

Durrant, C. and Green, B. (2000) 'Literacy and the new technologies in school education: Meeting the l(IT)eracy challenge?' *Australian Journal of Language and Literacy* 23, 2: 89–102.

Education Law of the People's Republic of China (1995) [Zhonghua Renmin Gong he Guo jiaoyu fa], China Legal Publishing House.

Garton, J. (1997) 'New genres and new literacies: The challenge of the virtual curriculum', *Australian Journal of Language and Literacy* 20, 3: 209–22.

Garvie, E. (1976) *Breakthrough to Fluency: English as a Second Language for Young Children*, Oxford: Blackwell.

Gu, M. (2001) 'The spirit of curriculum reform in mainland China', *Educational Century* (Jiaoyu Shiji), 3: 21–3.

Guo, D. and Zhang, J. (2002) Zhuti keli yanjiu: Geliefu Luji [Typical Film Lesson Research: Gulliver's Travels], Shenzhen shi Nanshan dui guoyu xuexiao keti zu Shenzhen [Nanshan Foreign Language School Film Study Group].

Hayhoe, R. (1992a) *Education and Modernization: The Chinese Experience*, New York: Pergamon Press.

—— (1992b) *Cultural Tradition and Educational Modernization: Lessons from the Republican Era. Education and Modernization: The Chinese Experience*, New York: Pergamon Press, 47–72.

Jin, F. (1980) *Sange heshang* [Three Monks] Ah Da. Shanghai: Shanghai Animation Studio.

Jin, Z. (1981) Sige xiao huoban [Four Buddies], Lu Wei, Qiqin gaowa. Beijing: Children's Film Studio.

Keane, M. (2001) 'Redefining Chinese citizenship', *Economy and Society* 30, 1: 1–17.

Lan, L. (1955) *Zuguo de huadao* [Flowers of the Motherland], Y. Gong. Changchun: Changchun Film Studio.

Lankshear, C. and et al. (1997) *Changing Literacies*, London: Open University Press.

Law, W. W. (2000) 'Education legislation in the People's Republic of China', *Centre of Research on Education in China*, Quarterly Newsletter 1.

Lei, F. (1990) *The Diary of Lei Feng*, Beijing: Liberation Army Art and Literature Press.

Light, P. and Littleton, K. (1999) *Social Processes in Children's Learning*, Cambridge: Cambridge University Press.

Ma, J. (1995) 'The social role and function of examination as seen from the reform of China's University Entrance Examination', in G. A. Postiglione and W. O. Ledd (eds) *Social Change and Educational Development: Mainland China, Taiwan and Hong Kong*, Hong Kong: Centre of Asian Studies, University of Hong Kong, 290–7.

Pepper, S. (1996) *Radicalism and Education Reform in 20th Century China: The Search for an Ideal Development Model*, Cambridge: Cambridge University Press.

Postiglione, G. A. and Lee, W. O. (eds) (1995) *Social Change and Educational Development: Mainland China, Taiwan and Hong Kong*, Centre of Asian Studies Occasional Papers and Monographs No. 115, Hong Kong: Centre of Asian Studies, University of Hong Kong.

Qian Bin and Yi Dan (2002) *Baseball Boy*, Director Qi Jian. Beijing: Children's Film Studio.

Rosen, S. (1992) *Women, Education and Modernization: The Chinese Experience*, R. Hayhoe. New York: Pergamon Press, 255–84.

—— (1995) 'Women and Reform in China', in G. A. Postiglione and W. O. Ledd (eds) *Social Change and Educational Development: Mainland China, Taiwan and Hong Kong*, Hong Kong: Centre of Asian Studies, University of Hong Kong: 130–8.

Sayers, Jane and Sternfeld, Eva (2001) 'Environmental Education in China' *Berliner China-Hefte* 21: 42–55.

Shi, J. (1995) 'China's Cultural Tradition and Women's Participation in Education', G. A. Postiglione and W. O. Lee (eds) *Social Change and Educational Development: Mainland China, Taiwan and Hong Kong.* Hong Kong: Centre of Asian Studies, University of Hong Kong, 139–49.

Tang, Q. (ed.) (2002) *Dianying yu huan bao* [Motion Pictures and Environmental Protection] Jiangxi Pingxiang shi shiyan you'er yuan [Pingxiang, Jiangxi, Pingxiang Experimental Kindergarten].

Xi, J. (ed.) (2000). *Baininan zhongguo ertong* [Chinese Children in the Twentieth Century], Guangzhou: Xinshiji chubanshe.

Yang, D. (2000a) *Education Evolution in China (III): Problems and Arguments*, China Education and Research Network, 2002.

—— (2000b). *Educational Evolution in China (I): Educational Evolution and Reform*, China Education and Research Network, 2002.

Yau, E. Ching-mei (1990) *Filmic Discourses on Women in Chinese Cinema (1949–1965): Art, Ideology, and Social Relations*, Los Angeles: University of California.

Zhu, W. (1992) 'Confucius and Traditional Chinese Education: An Assessment', R. Hayhoe (ed.) *Education and Modernization: The Chinese Experience*, New York, Pergamon Press, 3–22.

Part III
Reinventing domestic space

7 Building for the future family*

Sally Sargeson

Oh for great mansions, with thousands of rooms,
Giving welcome shelter to the earth's poor,
Unshaken like the mountains in the storm's uproar ...
(Du Fu, 'Ode to my cottage,
unroofed by autumn gales', 1985)

This chapter examines how young women's aspirations for, and efforts to acquire new housing are contributing to important changes in the economic and cultural conditions of village life. Specifically, it argues that young women have given impetus to the following interrelated trends. In the wealthier regions of China, including the Zhejiang villages that are the focus of this study, young women often stipulate that they will only marry a man who owns a new mansion. Most mansions are occupied by nuclear households. Their construction has necessitated the rescheduling of intergenerational property transmission and the migration of labour, and spurred the marketisation of China's countryside. The eclectic architectural designs of the new mansions intentionally signify the suburbanisation of village communities, spatially reconfigure family relations and re-engender the domestic sphere.

My representation of women as agents of these changes is a preliminary attempt to respond to the recent challenge put forward by Arif Dirlik. Dirlik exhorted researchers to attend to the ways that individuals – 'circumscribed by the very conditions they would transform' – create distinctive cultures of consumption within and outside the realm of global capitalism (2001: 23). The proposition that people intent on their individual goals collectively create the cultural practices that sustain capitalism is not novel (Creed 2000; Douglas and Isherwood 1979). What makes Dirlik's formulation particularly relevant to

*Field research was funded by an Australian Research Council Small Grant, and Pacific Cultural Foundation Grant SC8105. The research methodology, profile of survey respondents and research sites are described in detail in Sargeson (2002). I am extremely grateful to Anne-Marie Medcalf, whose insightful comments on an earlier draft of this chapter helped me to clarify my argument.

scholars concerned with the lives of women in contemporary China is his argument that while consumption might offer individuals a means of temporary liberation and self-expression, it simultaneously enmeshes them in complex capital, labour and product markets. I illustrate Dirlik's argument by showing how young women's pursuit of housing and family ideals is helping to embed Zhejiang villages in global markets. At the same time, of course, the lives of rural women are being transformed by the very processes of property accumulation and consumption that they are facilitating.

However, in representing women as agents of these changes, my argument clearly is at odds with influential paradigms that have dominated scholarship on gender, marriage and household formation in China. In those paradigms, the marriage of women was viewed, first, as an exchange of productive labour and reproductive potential among patrilineal households, then as a moment for demonstrating prestige, exchanging wealth and transmitting property between generations. For this reason, it is instructive to begin this study with a brief review of how theories of marriage, household formation and property transmission have altered in response to changes in China. I then draw on my field research into rural housing to show that the housing boom in Zhejiang Province is being driven, in part, by women's residential aspirations and preference for independent, nuclear households. The following sections explore how young women's demand for mansions has encouraged labour migration and the earlier division of family wealth, and altered the material culture and domestic life in villages.

Changing paradigms of marriage and property transmission in China

The key features of the original paradigm of the 'orthodox' Han Chinese household are well known. Virilocality (the bride marrying into the groom's family), patrilineality (inheritance through the father's line) and patriarchy (male dominance) are the cornerstones on which the household is founded. For much of the twentieth century, Western scholars assumed that there was little variation in the means by which new members were recruited. After parents concluded negotiating the payment of brideprice and dowry and the performance of appropriate rituals, a bride would be taken to her husband's home. Initially as an 'outsider', then as a junior member of the subordinate sex in his family's household, she would contribute to patrilineal extension and the accumulation of joint assets. Unless friction or poverty forced division of the domestic group, the joint, extended household could be expected to endure until after the death of the father, when his sons would inherit the family's property (Fei 1983: 26–8; Freedman 1966; Baker 1979). This paradigm of marriage and household formation reflected the androcentric, functionalist assumption, commonly held by early British and French anthropologists, that marriage primarily served to exchange the productive and reproductive potential of women between property-owning patrilines (Watson 1982). Women played no role in the transactions that created and sustained households.

In the 1970s, 1980s and 1990s, the 'typicality' of some components of the paradigm was called into question. Historians, anthropologists and sociologists demonstrated that in many cases, brideprice and dowry were paid concurrently. The dowry remained the property of the bride, while a component of the brideprice was retained by the couple as conjugal property. Joint, extended families, stem families and simple conjugal units were all common household forms, and many individuals would have experienced each of these structural permutations in the course of their life (Cohen 1978; Ebrey and Watson 1991; Davis and Harrell 1993). Notwithstanding the idealisation of several generations residing under one roof, family division and the partition of property frequently occurred before, rather than after, the father's death (Wakefield 1998). Indeed, scholars like Margery Wolf (1972) argued that neither the patrilineal household nor the lives of women were of one piece. By emotionally bonding their sons to them, mothers effectively created their own loyal sub-cell within the larger household unit. Household division often was instigated by women's efforts to secure a share of the household estate for what Wolf called their 'uterine family' (Wolf 1972: 158–70). Hence, although women might enter their husbands' households as subordinates, they certainly gained in stature, security and agency when they became the mothers of sons.

Furthermore, scholars showed that whatever empirical accuracy the paradigm once possessed was diminishing over time. In the first few decades of the twentieth century, the average household had more than five members, with up to half of all households comprising an extended family. In 1982, the average household held only 4.43 people. By 2000, this number had further declined to 3.4, and more than three-quarters of rural domestic units contained a simple nuclear family (Benjamin *et al.* 2000: 94–5; Du and Tu 2000: 85; China Statistical Bureau 2001). Evidently, an increasing percentage of families were dividing at, or shortly after, the marriage of a son. Family size and form were not the only things to have changed. Many young people were choosing their own spouses. Village and surname endogamy were no longer considered to be taboo, so marriage was not inevitably associated with women's removal from their natal settlement (Parish and Whyte 1978).

Yet despite the transformation of marriage practices, the monetary value of marital payments was escalating rapidly. In areas where eligible women were scarce and there was strong competition for 'good' marriage partners, families were paying huge brideprices, whilst in economically developed areas, parents keen to marry their daughters into reputable families were providing them with lavish dowries. In both types of transfer, most of the marital payments were passing directly to the young married couple to allow them to purchase housing and furniture (Yan 1996).

Housing has long been one of the most important investments made by rural families, and it also has played an important social semiotic function in their arrangement of marriages (Knapp 1999). Martin Yang wrote that in Shandong in the 1940s, 'a family may have enough houses for all its members to live in, but they keep on buying and building new ones and acquiring land for the future generations' (Yang 1947: 46). Yang also observed that parents negotiating the marriage of a daughter judged the status and economic standing of would-be spouses by the condition of their families' homes. As an indicator of a family's situation, the size and condition of housing became of even greater significance during the Maoist period, because land ownership, the wearing of jewellery and other marks of distinction were disallowed (Gao 1983; Xin 2000). What changed in the 1980s and 90s, though, was that marital payments, together with the savings from young men's wages, were being used to finance the construction of massive new mansions intended for the occupation of newly-weds (Shi 1997: 143–4; Wang and Murie 1999: 209; Murphy 2001).

Jack Goody's proposition, that different economic and social systems follow quite distinctive logics in utilising marital payments and inheritance to circulate property, provided a potentially useful framework for theorising changes in marriage, household formation and inter-generational wealth transmission in China (Goody 1990, 1998). Goody argued that in classless societies practising shifting cultivation in Africa, payments of bridewealth reallocated the wealth necessary for the arrangement of marriages laterally among households with children of marriageable age. In Europe and Asia, where complex divisions of labour were associated with intensive agriculture, industry and commerce, economic and social status inequalities were perpetuated and family wealth conserved in the form of productive assets by the vertical transmission of property, through sons' inheritance and daughters' dowries.

Applying Goody's theorisation to explain changes in dowry and brideprice in the Guangdong delta in the 1980s, Helen Siu (1993) suggested that marriage customs and methods of intra-familial property transmission were being altered in response to China's market transition. Siu argued that marital payments 'involve not so much the exchange of material goods and prestige between the families of bride and groom as the intense and rapid devolution of property to the conjugal couple at the time of marriage itself' (Siu 1993: 170). This was precipitated, Siu reasoned, by villagers' concerns about 'continuation of the house' in the context of the revival of a market economy. The collective investment in new housing was a 'family strategy' to acquire prestige, expand social networks, strengthen children's allegiance to their parents and reinforce rights to settlement and farmland.

However, Goody's proposition that families utilise marital payments and inheritance to conserve their assets is, to a large extent, contingent on the assumption that the rights of beneficiaries to exchange and profit from those assets will be protected by private property rights institutions. In rural China, some collective property rights still take priority over the property rights of individuals. Individuals do not own the land on which their village houses are situated, for all rural land is the collective property of villagers (Ho 2001). Certainly, houses in the countryside are owned by individuals and can be sold and rented. But rural real estate markets are suppressed by legislation, specifically designed to conserve agricultural land, that prohibits villagers who sell or rent their homes from immediately applying for another site on which to build

(Sargeson 2002). As a consequence, the sale and rental of rural housing is common only in the vicinity of cities. Nor can rural dwellings easily be mortgaged. Contrary to Siu's suggestion, house owners are not automatically entitled to contract farmland or receive subsidies, benefits or dividends funded by the village's collective assets. Hence, in contrast to Goody's prediction that intergenerational transfers are intended to preserve a family's ownership of productive property, in rural China the expenditure of marital payments on a new dwelling transforms family wealth into an *unproductive* asset.

Economically unproductive, perhaps, but Siu argues that new housing is necessary to ensure the *reproduction* and prestige of the family. And, notwithstanding a caveat that members of a family might disagree over their collective values, goals and strategies, her argument implies that it is the patrilineal family whose reproduction is being ensured. This begs investigation. Precisely whose 'house' is to be continued? Who insists that new mansions must be built? Who initiates early family division, and why?

Recent research suggests that young women increasingly are transacting their own marriages and household arrangements, rather than being the objects of others' transactions. In Shaanxi, Yan Yunxiang (1996) found that young women had begun to take it upon themselves to inspect the quality of potential bridegrooms' houses and then negotiate the size and content of marital payments with both their own parents and the groom's family. Not surprisingly, Yan's informants downplayed women's agency, saying that the brides were acting as pawns of their husbands-to-be, eager to acquire a share of family wealth and village land. Zhang Weiguo (1998) drew different conclusions from his study in Hebei. Zhang found that village women controlled much of the expenditure of marital payments and, once married, they decided how household income would be spent.

My own investigation of housing construction and household formation supports Siu's contention that villagers are indeed building to ensure 'continuation of the house', but, in keeping with Yan's and Zhang's findings, it shows that in many instances it is young women's housing and family ideals that are being constructed. The mansions that are springing up across the Zhejiang landscape express women's desire to emancipate themselves from their husband's family and identify them and their families as 'modern', independent participants in the capitalist economy. At the same time, the resources needed for ongoing construction urge villagers to participate in ever-widening markets for labour, credit, material goods and 'life-styles'.

My argument draws on three sources of information. Over more than a decade, I have been visiting and conversing with two generations of women from a few families in a village in north-eastern Zhejiang. To assess the representative nature of their actions and attitudes, in 2000 I conducted a random survey of 296 households and conducted interviews with members of 40 households in four villages in northern, central and south-western Zhejiang. I also interviewed the village chiefs, Party Secretaries and women in charge of family planning in the surveyed villages, and officials in the city and town land administration and

Plate 7.1 Villagers' housing, Hangzhou, 1999 (photograph by author).

construction bureaux administering those villages. The average size and composition of the households surveyed were consistent with national averages. The villages also presented a broad spectrum of households' economic circumstances, with average per capita annual incomes ranging from 14,528 yuan in the wealthiest village to 2,900 yuan in the poorest village. My third source of data comprised government documents, statistical yearbooks and press reports on household formation and housing construction in rural Zhejiang. Based, as it is, on research in one affluent coastal province, the findings from this study cannot be extrapolated to explain trends in China's central and western regions or in urban centres. Nevertheless, my research demonstrates that at least in this part of the countryside, women are attempting to secure some control over their married lives and the future of their children. It also illuminates the (sometimes unintended) consequences of women's actions for the economy and culture of rural Zhejiang, and for relations within the home.

Tracing women's agency in the rural housing boom

Every traveller to the Zhejiang countryside can see that a rural housing boom is underway. What they are unlikely to realise is just how long the boom has lasted and how much housing space has been created. As soon as farming incomes increased and building materials became available in the early 1980s, villagers set about satisfying accommodation demands that had been suppressed throughout the Maoist period. Within a few years, land administrators and researchers warned that both land and capital were being wasted by the annual construction of more than 50 million square metres of floor space (Zha 1990). Notwithstanding a drop in the rate of growth of rural incomes and government efforts to rein in construction, official statistics show that the average per capita living space of Zhejiang villagers continued to increase in the 1990s, reaching more than 40 square metres by the end of the decade, four times more than the per capita space available to urban residents and one-third more than the rural average (Zhejiang sheng tudi guanli ju 1999; *Zhongguo gengdi wanli xing* 1998: 471; *Zhejiang tongji nianjian 1999*: 184). Mansions in the rich hinterland of the provincial capital, Hangzhou, loomed six storeys tall and contained several hundred metres of space.

There is ample evidence that people in each of the five case-study villages participated enthusiastically in the housing boom. More than half of all households built at least one new house between 1990 and 2000. Some households had built, demolished and rebuilt two or even three times during this period. A handful admitted to illegally owning multiple new residences. Nevertheless, construction continues. Why?

One thing, at least, is certain. Demand for new housing is not correlated solely with the age of habitations or a shortage of space. Most people living in dwellings that had been put up more than six years earlier said that as soon as they had sufficient savings, they would build again. Yet by their own admission, the average per capita floor space of respondents' houses had increased from 41 square metres in 1995 to 71 square metres in 2000.

Official accounts explain the housing boom as a product of peasants' residual 'feudal' thinking and irrational competition for 'face'. In the words of Zhu Yinchuan, Head of the Bureau of Land Administration in Hangzhou, 'many villagers who have been farming their entire lives have been building houses their entire lives, and the little profit that they have ploughed from the soil largely has been spent on house-building' (*Zhongguo guotu ziyuan bao* 2000: 1). So keen are some villagers to outdo their neighbours, wrote Zhu, that they demolish sound houses inhabited for only a few years in order to replace them with ever larger, taller and more exotic buildings. Families who cannot afford to rebuild are considered 'impoverished', even though they inhabit a massive new villa. Zhu omitted to identify young women's housing ambitions as one of the factors driving residential construction in Zhejiang. Yet time and again when I queried people's motives for building I was told, 'No woman would marry a man without a new house.'

This bald assertion is remarkable on three counts. For one, it demonstrably is untrue. Many people in the western regions of rural China lack the wherewithal to construct any sort of new housing. Newly-weds must, perforce, live in dilapidated accommodation. The second remarkable point is that it contains an acknowledgement that most women do, indeed, decide whom they will marry. Many factors have combined to accommodate women's freedom of choice in marriage. In most families, at least two generations have now been born since national legislation was passed to grant women the right to decide whether, and whom, they will marry. Novels, newspapers, television programmes and popular music and, to a lesser extent, propaganda and educational materials, have promoted the idea that marriage should be a romantic, voluntary and mutually satisfying union (Friedman 2000). Although market reforms have not eliminated gender discrimination in agriculture, industry and business, village women now enjoy a wider variety of job opportunities. Many young women move to cities and towns where they become economically independent and are relieved of parental supervision of their social life. Further, throughout China there are considerably fewer females of marriageable age than there are males (*New York Times* 2002). As economists from the Chicago school might put it, this places young women in a strong bargaining position in the 'marriage market' (Grossbard-Scechtman 1995: 101–7).

The third notable point in the assertion above is that housing is believed to be a crucial criterion in women's marital behaviour. On survey questionnaires, 25 respondents wrote that they had built their new houses solely because their son was intending to wed. In answer to my query about how house-building is linked to marriage, most respondents stated that women decide between suitors partly on the basis of the age and quality of their housing. Indeed, so directly do some villagers connect marriage and housing construction that one survey respondent reasoned, 'A new house shows that a family has an unmarried son. Without the son, they would have no need to rebuild.'

But if men and their families put up new houses as a means to acquire a bride and all that she might provide, women are demanding houses with a view to achieving their own goals and their ambitions for their 'uterine family'. Villagers explained that the possession of a mansion demonstrates to a woman that her suitor and his family have income, access to credit, and sufficient social connections and ability to navigate the bureaucratic obstacles that confront house-builders. After all, they pointed out, 'You can tell what a family's situation is like if they live in a dump.' Young women said that they were reassured that they would find comfortable, hygienic and attractive accommodation in a new house. They also explained that when they had married, they had wanted a private, intimate space for their husbands and themselves, and a measure of independence from their mothers-in-law. Finally, men and women both reasoned that if a woman marries into a family with a new house, she can be confident that she will not immediately be saddled with the cost of constructing the house of her dreams: 'A new house tells a woman that if she marries into that family, there will be no need for the newly-weds to borrow in order to build.' Unencumbered by housing debts, she and her husband will be able to save, invest in more lucrative ventures, pay school fees and so provide for her progeny.

When it comes to young women's housing preferences, size matters. Brides' desire for an autonomous space has led to entire floors being given over to newly-wed couples. Hence, in two- and three-generation households, I found the vertical duplication of functional spaces. 'On the first floor there is a kitchen, dining room, games room and bathroom. Upstairs are three bedrooms and a living room and bathroom. On the third floor is a living room, two bedrooms and a bathroom.' In wealthier houses, kitchenettes are installed 'upstairs' for the convenience of young couples. Over one-third of the surveyed households that lived in a new home mentioned that they had rebuilt specifically to create more space for school-age children. Yet most respondents acknowledged that at least one-third of the rooms in their new homes were unused. Perhaps one day, they mused, the empty rooms might be inhabited by their child and its spouse.

Increasingly, however, young women want not just a floor to themselves, but a house of their own. In four of the five case-study sites, the great majority of households divide when a son marries. Young couples then move into their own, purpose-built, homes. In the four villages where early division is common, informants said the creation of neo-nuclear households grants young couples a high degree of autonomy and eliminates friction over the increasingly divergent life-styles led by older and younger generations. This generally was illustrated by reference to the minutiae of everyday domestic life. As one young woman put it: 'It's simply not convenient for the older and younger generations to live together. We eat different sorts of food. Old people like softer foods, whereas we like crisp textures. Its much better to separate.' Other women mentioned that early division precludes intergenerational arguments over television programmes, music and bedtimes. A few respondents explained that division can be caused not by youngsters' desire to set up an independent household, but rather by the refusal of the elderly to move into the huge, 'empty' dwellings preferred by young women. Only in the poorest locality did a few respondents say that household division sometimes is precipitated by economic conflict. One old miser complained, 'We are always scrimping and saving, whereas young people waste money. If my sons had their way, they wouldn't divide. They'd want us to support them and look after their kids. But I think they should stand alone and look after themselves.'

Against the normative practices of those four villages, the post-marital residence and property transmission customs in the fifth case-study village provide an instructive contrast. The fifth village is highly industrialised, has a thriving private business sector, and is located 10 kilometres from Hangzhou city. Here, marriage only precipitates household division in families who have two or more adult children. Given that the current cohort of newly-weds predominantly belong to one-child families, division is rarely necessary. In keeping with the 'orthodox' paradigm of household formation, most young couples take up post-marital residence with parents. At odds with the orthodoxy, though, is that fact that uxorilocal marriage is also relatively common – that is, the man marries into the woman's family, for women who are loath to leave their parents can easily find men who are willing to marry into such a rich community. In both types of marital union, brides' housing aspirations are satisfied by their occupation of self-contained apartments in multi-storeyed family mansions.

What explains these apparently anomalous practices? Before offering an answer this question, it is worth mentioning a second feature of life in this village that diverges from the customs of other research sites. Inheritance, rather than marital payments, is the main mechanism for transmitting wealth between generations in the fifth village. Yet in the light of Goody's theory, it is paradoxical that it is precisely this fifth village that offers the strongest economic incentives for early household division. Villagers have been compensated generously for Hangzhou city's resumption of village land and houses. Their factories employ a large population of immigrant workers who pay premium rent for rooms. Why, then, do newly-weds forgo the opportunity to earn rental income or possibly receive compensation for the resumption of their house? Villagers initially explained both their post-marital residential arrangements and their inheritance practices as 'local customs'. But further questioning revealed that these were consequences neither of cultural conservatism nor of parents' efforts to bind their son's allegiance. On the contrary: unlike other wealthy villages where infants are cared for by non-working mothers and grandmothers, almost all adult women in this locality work full-time. Women said that co-residence in a stem household allows all adults to share responsibility for childcare and maximises family savings and business investment. In short, women's concerns for the care and future prosperity of their 'uterine families' are decisive in sustaining stem households, encouraging the formation of uxorilocal unions and building up family capital that is transferred as inheritance.

The links appear unambiguous. Brides' marital demands are one of the sources of the rural housing boom in Zhejiang. Empowered by legislation and employment, an unequal sex ratio, and a culture of competitive consumption, young women are stipulating the physical conditions into which they will marry. Their demands include personal comfort and the provision of space for individual privacy, conjugal intimacy and children. As the size of their houses increase, the size of their households has shrunk. Women's desire to create their own household – one in which age cohorts enjoy independence and opportunities – trumps efforts by patrilineal families to shore up their prestige, solidarity and authority over the younger generation through the bestowal of marital payments. I shall argue in the following section that women's housing aspirations are also propelling credit circulation, rural–urban migration and the redistribution of family wealth between the generations and between sexes.

Who pays? Who profits? Whose house?

There is no doubt that housing consumes a major portion of rural families' income, and that much of the credit informally circulating in the countryside is associated with residential construction and marriage. The average cost of building a new dwelling is equivalent to between seven and ten years' combined income for a married couple. High-income villagers have no difficulty affording mansions and even urban apartments to accommodate their newly-wed children. Indeed, anticipating the inevitability of post-marital division and subscribing to the idea that it is desirable to give a new couple a debt-free start to married life, many prosperous parents put up houses for boys who still are at school (Knapp and Shen 1992: 68).

For the less wealthy, however, the impending marriage of a son might portend financial ruin. Not only must they upgrade their own habitation in order to demonstrate their economic and social standing to potential in-laws, but to keep abreast of the competition they also must help to construct a mansion for the occupancy of their son and his bride. One elderly woman whom I accompanied as she hurried from her job as a cleaner in the village offices to spend the last hours of daylight hoeing her contract fields said that she and her husband had built their three-storey house in order to facilitate her son's marriage. They fitted out the third floor apartment with wallpaper, air-conditioning, television, refrigerator and new lounge and bedroom suites. Their savings exhausted, she and her husband took up residence on the ground floor among unpainted concrete walls and the furniture from their old house. Although her son and daughter-in-law are both doing well in private business, they make no contribution towards household expenses because they are saving to build their own new house. Another anxious parent moaned that she and her husband would never be able to save up to build again in time for her son's marriage: 'We only earn around 12,0000 yuan a year, and just in the past six months we have had to give 3,000 or so to relatives that are building their own houses and marrying. So we can't even repay the 80,000 we borrowed to put up this place!'

About one-quarter of survey respondents remarked that the exigency of saving for a house and marriage necessitates rural–urban migration. Young and middle-aged males are disproportionately represented in China's 'floating population' and their remittance payments to the countryside are channelled into house-building (Chan 1999: 57–8; Davin 1999: 87–8; Zhou 1997: 237). By comparison, except for those who come from villages stricken by poverty or natural disasters, unmarried women remit comparatively little money to their families. In the case-study sites, new mansions were built with remittances from parents of both sexes. In the most affluent village, much of the capital for housing construction came from profits earned by couples who had set up dumpling (*jiaozi*) restaurants as far afield as Guangzhou and Chengdu. In the poorest village, new houses were inhabited by the aged parents and children of people that had 'gone out' to work in factories and on building sites so they could repay housing loans.

Who stands to gain from the trend towards borrowing, remitting and investing marital payments in new housing? At first glance, the answer seems obvious. In contributing towards a son's marriage and housing for his family, parents transfer a substantial amount of family wealth to their male offspring. As most brides move to the houses owned by their husbands or his parents, it stands to reason that their right to occupation might well be conditional on their maintenance of good marital relations (Wang 1999; Zhao 2001). And as in the past, so today discriminatory inheritance practices tend to favour male beneficiaries (Davis 2000). In short, young men appear to gain most from housing investments.

To some extent, the discriminatory impact of such customary practice is mitigated by legislation. Women's equal rights to property are spelled out in the Chinese Constitution and a raft of civil and family law, including the recent Law on the Protection of Women's Rights. The Law on Contracting Village Farmland and the Inheritance Law grant women the right to contract land and house sites, and to own, inhabit, inherit and benefit from joint family property. The Inheritance Law also provides that spouses' inheritance rights take priority over the rights of children, parents and siblings. As women tend to be the primary caregivers in families, their interests are represented in the stipulation that family members who care for property owners should be recompensed from their estate.

On the other hand, legislation that individualises property rights may have some negative implications for women's claims to marital property. Ironically, this is the case with Articles 17, 18 and 19 of the revised Marriage Law of 2001. Unless husband and wife sign a written agreement to the contrary, the property owned by each party before marriage remains their personal property, while all income from wages, businesses, agricultural production and intellectual property, and assets, inheritance and gifts obtained during the marriage become the joint property of husband and wife. Yet as I have pointed out, in many cases young women make no financial contribution towards the construction of their post-marital residence because they prefer to marry a man who is already in possession of a new house. Although marriage to a propertied man promises a woman a life initially free of housing debt, in the absence of a document conferring joint ownership, it confers on her no rights in her husband's house.

Two factors might counterbalance the potentially adverse effects on women of this individualisation of property rights. First is the instruction, in Article 39 of the Marriage Law, that in adjudicating property disputes in divorce cases courts must evaluate the needs of all parties and 'follow the principle of favouring the children and the wife'. From the fact that around 70 per cent of divorce cases are pressed by women, many of whom are rural residents disgruntled about property issues, one can assume that at least some village women have confidence that courts will indeed protect their interests (*Shanghai Star*, 10 October 2000; *People's Daily*, 6 November 2001).

The second factor is the capacity and willingness of young women to negotiate their housing entitlements as part of a marital agreement. Consider the disparate routes by which two informants, Aihua and her prospective daughter-in-law, Jieming, achieved home ownership. There is no denying that Aihua had worked hard to achieve her own status as a homeowner. I had observed her slaving, saving and scavenging the materials to erect a modest, two-storeyed village house when I lived in Hangzhou from 1992 to 1993 (Sargeson 1999: 215–19). And I knew that one of Aihua's main motives for building her house was to attract a bride for her son Tianshan who, she confided, possessed few attractive qualities. The village house was also intended to provide Aihua and her husband, who have neither social security benefits nor savings, with a home to which they could retire. By 1999, Aihua's house had grown an extra storey, but it remained uninhabited. Aihua's entire family had migrated to work in the sprawling industrial suburbs of Shanghai. Tianshan's fiancée, Jieming, was still in the village filling dressmaking orders. She said she would marry only when she and Tianshan were given their own apartment in Shanghai.

A Shanghai apartment! Aihua's husband balked at the prospect of incurring such a huge debt in his old age, though with an eye to spiralling property prices, he conceded that an apartment would be a good investment. Aihua, though, was outraged. She insisted that the money she had saved for Tianshan's marriage should be spent on jewellery, presents and feasting for village relatives. Jieming should move into the house Aihua had built and concentrate on expanding her dressmaking business. How could she and her husband ever retire back to the village if they had to borrow to buy urban real estate? Yet even someone as determined as Aihua could not prevail against her daughter-in-law's wishes. Tianshan and Jieming now live in a tiny high-rise nest in Pudong. Aihua's longed-for retirement has been deferred indefinitely, while she and her husband help Tianshan pay for the apartment. Nevertheless, Aihua unconsciously refers to the apartment as 'theirs', rather than 'his' or 'ours'. The resolution of Jieming's housing demands resulted in a reallocation of family wealth among the sexes, as well as among the generations (see also Li 1999: 252).

As Hann remarks, 'To speak of property . . . is to engage with a range of issues of global political economy in the contemporary world' (Hann 1998: 2). In the case-study villages, the necessity to finance construction presses villagers into indebtedness, migration and work in metropolitan centres. Many sojourners remit the bulk of their earnings to construct a house intended to provide them with a sanctuary from a life of itinerant wage-labour. Exposed to advertising and market 'intelligence', others are tempted to invest in urban real estate. Inheritance customs that favour males have not been eliminated by the ambivalent efforts of the Chinese state, first, to enshrine legally women's rights to marital property, and second, to protect the private property relations that are considered central to the operation of markets. Marriage is one of the moments when young women can intervene to secure rights to housing. The case of Aihua and Jieming indicates that their housing ambitions might be achieved at the expense of their parents-in-law.

Rebuilding village cultures

In demanding new mansions, and in purchasing the furnishings, labour-saving appliances, fittings and ornaments to install in their mansions, women are contributing to the integration of villages into ever-widening circuits of cultural exchange. A case in point is the manner in which architectural fashions travel the routes mapped by investment capital and migrant labour. Respondents delight in the synthesis of architectural styles they have created in their new mansions. In the rebuilt section of one village, courtyard gates make explicit reference to the curled, cascading tiled roofs of old housing compounds, while the houses inside display such 'foreign' decorative motifs as sweeping semi-circular entrance stairs and moulded baroque architraves. In another wealthy village, regular grid pattern streets and uniform rows of tall town-houses reflect the power of the local planning authorities and the urbane ambitions of the inhabitants. In a third locality, planners have ignored the usurpation of farmland and fishponds by walls that encircle free-standing villas, paved courtyards, water features and rose-beds (see Plate 7.2). In the poorest village, the completion of even simple cubist brick structures awaits the receipt of remittance payments from itinerant family members. Yet here, too, one hears of plans for future ornamental flourishes. In so far as villagers seek alternatives to the residential orthodoxies presented by planners and marketed by construction firms, their quest leads them to look to foreign soap-operas and suburban developments for models of their dream mansion.

The global and national cultural flows propelled by the construction of mansions have local economic and political impacts. Regionally distinctive building skills have been supplanted by construction methods and materials marketed by corporations headquartered in cities. New houses primarily are built by extra-local contractors of prefabricated concrete slabs, steel beams, kiln-dried brick, ceramic tiles, and aluminium-framed plate-glass windows. Although construction standards and sanitation regulations are observed only rarely, they serve as an institutional touchstone in local governments' resolution of the many disputes that arise between owners and builders. The necessity to investigate and adjudicate conflicts between neighbours over the height, orientation and floor area of their new mansions has triggered the expansion, supervision and training of bureaucracies in counties and towns (Xie *et al.* 1999).

The commercialisation of rural housing has not (yet) resulted in a re-valorisation of local heritage by villagers. Not one respondent said they preferred the local over imports, or the old to the new. On the contrary, they repeatedly drew unfavourable comparisons between the 'messy', 'dirty', 'dark' and 'unhygienic' conditions in older houses and the cleanliness, light and spaciousness of contemporary dwellings. No one mourned the loss of the roofed verandahs and 'sky well' courtyards that protected old houses from rain and sunlight and provided their inhabitants with semi-public spaces for work, social interaction, play and storage. Old settlement patterns similarly are disparaged. The poorest of the case-study villages comprises dense clusters of houses interwoven by winding cobbled and dirt paths. At corners and where houses are recessed, these paths widen to form open spaces where, on summer evenings, people gather to chat with passers-by while they shell beans, mend tools or watch over children. But residents bitterly complain that the town government has not yet demolished both housing and paths in order to build straight, broad all-weather roads – roads that simultaneously will provide vehicular access to new mansions and discourage the casual gatherings that sustain interaction and flows of information among villagers.

Why this outspoken rejection of local architectural traditions? In reproducing the built form of commercially branded suburban utopias – 'Prosperity Mansions', 'Swiss Village' – women in particular seem intent on overturning old urban prejudices that identify the rural with agricultural production and parochialism. Several women mentioned that mutual respect and pride in their community had been fostered by the 'urbanisation', 'beautification' and greater 'sophistication' that came with the construction of new dwellings. The nearer

Plate 7.2 Contemporary 'European-style villas' in the Zhejiang countryside, 2000 (photograph by the author).

their proximity to cities and the higher their exposure to commercial media, the more likely were women to describe even relatively new houses as 'dilapidated' or 'backward'. The three-storey rectangular concrete structures thrown up in the 1980s and early nineties were disparaged, even by their owners, as ugly, poorly designed and anachronistic: 'I'd like a prettier house. This is really old-fashioned. The houses got bigger in the nineties but now people are less concerned with the size and height of a house and more concerned with external appearance and modern interior designs.'

It is something of a commonplace that the stylistic referent and spatial form of houses 'acts as both behaviour setting and mnemonic for idealized concepts of the domestic unit that resides within' (Lawrence-Zuniga 1999: 158). The truism aptly sums up the life-style changes that are being wrought in village mansions. Once, Chinese domestic interiors were hierarchically encoded (Blanton 1994; Knapp 1999: 181–2). Now, domestic space is demarcated less by ritual, generational and gender hierarchies than by perceptions of public and private space, and by the prioritisation of consumption over productive activity.

Few mansions contain a formal reception room. The only vestige of the central hall that once functioned as the stage for public reception, ethical instruction and kinship ceremonial is to be found in the occasional placement in the centre of a living room of a sideboard above which hang ancestral photos. The significance of such photos is, however, frequently undermined by the proximity of colourful studio portraits of the living family, or reproductions of oil paintings and calligraphy. Hierarchical spatial sequences are further disrupted by the placement of asymmetrical living rooms off the central axis of the house (Jing 1999). Containing sofas, console for television, VCR and karaoke, lifestyle signifiers like exercise equipment and water-purifiers, aquariums, cabinets displaying glassware, bottles of liquor and ornaments, these rooms are designed and furnished to facilitate casual social interaction among the few members of each nuclear family unit within the households, Upstairs, the concept of marriage as a romantic union is expressed in the provision of designated parents' suites that provide retreats from the eyes and ears of other family members. Only one of the dozens of newly-weds' bedrooms I have seen contained a 'traditional' curtained wooden bed inherited from the couple's forebears. All others were store-bought fashion statements.

Women's pursuit of their housing ideals not only alters village cultures and home life. Spatially, women's domestic roles are also being reconstituted. Along with other productive activities, women's contributions towards the household economy increasingly tend to be carried out in segregated work spaces hidden from public view: in laundries, sewing rooms and small kitchens that disallow social gatherings. I was told on many occasions that one of the best features of new houses is the provision of ample cupboard space and ground-floor garages that conceal the containers, chemicals, appliances and equipment used in the home and courtyard. And, as Habermas (1989: 43–51) observed of the houses of the European bourgeoisie, the spatial structuration of privacy and consumption in village mansions reduces the number of occasions when women can take their 'inside' chores outside.

In the most affluent of the case-study villages, a woman who had a washing machine blushed when she confessed that she still preferred to take her washing to the village pond. When her husband scoffed, she excused herself by saying, 'It saves water! And I like to see what's going on, who is walking past.' But while dirty, productive activities are sequestered from the life of household and community, women's maternal, nurturing and pedagogic roles are newly privileged by the allocation of purpose-built spaces. For the first time in rural domestic life, specific domains are being designated as nurseries, children's bedrooms, playrooms or 'child's study'. Mothers are acting as the tutors of the future family. In short, appropriation of the built forms of modernity is re-engendering the domestic role of village women.

Conclusions

Old paradigms of marriage and household formation in China tended to overlook the will and capacity of individual members of the family to exercise some control over their lives. This tendency was particularly evident in studies of rural marriage and household formation. And no individual members of the rural family have appeared less likely to take control of their marriage and shape the size and structure of their household than young women, so often depicted as the objects of marital exchange, vehicles for the reproduction of patrilines or achievement of status aspirations, and victims of sexual oppression and exploitation. Studies such as those by Margery Wolf (1972) added tone, colour and texture to that monochromatic representation, showing that middle-aged mothers wielded considerable influence over their sons and, through them, over other household members.

From the vantage point of an investigation into the factors that are propelling the 'rural housing boom' in Zhejiang Province, however, I have found that women on the verge of marriage are now in a strong bargaining position. They choose whom they will wed, and in the process of making that choice they negotiate the physical conditions and household forms in which they will live. Conversely, the mothers of marriageable sons might well lose out in negotiations with prospective daughters-in-law over marital payments, post-marital residence and household form. Admittedly, it is impossible to demonstrate the extent to which young women directly influence the decisions taken by potential spouses and their families with respect to housing. After all, the acquisition of a dwelling might entail years of saving, complicated financial transactions, government authorisation and commercial contracts. But there is no question that the popular belief that 'no woman would marry a man without a new house' motivates many village families to build, renovate, divide and rebuild.

This study found no evidence to support the hypothesis that the trend towards devolving family wealth at marriage rather than after the death of the patriarch, and the conversion of marital payments into the built form, is a response to rural industrialisation and marketisation in China. On the contrary, it is apparent that village families do not expect to protect and enhance their productive property through time by transforming it into residential housing. The complex property rights regime in the countryside and limited market demand for rural housing actually discourage investment in rural real estate. In the one case-study village in which industry and commerce is highly developed and housing is, indeed, a lucrative investment, newly-weds co-reside with parents and wealth is inherited. Nor is there any reason to conclude that the construction of housing for newly-weds is an outcome of efforts by patrilineal families to ensure continuation of their house. Rather, all the evidence suggests that the changes in the methods of intra-familial wealth transmission and the outlay of wealth on housing are related to young women's marital demands. And those demands, in turn, reflect women's efforts to gain some degree of autonomy and control in their own homes.

It is also clear that young women's housing demands have consequences that extend well beyond negotiations over marital payments and the building activity of individual families. They are giving impetus to labour migration, the remittance of monies for residential construction and, on occasion, villagers' investment in urban real estate markets. Young women's preference for a home of their own is contributing to the growing incidence of nuclear households and the creation of life-styles distinct to different generations within villages. The material culture of villages is being transformed, as indigenous architectural traditions are being superseded by designs and materials purchased from urban and international firms. And commercially produced housing designs import new concepts of privacy, leisure, conjugal intimacy and childhood into village life. Finally, in the process of negotiating their post-marital life, young women are remaking themselves and their families in the image of idealised 'modern' units of consumption and are re-engendering the domestic realm.

Viewed from the 'frog-in-the-well' perspective of women, marriage, household formation and the rural housing boom, then, the rapid growth of China's markets is seen to be impelled not just by the reformist zeal of government and by entrepreneurial endeavour, but also by complex cultural forces. However, as Dirlik points out, in negotiating some degree of emancipation from the obligations imposed upon them by patrilocal residence and patrilineal reproduction, in transacting their entitlement to housing and in acquiring the structures and styles of modern domesticity, young women render themselves and their future families more vulnerable to the storms of globalised markets.

References

Baker, H. D. R. (1979) *Chinese Family and Kinship*, London: Macmillan.
Benjamin, D., Brandt, L. and Rozelle, S. (2000) 'Aging, Wellbeing and Social Security on Rural North China', in C. Y. C. Chu and R. Lee (eds) *Population and Economic Change in East Asia*, New York: Population and Development Council.
Blanton, R. (1994) *Houses and Households: A Comparative Study*, New York: Plenum Press.
Chan, K. W. (1999) 'Internal Migration in China: A Dualistic Approach', in F. N. Pieke and H. Mallee (eds) *Internal and International Migration: Chinese Perspectives*, Richmond: Curzon Press.
China Statistical Bureau (2001) *Statistical Yearbook of China*. Available online at <http://www.stats.gov.cn/english/index.htm> (accessed Aug. 2002)
Cohen, M. (1978) 'Developmental Process in the Chinese Domestic Group', in A. P. Wolfe (ed.) *Studies in Chinese Society*, Stanford, CA: Stanford University Press.
Creed, G. (2000) '"Family Values" and Domestic Economies', *Annual Review of Anthropology* 29: 329–55.
Davin, D. (1999) *Internal Migration in Contemporary China*, Houndmills: Macmillan.
Davis, D. S. (2000) 'Reconfiguring Shanghai Households', in B. Entwisle and G. E. Henderson (eds) *Re-Drawing Boundaries: Work, Households and Gender in China*, Berkeley: University of California.
Davis, D. S. and Harrell, S. (eds) 1993) *Chinese Families in the Post-Mao Era*, Berkeley: University of California Press.
Dirlik, A. (2001) 'Markets, Culture and Power: The Making of a "Second Cultural Revolution" in China', *Asian Studies Review*, 25: 1, 1–34.
Douglas, M. and Isherwood, B. (1979) *The World of Goods: Towards an Anthropology of Consumption*, London: Athlone Press.
Du, F. (1985) *Tu Fu: One Hundred and Fifty Poems*, trans. Wu Juntao, Xian: Shaanxi Renmin Chubanshe.
Du, P. and Tu, P. (2000) 'Population Ageing and Old Age Security', in X. Z. Peng with Z. G. Guo (eds) *The Changing Population of China*, Oxford: Blackwell.
Ebrey, P. B. and Watson, J. L. (eds) (1991) *Kinship Organization in Late Imperial China 1000–1940*, Berkeley: University of California Press.
Fei, X. T. (1983) *Chinese Village Close-up*, Beijing: New World Press.

Freedman, M. (1966) *Chinese Lineage and Society*, London: Athlone Press.

Friedman, S. L. (2000) 'Spoken Pleasures and Dangerous Desires: Sexuality, Marriage and the State in Rural Southeastern China', *East Asia: An International Quarterly*, 8.4.

Gao, X. S. (1983) 'Li Shunda Builds a House', in Lee Y. (ed.) *The New Realism*, London: Hippocrene Books.

Goody, J. (1990) *The Oriental, the Ancient and the Primitive: Systems of Marriage and Family in the Pre-industrial Societies of Eurasia*, Cambridge: Cambridge University Press.

—— (1998) 'Dowry and the Rights of Women to Property', in C. M. Hann (ed.) *Property Relations: Reviewing the Anthropological Tradition*, Cambridge: Cambridge University Press.

Grossbard-Scechtman, S. (1995) 'Marriage market models', in M. Tommasi and K. Ierulli (eds) *The New Economics of Human Behaviour*, Cambridge: Cambridge University Press.

Habermas, J. (1989) *The Structural Transformation of the Public Sphere: An Inquiry into a Category of Bourgeois Society*, Cambridge, MA: MIT Press.

Hann, C. M. (1998) 'Introduction: The Embeddedness of Property', in C. Hann (ed.) *Property Relations: Renewing the Anthropological Tradition*, Cambridge: Cambridge University Press.

Ho, P. (2001) 'Who Owns China's Land?' *China Quarterly* 166: 394–421.

Jing, Q. M. (1999) *Zhongguo quantong minju [Traditional Chinese Dwellings]*, Tianjin: Tianjin daxue chubanshe.

Knapp, R. G. (1999) 'Cangpo Village, Zhejiang: A Relict with a Future?', in R. Knapp (ed.) *Chinese Landscapes: The Village as Place*, Honolulu: University of Hawaii Press.

Knapp, R. G. and Shen, D. (1992) 'Changing Village Landscapes', in R. Knapp (ed.) *Chinese Landscapes: The Village as Place*, Honolulu: University of Hawaii Press.

Lawrence-Zuniga, D. (1999) 'Suburbanizing Rural Life-styles through House Form in Southern Portugal', in D. Birdwell-Pheasant and D. Lawrence-Zuniga (eds) *House-Life: Place and Family in Europe*, Oxford: Berg.

Li, Z. M. (1999) 'Changing Land and Housing Use by Rural Women in Northern China', in I. Tinker and G. Summerfield (eds) *Women's Rights to House and Land: China, Laos, Vietnam*, Boulder, CO: Lynne Rienner.

Liu, X. (2000) *In One's Own Shadow: An Ethnographic Account of the Condition of Post-reform Rural China*, Berkeley: University of California Press.

Murphy, E. T. (2001) 'Changes in Family and Marriage in a Yangzi Delta Farming Community, 1930–1990', *Ethnology*, 40, 3: 213–35.

New York Times (2002), 22 June.

Parish, W. L and Whyte, M. K. (1978) *Village and Family in Contemporary China*, Chicago: University of Chicago Press.

People's Daily (2001) 6 Nov. Available online at <http://www.english.peopledaily.com.cn/2001106/21/>.

People's Republic of China (1985) *Inheritance Law of the People's Republic of China*, approved 10 April.

—— (1992) *Law Safeguarding the Rights and Interests of Women of the People's Republic of China*, approved 3 April.

—— (2001) *Marriage Law of the People's Republic of China*, approved 28 April.

—— (2002) *Law on Contracting Agricultural Village Land of the People's Republic of China*, approved 29 Aug.

Sargeson, S. (1999) *Reworking China's Proletariat*, Houndmills: Macmillan.

—— (2002) 'Subduing "The Rural House-building Craze": Attitudes toward Housing Construction and Land Use Controls in Four Zhejiang Villages', *China Quarterly*, 172.

Shanghai Star (2002) 22 Oct. Available online at <http://www.chinadaily.ecom.cn/star/2000/1010/cn2-3.html> (accessed Nov. 2002).

Shi, Y. L. (1997) 'One Model of Chinese Urbanization: The Urbanization Process in Xiamen City's Caitang Village', in G. E. Guldin (ed.) *Farewell to Peasant China: Rural Urbanization and Social Change in the Late Twentieth Century*, New York: M.E. Sharpe.

Siu, H. (1993) 'Reconstituting Dowry and Brideprice in South China', in D. Davis and S. Harrell (eds) *Chinese Families in the Post-Mao Era*, Berkeley: University of California Press.

Wakefield, D. (1998) *Fenjia: Household Division and Inheritance in Qing and Republican China*, Honolulu: University of Hawaii Press.

Wang, Y. P. and Murie, A. (1999) *Housing Policy and Practice in China*, Houndmills: Macmillan.

Wang, Y. X. (1999) 'De-intensification and the Feminization of Farming in China', *Gender, Technology and Development*, 3, 2: 189–214.

Watson, J. L. (1982) 'Chinese Kinship Reconsidered: Anthropological Perspectives on Historical Research', *China Quarterly*, 92: 589–622.

Wolf, M. (1972) *Women and the Family in Rural Taiwan*, Stanford, CA: Stanford University Press.

Xie, D., Wei, Q. and Deng, Y. (1999) 'Nongcun jian fang de sikao yu jianyi' [Reflections and recommendations on rural housing construction], *Cunzhen jianshe*, 2: 26–7.

Xin, L. (2000) *In One's Own Shadow: An Ethnographic Account of the Condition of Post-Reform Rural China*, Berkeley: University of California Press.

Yan, Y. X. (1996) *The Flow of Gifts: Reciprocity and Social Relationships in a Chinese Village*, Stanford, CA: Stanford University Press.

Yang, M. C. (1947) *A Chinese Village: Taitou, Shantung Province*, London: Kegan Paul, Trench, Trubner & Co.

Zha, J. D. (1990) 'Zhejiang sheng cunzhen jianshe "zhili zhengdun" de qishi' [Revelations on the 'improvement and rectification' of rural construction in Zhejiang Province], *Chengxiang jianshe* 4: 22–3.

Zhao, Y. H. (2001) 'Domestic Violence in China: In Search of Legal and Social Responses', *UCLA Pacific Basin Law Journal* 211, accessed via <http://0-www.lexisnexis.com.au.prospero.murdoch.edu.au/cui/>.

Zhang, W. G. (1998) 'Rural Women and Reform in a North Chinese Village', in F. Christianson and J. Z. Zhang (eds) *Village Inc.: Chinese Rural Society in the 1990s*, Richmond: Curzon Press.

Zhejiang sheng tudi guanli ju (1999) *Zhejiang tudi ziyuan [Zhejiang's land resources]*, Hangzhou: Zhejiang kexue jishu chubanshe.

Zhejiang tongji nianjian 1999 [Zhejiang statistical yearbook 1999] (1999) Beijing: Zhongguo tongji chubanshe.

Zhongguo gengdi wanli xing [The great march of China's cultivated land] (1998) Beijing: Zhongguo dadi chubanshe.

Zhongguo guotu ziyuanbao (2000) 15 Nov.

Zhou, D. M. (1997) 'Investigative Analysis of "Migrant Odd-Job Workers" in Guangzhou', in G. E. Guldin (ed.) *Farewell to Peasant China: Rural Urbanization and Social Change in the Late Twentieth Century*, New York: M.E. Sharpe.

8   Women's work and ritual space in China

Anne E. McLaren

One of the central themes of this book is the question of what constitutes 'women's work' in contemporary China and how notions of 'women's work' have shifted in the course of the twentieth century. This issue is also one of the most contentious in the field of Chinese gender studies (Mann 1997, 2000; Bray 1997; Jacka 1997; Entwisle and Henderson 2000). Since antiquity, the Chinese have recorded notions of 'outer' work (perceived as male) and 'inner' work (perceived as female). Historians and sociologists have demonstrated the constructed and temporal nature of these notions of inner and outer. In this chapter I seek to continue the debate by enriching notions of 'women's work', usually considered narrowly as the production of goods and services, to include the function of women's ritual culture and domestic space in community perceptions of female labour. In particular, I will discuss the issue of women's agency and empowerment in their 'traditional' work sphere. Finally, I will pose questions about not only what women gained in the tortuous process of revolution and modernization, but also what they may have lost.

The general narrative about the gendered division of work in Chinese history begins with classical formulations of 'women's work' or 'womanly work' (*nügong*) and notions of the separation of the sexes.[1] In early China, women's work was regarded as of complementary status to that of men.[2] The Confucian notion that ruling a state began with ruling one's home lent dignity to notions of household governance and female management in the domestic sphere.[3] For early and medieval China, notions of what was appropriate work for women focused on spinning, weaving and sewing. 'Men till the fields and women weave' was the traditional formulation (Bray 1997: 180; Mann 2000: 19).[4] In this way men and women were seen to play commensurate and indispensable roles in maintaining family fortunes.

The perceived importance of 'women's work' may have declined in some regions as textile production became commodified from the Song (960–1279) period onwards. According to Francesca Bray, men came to dominate the commercial production of textiles by the seventeenth century. Now that women no longer produced cloth for sale on the market or to meet government taxation requirements, their social status declined accordingly (1997: 175ff).[5] Bray points out the unfairness of this perception. Women still continued to be heavily involved in providing cocoons and silk thread but, she argues, '[I]n China whoever sat at the loom was considered the real maker of the cloth' (1997: 257). By the late nineteenth century, the domestic space in which women lived and performed unpaid but essential work for the family came to be perceived by Chinese reformers, foreign observers, and increasingly by women themselves, as a site of seclusion and dependence (Bray 1997: 263).

Women's perceived lack of skill to perform remunerated labour was regarded as a social problem by leading reformers such as Liang Qichao (1873–1929) (Ono 1989: 26–8). Attempts were made to encourage women to work outside the home for the benefit of the nation. Visual media such as 'New Year prints'(illustrations of traditional images and motifs circulating in villages) exhorted women to take part in the national 'Self-strengthening' movement. One such print alludes to women's physical 'weakness' but nonetheless calls on women to stop sitting around idly, relying on men for their daily food (McIntyre 1999: 67–8, 76 fig. 6). Another print urges women to work together in a cottage textile industry. As Tanya McIntyre points out, this print is denuded of the usual 'domestic features', such as children, flowers, doorways and windows (1999: 67–9, 76 fig. 7), thus implying a 'modern' setting for the working woman. Another curious print of the same era has women, tottering on bound feet, lining up with rifles in military formation (McIntyre 1999: 64–5, 75).

Women's bound feet were the most obvious impediment to the emergence of women in the emerging modern workforce, but traditional notions of 'women's work' were another serious burden (see also Edwards, this volume). It is important to note that the dominance of the inner/outer model of labour did not mean that women never participated in 'outer' work, only that this sphere was not seen as natural to them. Young women and girls in Guangdong in the 1920s, for example, were commonly responsible for cultivating gardens close to the house, for the care of poultry and pigs, for pounding and grinding rice, selling produce at the market, assisting with bringing in the harvest, the raising of silkworms, spinning, weaving and sewing (Kulp 1925, repr. 1966: 252–3). Women's work remained crucial for the production of labour-intensive handicrafts, although, as Gates notes, this labour was 'nearly invisible' in the written record (1997: 122). In agricultural production, it was men who carried out most of the heavy fieldwork. For example, John Buck, who surveyed a number of regions in China during the 1920s, found a low participation of women in fieldwork in northern wheat regions and a slightly higher rate in rice regions (Jacka 1997: 23; Mann 2000: 27).[6] In the nineteenth and early twentieth century, the notion that it was shameful for women to engage in paid work outside the home precluded all but the poorest class of women from seeking work in western-style textile mills in urban areas (Huang 1990: 176; Hershatter 1986). After the founding of the People's Republic in 1949, the government sought to transform the traditional notion that women should not perform remunerated work outside the home. However, as many commentators have noted, government views were dominated by broad national concerns rather than specific goals to achieve women's emancipation.[7] The result is a certain inconsistency in official encouragement for women to work outside the home. As Jacka has argued (1997: 31), when 'left-wing' policy called the tune, women were urged to engage in non-domestic, remunerated labour. However, governments of a more 'right-wing' tendency were more concerned with providing employment opportunities for men than with encouraging women's participation in remunerated labour.[8]

One important consequence of the revolutionary and socialist era was a devaluing of 'inside' work, which was now regarded as work for the family as opposed to work for the collectivity (Jacka 1997: 34). In the mid-1990s, rural Chinese considered unremunerated household work as not falling into the category of '*gongzuo*' or labour (Henderson *et al*. 2000: 48). It was women who continued to carry out the greater part of domestic housework and childcare. Married women in the socialist era who performed salaried work in newly constituted work units (*danwei*) thus laboured under a cruel double burden (Harrell 2000: 74). Their traditional workload in the house remained much as before, at the same time as there was unprecedented pressure on them to work outside the house.

For many women, the revolution, for all its agonies, brought with it a sort of liberation. Nonetheless, there was a sense of loss as well. Lisa Rofel's informants in Hangzhou textile factories spoke to her of a sense of shame they felt when first forced to work 'outside' in paid employment (1999: 64, 70). It was not so much the notion of paid work that was the problem as the sense of 'exposure' when they worked outside their homes. The location of the work was of crucial importance. Rofel noted that a woman who managed a factory before 1949 lived over the factory and hence did not feel that she was working 'outside' her home (Rofel 1999: 73). Even in cases where women did work in part outside the home, as in the case of the Shaanxi women interviewed by Gail Hershatter, the convention that 'virtuous' women stayed at home led women to describe themselves as living in seclusion even when this was not entirely the case (Hershatter 2000: 81). In the revolutionary period shy peasant women were patiently coached by the Women's Federation to perform 'external' roles such as public speaking (Hershatter 2000: 86–7). For these women, the revolution meant the shedding of one identity and the painful acquisition of another one.[9]

There were other losses. When women left homes for factories and collective enterprises they left behind not just their households but also a whole community of women with whom they had toiled and felt a sense of fellowship. Before the revolution, senior women had largely governed the female domains of labour (Ko 1994: 190–2; Bray 1997: 128–50; Stockard 1989: 31–47). In the new work units, men and women often continued to work in segregated spheres of activity, but this time women were controlled by cadres who were overwhelmingly male.[10] Within the home, women gradually shed their traditional ritual authority, including mediation between the household and supernatural forces through their care of the household gods. Waves of government campaigns against 'superstition' and 'extravagance' robbed them of traditional rites of passage such as elaborate marriage and funeral ceremonies, the patronage of female deities, the power to heal the household through charms, and to protect the family through sorcery. Also gone were the once powerful ritual arenas for the expression of women's grievance, such as bridal laments (McLaren and Chen, 2000; McLaren 2000, 2003). In the Pearl River delta region, young unmarried women lost the companionship of 'girls' houses', where they spent most of their teenage years (Stockard 1989; Watson 1994). As rural China modernized, women lost the community of women working and chatting together, a fellowship of peers that would meet in upper chambers, in inner courtyards, in the alleyways, by the banks of water channels, or at the street stalls in nearby markets. In this volume, Sally Sargeson notes the case of a woman in an affluent village in Zhejiang who, although she owned a washing machine, still took her washing to the village pond in order to 'see what's going on, who is walking past'.

There has been some speculation about the ritual and symbolic nature of women's work in the home but one finds only scattered mention in the scholarly literature. Here I will explore women's labour in the production of goods and services as interpreted through the framework of women's oral and ritual culture. My goal here is to better understand 'traditional' perceptions of 'women's work' in order to assess what women may have lost when they underwent revolution and modernization.

Women's ritual work in twentieth-century China

Daniel Kulp noted that ritual and religious duties were important duties of women he observed in Phoenix Village, Guangdong, in the 1920. These ritual duties were intimately allied with the prosperity and well-being of the family. He lists the following as part of the training given to girls and young women:

> How to worship, what shrines and for what purposes; kitchen gods for prosperity in the home; the sky god for a good marriage; on the eighth month, the moon god; Guan Yin, Goddess of Mercy, for those who are sick; visit the graves of the ancestors at Tsing Ming [the Qingming Festival of the Dead], spring festival, and worship with mother by shooting off fire crackers and burning yellow paper as money for the spirits; burn silver money when the men are performing the ceremonies of ancestral worship in the Ancestral Hall or Temple or in the home at the following times; the fifth month, the middle of the seventh month, autumn festival, and the eleventh month or winter festival.
>
> (1925; repr. 1966: 251)

He also notes with disapproval the constrictions placed on the behaviour of girls: 'Girls must learn that they cannot play, sit or eat with boys; that they cannot talk with strangers; cannot worship ancestors themselves; must not disobey parents; must not quarrel; must not walk on the street alone nor eat things on the street' (Kulp 1925, 1966: 254). He concludes, 'Thus their entire education is for participation in familist activities in their narrowest spheres' (Kulp 1925, 1966:

254). His view was echoed by many other foreign observers and became a central part of the condemnation of Chinese tradition by Chinese intellectuals, both male and female, caught up in the May Fourth reformist movement (1915–27). For Kulp, other foreign observers, and May Fourth intellectuals in general, the confinement of women to domestic space and their training in purely 'familist' concerns demonstrate the 'narrow', confining nature of the treatment of women and hence the urgent need to reform the traditional Chinese state. In this analysis, Kulp ignores the function and importance of women's ritual and religious roles in community perceptions of the value of women's labour.

The weak, uneducated Chinese woman, with her bound feet and sequestration within the home, became a potent symbol of Chinese shame and backwardness in the twentieth century. Successive decades of scholarship on Chinese modernity have accepted this paradigm uncritically. Recent path-breaking work by Dorothy Ko (1994) has led to a fresh assessment of the dominant image of 'the Chinese woman as victim'. Ko asks different questions of her historical data, including the issue of women's perceived 'vested interests' and complicity with a system that seemingly kept them in subordination. Where scholars have looked, often in vain, for signs of female resistance to historical injustice, Ko looks instead for signs of women's 'contestation and negotiation' with the social processes that sought to constrict and define them (1994: 8).

Ko's important book deals with communities of elite women in the lower Yangtze delta during the seventeenth century. She is able to demonstrate how these women built up communities based on letter-writing and shared activities and interests. These communities valorized women's activities within the home, allowed for 'diversity and plurality of expression', and thrived precisely because they were not subversive of the status quo (1994: 292). Ko is fully aware of the limitations of her focus on this 'tiny and highly atypical group of men and women' for the study of Chinese women in general (1994: 296) but demonstrates convincingly the huge gap between Confucian ideology and actual practice for her group of elite women.

Did rural non-elite women also have 'vested interests' in the existing system? Are there signs of 'contestation and negotiation' with oppressive patriarchal structures? Here I will ask what role women's oral and ritual culture played in individual and community perceptions of a woman's value and the worth of her labour. This is a question rarely asked, not least because of the general lack of recognition that women do in fact have an oral and ritual culture that is not just one of 'assisting' at the rituals important to men and the lineage. Women's oral culture has little or no place in 'scriptural Confucianism' – that is, formulations in the classics, memoirs of the literati, stipulations of the state and similar. However, this does not mean that a rich oral and ritual culture associated with women did not exist. In recent decades, anthropologists have explored rituals involving either female deities or fertility cults (Sangren 1983; Cahill 1993; Baptandier-Berthier 1994, 1996; Shahar and Weller 1996; Gates 1996: 177–203) and women spirit mediums and healers (Cass 1999: 47–64). One finds occasional mention of household deities but little analysis (e.g. Feuchtwang

1974). Many studies refer briefly to links between ritual culture in general and women's labour – for example, cooking and the God of the Stove (Chard 1995) and ritual and sericulture (Mann 1997: 151–9; Bell 1994: 196–201; Bray 1997: 251). Emily Ahern has noted the 'pollutive' and 'dangerous' nature of women's ritual role, especially in funeral rites (1975). However, in the absence of a comprehensive study of women's role in Chinese ritual culture, it is hard to assess the extent to which women's ritual culture related to their productive labour. It is also difficult to assess how women's 'ritual work' was perceived within the community. The case of women's ritual culture in Korea may well be instructive here. As Laurel Kendall argues in her book on Korean women shamans, women's rituals have been commonly regarded as 'peripheral' cults, remnants of a 'primitive' or 'discredited ancient faith' (1985: 24). In contradistinction to the perceived marginal and 'primitive' nature of women's cults, Kendall argues that the women's rituals she investigated 'are integral components of Korean family and village religion. Women and shamans perform essential ritual tasks that complement men's ritual tasks' (1985: 25).

Serving the patriline

In this section I will discuss four case studies based on recent fieldwork that illustrate the intersection between oral arts, ritual culture and the daily tasks defined as 'women's work' in rural China. The first two examples are of ritual practices widely prevalent in pre-1949 China but which exist now only in the memories of the elderly. These examples offer insights into how women's domestic labour was perceived before the establishment of the People's Republic. The second two case studies, however, are examples of the reinvention of women's ritual culture in the new economic conditions of the reform period.

The first case-study discussed here is based on my fieldwork into the oral and ritual culture of the women of Nanhui County, located south of the Pudong region of Shanghai. In pre-revolutionary China, bridal laments ('weeping on being married off' or *kujia*) were known over broad regions of the country. Laments mark the rite of passage as the bride leaves her family to live in the household of her husband, subject to the governance of her parents-in-law. This was a traumatic time for the young bride, who had little say in the choice of bridegroom. As she departed, the bride took with her a dowry painfully acquired by her family over many years. On the size and quality of the dowry hinged the sort of welcome accorded to the bride by the husband's family. Although the dowry included items purchased in village shops, the bulk of the goods were textiles made by the girl and the women in her family, such as bedding, coverlets and bolts of cloth. In the Nanhui bridal laments, which took place in stages throughout the three days before she departed her home and were observed by both male and female family members (McLaren and Chen 2000), the bride often refers to her dowry in terms of great anxiety. She also refers to her own skills for weaving and household management in terms of hyperbolic self-deprecation. It is in these two aspects of the laments that one can find striking examples of how the bride constructs her own perceptions of 'women's work' and women's talent and skills. The laments also project a clear sense of the scope of the female domain of labour and the importance of the governance of that domain by senior women.

In the lament called 'Thanking the Sister-in-law' (*Xie Saosao*), the bride bids farewell to the wife of her older brother, who may have lived in their household for several years. In Nanhui, the oldest brother and his wife (*saosao*) are accorded particular power in the household and the oldest brother has the authority to approve the size of the dowry. In her address to the sister-in-law, the bride thanks her for teaching her the finer techniques of spinning and weaving cotton and for her generosity in providing cloth for her trousseau. As for the perceived value of the women's labour, it lies clearly in the 'face' it gives the family – that is, the display that can be made of the finely crafted dowry items:

> Thanks to you, many thanks.
> It is you who, setting store on our relationship, have given me much,
> Valuing our relationship, you have given me many favours …
> You gave me indigo printed cloth to add to my trousseau,
> You gave me satin coverlets and helped my father spread out the bedding to add to the show.

The bride praises the impeccable weaving of the sister-in-law and her kind teaching:

> In weaving, you weave close and fine.
> It is you, sister-in-law, who teaches me to take pains in spinning and weaving.
>   (Ren 1989: 74–5, 'Thanks to the Sister-in-law', lines 1–6, 14–15)

However, elsewhere the bride will refer ceaselessly and comically to her own poor mastery of the skills regarded as 'women's work', particularly cooking, spinning and weaving:

> I don't know how to use the shuttle on the loom, nor do I know how to weave cloth,
> As for the shuttle of poplar wood, I know not which is front and which back,
> As for the bamboo pole [on the cotton spinner], I have no idea how to hold it,
> Four-pointed palm leaves [used in wrapping sticky rice]; I don't know how to arrange these.
>   (Ren 1989: 23 'Filling the Box' lines 377–81)

The bride claims she is too frail to bear heavy burdens like the senior women of the groom's house. They will surely mock her.

> At their house, the Dama [wife of husband's elder brother] has shoulders of bronze and a waist of iron

In one pannier on her shoulders she can carry three *mu* of wheat …
But I, your daughter, have shoulders of beancurd and a waist of sticky
    rice …
When I carry even three *qian* of beancurd, I wobble this way and that …
                    (Ren 1989: 29, 'Filling the Box' lines 495–6, 499, 500)

Her nightmare rehearsal of what it will be like cooking for her parents-in-law
will resonate with the experience of many a young bride in China and elsewhere.
In this lament, the bride imagines the huge pots and ladles in the spacious
kitchen of the groom, and the huge stove with many burners guarded by the
Stove God icon. She then expresses anxiety at her own lack of skill:

Their chopstick holder is made from select timber,
A pair of ivory chopsticks is placed at the centre,
Silken towels hang on shiny hooks,
The rice of the sister-in-law [Dama] is fragrant as sticky rice,
The gruel she makes is sweet as dates.
Her beancurd tastes like salty meat,
But the rice I make has grass and seeds in it, My skin is too rough and dirty,
    how can I be a match for this?

                                                        (lines 47–50)

In the bottom are river snails,
In the middle is raw rice,
The rice is cooked on the top and raw underneath.
I eat the hard uncooked rice,
The mother-in-law likes her rice a little hard,
The father-in-law likes his rice a little soft,
So how can I manage, how can I cook for them?
                                                        (lines 58–68)

These laments demonstrate the importance of the acquisition of female domestic
skills for the 'face' of her natal family and for the proper functioning of the
marriage system, which relied on the importation of female labour through
marriage. The bride's work here is constructed primarily as service to the
parents-in-law and adaptation to their household customs and protocols. Above
all, the bride fears the carping judgement of the senior women in the household.
Women here are assessed by their physical strength, and competency at
household skills and diplomacy. The hyperbolic and often comic protestations of
the bride at her ineptness need not be taken literally. Nonetheless, the anxieties
of the bride, at this crucial turning point in her life, are very real.

Another women's cult that reflected the anxiety of young women about
marriage is the cult to the Maiden of the Lavatory. One of the humblest tasks
carried out by women in China was the carrying of the buckets of human waste
from the house to a manure pit. In the case of the lower Yangtze delta, the

manure pit is a clay vat sunk deep into the ground in land at the rear of the residence. After a few days it can be used as fertilizer, an essential ingredient in crop production. The second case to be examined here deals with a cult surrounding women's essential work in supplying the manure pit. From 1999 to 2000, Chen Qinjian of East China Normal University, Shanghai, carried out an investigation of the cult to the Kengsan Maiden, the Goddess of the Lavatory, in two villages in Songjiang County outside Shanghai.[11]

In these villages the goddess of the pit is known as Keng San *guniang* or Lavatory Pit Third Maiden.[12] It is believed that this cult was prevalent in many areas of China before 1949.[13] Chen interviewed women in their forties and fifties who had participated in the Keng San Maiden cult in their youth. The ritual performance was carried out annually on the fifteenth day of the Chinese New Year, a day that marks the formal end of New Year celebrations. The activity is called by the participants 'Inviting [down] the Kengsan maiden' (*qing Kengsan guniang*). Only young unmarried girls took part in the cult. The girls meet in the living room of someone's home. Rice bran is scattered on the dining table. Two girls would then take an empty bamboo basket used for holding rice and carry it to the lavatory pit. They would stand on both sides of the basket and hold it with one finger only. At the pit they would chant a formulaic dialogue of question and response, calling on the Maiden to descend into their basket. After some time, both feel that the basket has become 'heavy'. This is taken as a sign that the Maiden has descended into the basket. They then bear the bamboo basket back to the living room. It is now regarded symbolically as a sedan chair, used to carry statues of deities from temples or the bride to her new home.

Having 'descended' into the basket, the Maiden is now called on to display her power. A headband worn by women is placed around the rim of the basket, which is now inverted over the tabletop on which bran is scattered. A chopstick or hairpin is inserted through both basket and headband, with the pointed end hanging down loosely. The two girls hold the basket with two fingers over the table and the pointer then moves 'on its own' over the rice bran and is seen to sketch patterns or write characters in response to questions put by the devotees. A third woman interprets the 'sketching' of the deity. It is not necessary to be literate to interpret the 'writing' of the Maiden. Most of the questions put to the deity concern personal matters, especially who will be their future husband, whether their married life will be happy and their future children. When the deity is deemed to be 'tired', she is taken back to the lavatory pit as before.[14]

The Maiden of the Lavatory was only one of many female household deities venerated by women in this area before 1949. On the fifteenth day of New Year, rituals were also carried out to the Door Corner Maiden (*menjiao*), the Firewood Storage Maiden (*chaicang*) and Wall Corner Maiden (*bijiao*). The Maidens were said to be everywhere in the dwelling; however, the Lavatory Goddess was regarded as the most efficacious. She is attributed with every kind of magical power, exceptional wisdom, a kind heart, and a willingness to help others. Invoking the maidens brings protection of the family from pestilence and disaster. The young female spirits are called Maidens (*guniang*) rather than deities (*shen*) or Buddhas (*pusas*) to indicate the intimacy of their relationship with the young practitioners. Some of those interviewed also spoke of how village youths would come and disrupt their ceremony by throwing tiles and bricks into the pit, splashing manure over their clothing. It was noted that the Lavatory Goddess would not make an appearance while these hooligan antics were going on and the woman would be forced to call down another deity instead (Chen 2001).

This little-known cult of the Lavatory Goddess shows how even very humble activities, such as the removal of human waste, were infused with ritual significance in traditional village settings. The cult reflected issues of extreme concern to these young girls and allowed them to seek the blessings of a deified model of themselves. In a society that set taboos on the discussion of male–female relations, there was nowhere for a young woman to go to spill out her hopes and fears and seek consolation except amongst young girls in the same predicament. The success of the ritual relied on the degree of solidarity felt by the participants and expressed their common anxieties. Unlike the bridal lament, which was enacted before the whole family, the cult to the Maiden of the Lavatory Pit was performed by and for young women and involved their most intimate and personal questions.

Reinventing the patriline in the reform period

The cult to the Lavatory Goddess and the Nanhui bridal laments live on today only in the recollections of middle-aged and elderly women. They provide a valuable glimpse of the symbolic construction of 'women's labour' in pre-modern China. My next two examples, however, are instances of revived and 'reinvented' rituals. These examples offer a striking illustration of the way that women have reinvented rituals once considered to be the prerogative of men alone, including ancestral rituals intended to perpetuate the patriline. Both examples come from southern coastal provinces.

Li Yongji (1996) carried out research into the lineage rituals of Jiayuan village, Zijin County, Guangdong, beginning in the late 1980s. Throughout China women were not supposed to take part in the sweeping of the tombs or worship in the ancestral temple. This was true for Jiayuan village as well; women were not even allowed to observe the rituals. After the males returned from sweeping the tombs, they would dine at the banquet table. Women were not allowed to sit down at the banquet and busied themselves serving the men. Once the banquet was finished, the women ate the leftover food in the kitchen (Li 1996: 119).

In the 1980s the ancestral rituals were revived in Jiayuan village but the changed environment of socialist China shaped the revival in surprising ways. Families of means (families of cadres and business bosses) started to rebuild the lineage tombs. Tomb-building became an aspect of conspicuous consumption as wealthy families competed to construct lavish tombs and memorial stones (Li 1996: 120). However, the male cadres and business bosses were reluctant to play too prominent a role. Li notes that 'due to political considerations, they relied mainly on their mothers or wives to carry this out' (1996: 119).

Women have been important not only in the reinstatement of lineage rituals but also in the rebuilding of many temples smashed during the Cultural Revolution. Some of these new temples are devoted to female deities. Sometimes a local woman will claim to have a vision calling for the building of a particular temple (Li 1996: 120). There are even cases where certain older women are said to be transformations of the deities concerned or to have received special skills from the deity, or to have become 'wives' of the deities (Li 1996: 121). Senior women in the village played a leading role in initiating younger women in this reinvented 'women's ritual culture'. In Jiayuan village, four women were most active in local religious activities, two of them in their sixties and two in their thirties. Their chief advisers were women in their seventies who had previous experience of 'seeking help from the gods and asking questions about the future' (Li 1996: 120). The younger women seek advice from the older ones on how to proceed then go around to every household to get financial support. Women gathered funds to rebuild temples such as the Five Crops Temple (Wugumiao) (Li 1996: 121). Women who donated more than 10 yuan to this project had their names engraved on a stone memorial. The men played a supportive role behind the scenes. For example, since the older women were illiterate, they relied on their literate menfolk to help with the stone engravings. Li observed that although cadres did not take direct part they gave tacit support to these activities.

Jiayuan women also play a leading role in the reinstatement of rituals inside the household, including worship of the God of Heaven (Tianshen) and a hierarchy of other deities. The rituals are costly and involve feasting, incense and fireworks. Women, not men, preside over these household rituals, with children and husbands helping out (Li 1996: 122). Because of the interruption of several decades in transmission of these rituals, there is a degree of reinvention and re-creation. For example, the women do not know that the deity, Shuimu niangniang, was traditionally a disciple of the Buddhist deity, Guanyin. They offer her pork and chicken as offerings to her when vegetarian offerings are more ritually 'appropriate'. Modern ideas are added to the old in a fascinating pastiche of ritual practices. For example, in the past the Earth God was only given one birthday celebration on the second day of the second month, but now the ritual has been expanded by a woman called Deng who has set up three ritual acts for this deity. Another woman presiding over this ritual decided to bake a birthday cake for the god. As Li notes, 'women have reinvented this deity in line with contemporary logic' (1996: 122).

The ritual activities are shaped by the new consumer expectations of the reform era. The expenditure on festivals and celebrations is becoming quite burdensome for some families. If only incense is used then the expenditure is small, but if a banquet is required then it becomes quite costly. Given the sheer number of deities who need propitiation, this can come to a few hundred yuan in a year. Those who can most afford this sort of expenditure are the managers of businesses, and so it is wives of the affluent who are the most active. Jiayuan village has one Christian family. This family goes to church once a week and does not participate in the reinvented rituals, arguing that they save a lot of money that way (Li 1996: 123). Li concludes that the revival and reinvention of these rituals by women presents a challenge to the traditional patriarchal way of life. However, it is unclear whether the reinvented rituals assist women's status in other ways within the community. One could also view the phenomenon as the adaptation of the women's ritual work for the household to the new conditions of reformist China.

In the case of Jiayuan, the emergence of entrepreneurship and a consumer culture were critical factors in women's ritual enterprises. Festival activities made a comeback as well; for instance, the community ritual performances known as *jiaohui*, which involve theatrical troupes, dragon dances, fireworks, lantern shows and processions of images of the local deities through village streets (Li 1996: 116). These rituals and festivals are intimately associated with affluence and conspicuous expenditure. What is striking is the way that women have chosen to engage in ritual activities that consolidate the ancestral cult of the patriline. However, women are no longer marginal players but managers and inventors of ritual occasions.

Another example of the revival and reinvention of women's ritual is Dazuo village in Hui'an County, Fujian. Qiao Jian and Chen Lili, who have carried out fieldwork in Dazuo, note that women play a leading role in all of the four levels of religious activities in this village – individual, family, lineage and regional (1994: 763). The economic conditions of Dazuo differ significantly from those of affluent Jiayuan. Dazuo is close to the coast and the main traditional source of employment was fishing. However, the catch has declined in recent years and some of the men have sought jobs in Taiwanese fishing boats. Another key industry in the region is stone carving. Many younger males look for apprentice posts as stone carvers. The majority of men are involved in fishing and stone carving. As a consequence, there is a dearth of men to take up agricultural and construction work, which now falls to women.

Qiao and Chen observed a highly gendered division of labour. Women alone did the following: washing of clothing, cleaning of toilet buckets, water carrying, sewing, ploughing, sowing seeds, planting rice shoots, adding fertilizer to soil, weeding, harvesting, mending of nets, transporting of goods, knitting goods for sale, carrying stone and sand used in production. Tasks performed only by men were the design of clothing, fishing far from the coast, working as a hired hand on a boat, or as a boat repairer, concrete labourer, stone engraver or explosives technician in construction work (Qiao and Chen 1994: table 1, 765–6). They point out that this pattern of work is unusual in south China where men generally do the heaviest work, such as ploughing. However in this village, 'the men not only do not participate in agricultural production but also consider this sort of labour shameful'. The locals rationalize this by saying that the shoulders of women are particularly strong and therefore they are good at carrying heavy things while the hands of men are very strong, so they are good at fishing (Qiao and Chen 1994: 766). Women in this village also take part in construction work, where they dig foundations and carry concrete and bricks. The men do jobs such as concrete and carpentry jobs requiring a level of training. They conclude that 'whatever is rough, requiring a low level of skill, time consuming and less profitable is undertaken by women, whatever requires a high level of skill, and is more profitable, is undertaken by men' (Qiao and Chen 1994: 767).

Fishing and stone carving bring in most of a family's income, which leads to a huge disparity in the income earned by men and women within the household. Qiao and Chen argue that this disparity in income across gender lines accounts for what they say is the 'extreme male chauvinism' and deeply patriarchal kinship structure of the area (1994: 767). However, they also point out that the social and economic role of women in the village is not necessarily lower than in other parts of China; nor is it true to say that they are subject to absolute domination (Qiao and Chen 1994: 767). This is perhaps because women tend to be the managers of the family finances. The men often work far from home and financial control is left up to the women. Another critical aspect of female dominance is the ritual culture of Dazuo.

In spite of the seemingly unfavourable economic circumstances for women, it is women, not men, who play a leading role in lineage worship at Dazuo (Qiao and Chen 1994: 773 ff). The same process of the reinvention of lineage rituals apparent in the Jiayuan example is found here as well. Formerly only the names of males who had married and had a son were entered in the ancestral tablets. Now the names of wives can be entered as well. The village women also take ritual control over the kinds of deceased household members who do not warrant entry into the ancestral tablets and temples. They do this by looking after personal gods known as *furenma* (Qiao and Chen 1994: 768). The *furenma* are figures of men and women made of paper, each representing a deceased family member or person known to the household. The ghosts associated with the *furenma* are often those who died 'unnatural' deaths, including those who died before marriage or who committed suicide. The paper 'ghosts' are arranged in a box or encased in glass and placed in an inner room of the house, not the formal living room, together with sticks of incense. Through the cult of the *furenma*, women can maintain the health of the household. Unhappy events such as sickness (especially the sickness of a son) are seen as a sign of the ghosts' displeasure (Qiao and Chen 1994: 769).

The cult of the paper 'ghosts' is associated with married women. Elderly village women can often be called ritual specialists or *shangshen*. These women are believed to have magical power to communicate with ghosts through the medium of a special 'ghost official'. In ritual ceremonies they fall into a trance and speak strange utterances in a performance known as 'yawning'. The ghost speaks through them in the archaic language of the region that only older people can understand. On awakening they cannot remember what they said. When asked about the experience of becoming a *shangshen*, the women often said that it happened during a period of sickness. They believe that if they become *shangshen* then they will be cured (Qiao and Chen 1994: 768).

Within the Dazuo community at large, it is the senior women, not the men, who preside over the birthday of the Earth God and other deities. Women even carry out rites for the well-being and safety of the fishing expeditions of the men. Men participate in these ceremonies but do not control them. For example, men carry a statue of Guanyin from the temple to the fishing boat, but it is women who preside over the actual ceremony (Qiao and Chen 1994: 773). Women also preside over the birthday celebrations of the god of war, Guandi (1994: 777).

Qiao and Chen conclude that the women preside over and organize virtually all of the significant ritual activities of Dazuo village and that men participate only marginally. In this region the women ritual specialists known as *shangshen* appear to have replaced the former male ritual specialists known as *jitong*. Particularly striking is the active participation of women in ancestral rituals, an activity without precedent in pre-1949 China. In this case one can assume that the preoccupation of men with fishing and stone engraving, activities that take them away from the village, has opened up a public and private ritual space in which women could find new forms of agency in a relatively harsh economic environment.

Conclusion

The revival and reinvention of tradition in China of the reform period has been a much noticed phenomenon (Siu 1989; Dean 1993; McLaren 1998). Here I have concentrated on women's rituals and work practices. I have argued that these gender-specific rituals comprised an important but ignored aspect of 'women's work' in pre-revolutionary China and, in some areas, have been reinvented in the contemporary reform period. Women's ritual work adds another symbolic dimension to popular perceptions of the nature of work. To date, our understanding of the conceptual underpinnings of Chinese notions of work in the pre-modern period has relied almost completely on classical formulations composed by men (Mann 2000). With further investigation into women's ritual work we will be able increasingly to enrich scholarly paradigms concerning the gendered division of labour in China. From this initial study, it appears that women's ritual work reinforced popular understandings of inner and outer domains and the separation of the sexes. Domestic space was the essential female ritual domain in the same way as clan temples and burial grounds were the typical male ritual domain. The sense here is not so much of marginality and exclusion as of the complementarity of ritual roles. From the evidence presented here, women were not simply marginal witnesses to ancestral rituals based around the needs of the patriline but active participants in other forms of ritual culture that both complemented male ancestral cults and validated women's governance of the domestic sphere. Women played an active role in initiating and performing this ritual culture, which varied from region to region in line with different social and economic conditions. That this female ritual power has been little noticed in the past is due to the fact that it was transmitted orally by mainly illiterate women, and only rarely recorded in China's 'scriptural' culture.

The 'coming out' of women from the home into public space led inevitably to the erosion of household rituals in which women were at the very centre. Once women worked in factories and fields, they were not present in the home to tend to the household gods, or at least not to the same extent. Tutelary gods did not preside over their factory floors. Throughout most of China, as the household gods vanished into the recesses of the collective memory of the elderly, so did memories of women's past ritual authority. In the palatial homes now found in coastal Zhejiang, few remnants of kinship rituals remain in the open plan living rooms of the new commodity culture (see Sargeson, this volume). Nonetheless, as Sargeson elegantly demonstrates, women's agency in configuring the new 'modern' domestic space is everywhere apparent. While women's rituals have seemingly vanished in 'modernizing' China, the opposite process is happening in some regions. The examples from Jiayuan and Dazuo discussed here are striking for the way they reveal women's determined reinvention of past rituals. These examples offer a surprising demonstration of women's agency in reshaping notions of the patriline in ways that accord women significant power both within the family and the local community.

It has been assumed that women were marginalized within the 'patriarchal' system of the imperial past and that the allocation of women to the 'inner' sphere meant their necessary exclusion from domains of authority and power. The question of whether this 'inner sphere' had its own form of authority and power, and how women may have exercised agency in that sphere, has been given much less attention. The examples discussed here point to the importance of women's ritual culture for enhancing bonds within communities of women and infusing notions of 'women's work', understood as both physical and ritual labour, with rich symbolic meaning.

The general breakdown of women's ritual culture that accompanied the revolution led to a state of confusion as to what tasks should be considered male and which female. However, the notion that labour was inherently gendered has rarely faltered. In the new China, men and women have competed to attach particular symbolic values to their own domains of work. As Lisa Rofel has noted, the weaving of silk, once performed only by men, became a prized job for women after the founding of the People's Republic. However, in the 1980s the pendulum shifted once more. Silk weaving become a socially devalued form of employment, much to the chagrin of older generations of women weavers who had 'liberated' themselves from their homes. In the reform era, as men leave the fields for lucrative jobs in township enterprises, agriculture, including heavy fieldwork, is being increasingly 'feminized'; that is, defined as 'inner work'. The complexity of constantly shifting gender boundaries here is a symptom of the conceptual confusion that arose when 'inner' work lost its symbolic value and its association with female governance and ritual power.

In some parts of rural China, however, women have been able to recuperate ritual power in new and surprising ways. In Dazuo village, women do the heaviest and dirtiest work, the kind performed by men elsewhere, but nonetheless exert considerable ritual power within their own sphere, which is constructed as both the family and the local community. In the case of Jiayuan village, wives of the local elites engage in ritual activities once monopolized by men. In this case, the elite males found it politic to let their wives handle religious issues that enhance family prestige, thus opening up a ritual space for their wives. In Dazuo women's ritual culture has extended its scope beyond the traditional one of the household to the wider village community. These cases illustrate how the reform period is offering many new opportunities for women, but as many of the chapters in this volume demonstrate, with each new opportunity, a new gendered boundary is also likely to emerge.

Notes

1 As Bray notes, there are three different characters used to represent the word 'work *gong*' as it applies to work performed by women. In one case the character *gong* refers to any kind of work, male or female; in another case the character for *gong* refers to meritorious work, often work performed by women to meet household tax requirements. A third character *gong* referred to women's work in textiles (1997: 184).
2 For notions of the separation of the sexes in ancient texts, see Raphals (1998: 195–213). Raphals prefers to speak of 'distinctions' between the sexes based on differences of function rather than strict physical separation (1998: 212–13). She also argues that formulations of inner and outer work in antiquity did not prevent women from engaging in a wide array of activities outside the home (see esp. 1998: 232–3). Studies of women in the later imperial period show that in practice the necessary 'distinction' between the sexes was applied quite flexibly. For the Song period, see Ebrey (1993) and the Qing Ko (1994).
3 For example, in the Book of Rites, the home is the sphere of women: 'men must not speak of internal [i.e. household] affairs' (cited in Raphals 1998: 232). The importance of women's domestic governance is signalled most strikingly in classic marriage rituals (Mann 1991: 208–10).
4 The actual situation was a lot more complicated than this canonical proverb would suggest, see Gates (1997: 123).
5 Bray's thesis may hold most true for the silk industry. However, in the cotton industry women were heavily engaged in the production of cotton for sale and tax purposes; see review of Bray by Elvin (1998).
6 There were exceptions to this general picture, particularly amongst Hakka women in south China; see discussion in Gilmartin (1994: 197–8).
7 This was true even for the very early period of the revolution (Gilmartin 1994: 219–25). For a critique of patriarchy under Chinese socialism, see Stacey (1983). See also Edwards, this volume.
8 The 'left-wing' periods are said to be 1949–52, 1957–60, 1966–78). 'Right-wing' periods are listed as 1952–57, 1961–65, 1978 to the present.
9 Croll gives many examples of this process (1995: 69–108).
10 As Edwards notes in this volume, women were also very underrepresented in the Chinese Communist Party.
11 This project was part of a large Sino-Japanese research project, 'Folk Customs of Village Settlements in Jiangnan, China'. Chen led the Chinese investigatory team. The report below is extracted from Chen (2001).
12 The Kengsan *guniang* may well be a latter-day manifestation of an ancient female deity, Zigu, first recorded in the fifth century AD. Sometimes the same deity is known as Sangu furen.
13 For further details see consult Ye and Wu (1990: 776, 724).
14 This ritual act parallels other fortune-telling activities known to Chinese folk culture involving a deity who 'writes' a cryptic message through a spirit medium on a

planchette or featuring a deity who 'descends' to a sedan chair. For an example of the latter with male practitioners, see Jordan (1972: 65–6).

References

Ahern, E. M. (1975) 'Power and Pollution of Chinese Women', M. Wolf and R. Witke (eds) *Women in Chinese Society*, Stanford, CA: Stanford University Press.

Baptandier-Berthier, B. (1994) 'The Kaiguan Ritual and the Construction of the Child's Identity', *Minjian xinyang yu Zhongguo wenhua: Guoji yantaohui lunwenji* [Popular Belief and Chinese Culture: International Conference Proceedings], Academica Sinica, Taipei, 2 vols, vol. 2, 523–86.

—— (1996) 'The Lady Linshui: How a Woman Became a Goddess', in M. Shahar and R. P. Weller (eds) *Unruly Gods: Divinity and Society in China*, Honolulu: University of Hawaii Press.

Bell, L. S. (1994) 'For Better, for Worse: Women and the World Market in Rural China', *Modern China* (April), vol. 20: 2, 180–210.

Bray, F. (1997) *Technology and Gender: Fabrics of Power in Late Imperial China*, Berkeley: University of California Press.

Cahill, S. (1993) *Transcendence and Divine Passion: The Queen Mother of the West in Medieval China*, Stanford, CA: Stanford University Press, 1993.

Cass, V. (1999) *Dangerous Women: Warriors, Grannies and Geishas of the Ming*, Lanham: Rowman & Littlefield.

Chard, R. L. (1995) 'Rituals and Scriptures of the Stove Cult', in D. Johnson (ed.) *Ritual and Scripture in Chinese Popular Religion*, Berkeley: University of California Press.

Chen, Q. (2001) 'A Performance Art Reflecting the Concerns of Chinese Village Women: An investigation into the cult of the Kengsan Maiden in two villages in Songjiang County', paper presented at the Thirteenth Conference of the Folk Narrative Research Association, University of Melbourne, Australia, 17 July 2001.

Croll, E. (1995) *Changing Identities of Chinese Women*, London and New Jersey: Zed Books, Hong Kong University Press.

Dean, K. (1993) *Taoist Ritual and Popular Cults of Southeast China*, Princeton, NJ: Princeton University Press.

Ebrey, P. B. (1993) *The Inner Quarters: Marriage and the Lives of Chinese Women in the Sung Period*, Berkeley: University of California Press.

Elvin, M. (1998) 'Review Essay: Francesca Bray's *Technology and Gender: Fabrics of Power in Late Imperial China'*, *Journal of Social History* 32: 403–10.

Entwisle, B. and Henderson, G. E. (eds) (2000) *Re-drawing Boundaries: Work, Households, and Gender in China*, Berkeley: University of California Press.

Feuchtwang, S. (1974) 'Domestic and Communal Worship in Taiwan', in A. Wolf, *Religion and Ritual in Chinese Society*, Stanford, CA: Stanford University Press.

Gates, H. (1996) *China's Motor: A Thousand Years of Petty Capitalism*, Ithaca, NY, and London: Cornell University Press.

—— (1997) 'On a New Footing: Footbinding and the Coming of Modernity', *Jindai Zhongguo funü shi yanjiu* 5 (Aug.), 115–35.

Gilmartin, C. K. (1994) 'Gender, Political Culture, and Women's Mobilization in the Chinese Nationalist Revolution, 1924–1927', in C. K. Gilmartin, G. Hershatter, L. Rofel and T. White (eds) *Engendering China: Women, Culture, and the State*. Cambridge, MA: Harvard University Press.

Harrell, S. (2000) 'The Changing Meanings of Work in China', in B. Entwisle and G. E. Henderson (eds) *Re-drawing Boundaries: Work, Households, and Gender in China*, Berkeley: University of California Press.

Henderson, G. E., Entwisle, B. *et al.* (2000) 'Re-drawing the Boundaries of Work: Views on the Meaning of Work (*Gongzuo*) in B. Entwisle and G. E. Henderson (eds) *Re-drawing Boundaries: Work, Households, and Gender in China*, Berkeley: University of California Press.

Hershatter, Gail (1986) *The Workers of Tianjin 1900–1949*, Stanford, CA: Stanford University Press.

—— (2000) 'Local Meanings of Gender and Work in Rural Shaanxi in the 1950s', in B. Entwisle and G. E. Henderson (eds) *Re-drawing Boundaries: Work, Households, and Gender in China*, Berkeley: University of California Press.

Huang, Philip (1990) *The Peasant Economy and Social Change in North China*, Stanford, CA: Stanford University Press.

Jacka, Tamara (1997) *Women's Work in Rural China: Change and Continuity in an Era of Reform*, Cambridge: Cambridge University Press.

Jordan, David K. (1972) *Gods, Ghosts and Ancestors: Folk Religion in a Taiwanese Village*, Berkeley and Los Angeles: University of California Press.

Kendall, Laurel (1985) *Shamans, Housewives, and Other Restless Spirits: Women in Korean Ritual Life*, Honolulu: University of Hawaii Press.

Ko, Dorothy (1994) *Teachers of the Inner Chambers: Women and Culture in Seventeenth-century China*, Stanford, CA: Stanford University Press.

Kulp, Daniel Harrison (1925, repr. 1966) *Country Life in South China: The Sociology of Familism*, Vol. 1, Phoenix Village, Kwangtung, China, repr. Taipei: Ch'eng-wen Publishing Co. 1966.

Li Yongji, (1996) *Xingbie yu wenhua: kejia funü yanjiu de xin shiye* [Gender and Culture: New Studies in Hakka Women] Guangzhou: Guangdong renmin chubanshe.

McIntyre, Tanya (1999) 'Images of Women in Popular Prints', in Antonia Finnane and Anne McLaren (eds) *Dress, Sex and Text in Chinese Culture*, Melbourne: Monash Asia Centre, pp. 58–80.

McLaren, Anne E. (1998) 'Chinese Cultural Revivalism: Changing Gender Constructions in the Yangtze River Delta', in Maila Stivens and Krishna Sen (eds) *Gender and Power in Affluent Asia*, London: Routledge, 1998.

—— (2000) 'The Grievance Rhetoric of Chinese Women: From Lamentations to Revolution', *Intersections: Gender, History and Culture in the Asian Context* (electronic journal), 4: 1–17.

—— (2003) 'Mothers, Daughters, and the Socialisation of the Chinese Bride', *Asian Studies Review* 27: 1 (March).

McLaren, Anne and Chen Qinjian (2000) 'The Oral and Ritual Culture of Chinese Women: the Bridal Lamentations of Nanhui', *Asian Folklore Studies*, Vol. LIX–2, 2000, 205–38.

Mann, Susan (1991) 'Grooming a Daughter for Marriage: Brides and Wives in the Mid-Ch'ing Period', in R. S. Watson and P. B. Ebrey (eds) *Marriage and Inequality in Chinese Society*, Berkeley: University of California Press.

—— (1997) *Precious Records: Women in China's Long Eighteenth Century*, Stanford, CA: Stanford University Press.

—— (2000) 'Work and Household in Chinese Culture: Historical Perspectives', in B. Entwisle, and G. E. Henderson (eds) (2000) *Re-drawing Boundaries: Work, Households, and Gender in China*, Berkeley: University of California Press.

Ono, K. (1989) *Chinese Women in a Century of Revolution 1850–1950* (first publ. in Japanese in 1978), trans. J. A. Fogel, Stanford, CA: Stanford University Press.

Qiao, J. and Chen, L. (1994) 'Funü yu zongjiao – Dazuocun de li' [Women and Religion – the Case of Dazuo Village], in *Minjian xinyang yu Zhongguo wenhua: Guoji yantaohui lunwenji*, Academica Sinica, Taipei, 2 vols, vol. 2, 763–80.

Raphals, L. (1998) *Sharing the Light: Representations of Women and Virtue in Early China*, New York: State University of New York.

Ren, J. *et al.* (1989) *Hunsang yishi ge* [Wedding and Funeral Ritual Songs] Shanghai: Zhongguo minjian wenyi chubanshe.

Rofel, L. (1999) *Other Modernities: Gendered Yearnings in China after Socialism*, Berkeley: University of California Press.

Sangren, P. S. (1983) 'Female Gender in Chinese Religious Symbols: Kuan Yin Ma Tsu, and the "Eternal Mother"', *Signs 9-1, Journal of Women in Culture and Society*, 4–25.

Shahar, M. and Weller, R. P. (1996) *Unruly Gods: Divinity and Society in China*, Honolulu: University of Hawaii Press.

Siu, H. (1989) 'Recycling Rituals:Politics and Popular Culture in Contemporary Rural China', in Perry Link, R. Madsen and P. Pickowicz (eds) *Unofficial China: Popular Culture and Thought in the People's Republic*, Boulder, CO: Westview.

Stacey, Judith (1983) *Patriarchy and Socialist Revolutions in China*, Berkeley: University of California Press.

Stockard, Janice E. (1989) *Daughters of the Canton Delta: Marriage Patterns and Economic Strategies in South China, 1860–1930*, Stanford, CA: Stanford University Press.

Watson, Rubie S. (1994) 'Girls' Houses and Working Women: Expressive Culture in the Pearl River Delta, 1900–41', in M. Jaschok and S. Miers (eds) *Women and Chinese Patriarchy: Submission, Servitude and Escape*, London and New Jersey: Zed Books and Hong Kong University Press.

Wolf, Margery (1972) *Women and the Family in Rural Taiwan*, Stanford, CA: Stanford University Press.

Ye, D. and Wu, B. *et al.* (1990) *Zhongguo fengsu cidian* [Chinese Folklore Dictionary] Shanghai cishu chubanshe.

Index